Catskill Mountain Guide

APPALACHIAN MOUNTAIN CLUB
BOSTON, MASSACHUSETTS

Map Cartography: Larry Garland
Cover Design: Belinda Desher
Front Cover Photograph: Nancy Battaglia
Back Cover Photographs: Peter W. Kick
Book Design: Amy Winchester

Library of Congress Cataloging-in-Publication Data is available.

The paper used in this publication meets the minimum requirements of the
American National Standard for Information Sciences—Permanence of Paper for
Printed Library Materials, ANSI Z39.48-1984. ∞

**Due to changes in conditions, use of the information
in this book is at the sole risk of the user.**

Printed in the United States of America.

Printed on recycled paper using soy-based inks.

10 9 8 7 6 5 4 3 2

For Ryan Peter Kick, with love.

Contents

Acknowledgments

I would like to recognize the following individuals for their assistance, enthusiasm, and encouragement: Dr. John C. Dwyer, historian; Jim Morton, lifelong Platte Clove resident; Glenda Gustafson, Catskill Center for Conservation and Development; Justine Hommel, historian, former president of the Mountaintop Historical Society; Alf Evers, author, historian; H. Neil Zimmerman, author, former president of the New York–New Jersey Trail Conference; Howard Dash, New York–New Jersey Trail Conference chairman and Catskill 3500 Club, conservation chairman; Mike Kudish, botanist, author, professor of forest history; Ken Rimany, director of Development and Outreach for the Association for the Protection of the Adirondacks; Adam Greenhalgh, curatorial assistant of the Clark Art Institute; Jim Beil, assistant director of Lands and Forests for the NYS Department of Environmental Conservation; George Profous, DEC Region 3 forester; Barbara Lucas-Wilson, DEC Region 4 forester; and New York State forest rangers Pete Evans, Dennis Martin, Patricia Rudge, Steve Preston, Stephen Scherry, and Frederick Dearstyne.

Special thanks go to June Sanson for proofing and research, and the editorial staff at the Appalachian Mountain Club, including the editorial director, Beth Krusi; series editor Blake Maher; former editor Mark Russell; and the creator of the maps for this series, Larry Garland.

Key to Maps

Catskill Forest Preserve

To the Owner of this Book

With the object of keeping pace with the constant changes in mountain trails, the Appalachian Mountain Club publishes a revised edition of this guide at intervals of about five years.

Hiking and climbing in the Catskill Mountains should provide a combination of outdoor pleasure and healthful exercise. Plan your trip schedule with safety in mind. Determine the overall distance, the altitude to be reached, and the steepness of the footway. If you are returning to the starting point the same day, allow ample time, as your morning quota of energy will have lost some of its get-up-and-go. Read the caution notes where they appear in this book. They are put there for your guidance and protection.

We request your help in preparing future editions. When you go over a trail, please check the description in the book. If you find errors or can suggest improvements, send a note to the committee. Even if the description is satisfactory, "Description of such-and-such trail is okay" will be appreciated. Do not be deterred by a lack of experience. The viewpoint of one unfamiliar with the trail is especially valuable. Address: Catskill Mountain Guidebook Committee, Appalachian Mountain Club, 5 Joy St., Boston, MA 02108.

Introduction

THE CATSKILLS

Welcome to the Catskills—The Land in the Sky. It is to these rocky hills and mountains between the Hudson and Delaware Rivers that the trails described in this guide will take you. Today the Catskill forest preserve contains nearly 300,000 acres in four counties—Greene, Ulster, Delaware, and Sullivan. Within the Catskills there are 35 peaks more than 3500 ft., 98 peaks more than 3000 ft., and more than 300 miles of state-marked hiking trails (including a 94-mile-long section of the Long Path). Slide Mountain (4190 feet) is the Catskills' highest peak. First occupied by Native Americans more than 5000 years ago, the Catskills of today look much the same as they did then, with a few important changes. These changes came in the form of the many early settlers who arrived in the area, who marked the landscape with evidence of their industry—a history that is written in the hills.

The Catskill region occupies 1500 square miles. Next to the Adirondacks, these are New York's highest and most rugged mountains and have the highest elevations. Four distinct regions—the escarpment (northeast), the southern, the central, and the western—define the Catskill plateau. There are several smaller topographic regions as well, many of which run east-west or perpendicular to the southward movement of ice during the Pleistocene epoch.

The profusion of streams that formed when the vast thickness of ice melted and retreated resulted in the erosion that produced the rugged character we see in the Catskills today. The plateau is drained to the north by the Schoharie Creek, a tributary of the Hudson via the Mohawk. To the east the Rondout, Esopus, and Kaaterskill Creeks join the Hudson. To the south and west the Delaware and Neversink rivers are the major watersheds.

The things that make hiking fun and adventurous have a lot to do with trees, slope, elevation, and the resulting sense of wilderness they offer—all things determined by geology. The Catskills were lifted up and out of a shallow sea during the Devonian period, approximately 400 million years ago. The uplift of the Devonian sediments took place in several stages, and the much later Miocene stage, 24 million years ago, and subsequent stages were influenced by several episodes of Pleistocene glaciation. Today the higher peaks are located where the uplift was greatest and where their conglomerate sandstones were able to resist erosion by the advance of the continental ice sheets and later by glacial meltwaters.

During this uplift, streams began to carve out the shapes of today's Catskills. A minimum of folding or faulting occurred, however, nor were the rocks changed by igneous or metamorphic activity. Later glaciation put its final erosive mark of character on the Catskills. Deep ravines, called cloves (from the Dutch word *kloove* meaning "a cleft or gash in the landscape") frightened early settlers. The cloves later inspired the artists of America's first school of painting—the Hudson River School of Landscape Painting—and the country's early writers—William Cullen Bryant, Washington Irving, James Fenimore Cooper—and others whose efforts shaped the literary and artistic climate of the new world.

High, flat plains offered attractive areas for early settlements. Remote, forested peaks provided Native Americans with winter hunting encampments and later, hideaways and forts for the various revolutionaries and counterrevolutionaries of the eighteenth century. As civilization reached the area, mountain houses and railroads appeared. The tanbark and bluestone-quarrying industries followed. The hiker owes a considerable debt to these historic developments (forgetting, for the time being, their ruinous impacts on the environment), because they resulted in the construction of footpaths, stagecoach and tote roads, railway beds, and later the marked hiking trails that have provided access to the Catskills' most remote and scenic destinations. Because these old and remote interior wilderness roads now form many of the upper-elevation trailheads, especially in the eastern escarpment area of the Catskills, it is possible to start hiking at relatively high elevations. This allows Catskill hikers to reach isolated summits and remote wilderness areas fairly quickly.

What is perhaps most interesting about the underlying geology of the Catskills is the vegetation that flourishes there. The region represents the southernmost occurrence of boreal coniferous forests on glaciated uplands in North America. In contrast with this summit forest of spruce and paper birch is the valley-forest type. Known as the Carolinian-zone forest, it consists of oak, hickory, occasional black birch, tulip tree, and, until recently, chestnut. According to Catskills forest historian Michael Kudish, "The proximity of the Carolinian and Canadian zones, especially in the eastern Catskills, together with the effects of humans over two centuries, produces a rich, diverse flora, and creates a vegetation so complex that it nearly defies explanation."

While they are unique historically and geologically, the Catskills have yet another distinguishing characteristic—their youth. Surrounding ranges that are visible from the Catskills are considerably older. To the east lie the 450-million-year-old Taconics, formed during a continental collision that displaced older sediments in a period called the Taconic Orogeny. South of the Catskills are the Shawangunks, and although they are close to the Taconics in age, their evolution is more related to the Catskills. Extensive sands and quartz-rich gravels were deposited in a shallow sea during the Silurian period, about 450 million years ago. Much later the resulting sandstones and conglomerates were uplifted and differentially eroded.

From many of the Catskills' higher peaks, views of the distant mountain ranges of southeastern New York are outstanding. From the resistant limestone of the Helderberg Escarpment, to the dissected plateau of the Catskills, and into the crystalline Hudson Highlands lying beside the younger folded rocks of the Appalachians, you can see the parts of the puzzle that make up the region's geological history.

HIKING IN THE CATSKILL REGION

The wide variety of trails in these mountains offers the hiker an excellent range of opportunities.

For residents of southern New York State, the special appeal of most of these trails is their proximity to New York City. The majority of the trailheads lie within two hours of the city.

There are two ways to enjoy the Catskills. The social hikers will find many walking groups that offer regularly scheduled hikes and trips. The New York–New Jersey Trail Conference (NY–NJTC) will put you in touch with many of these groups. Organizations such as the Catskill 3500 Club, the Appalachian Mountain Club, the Sierra Club, and chapters of the Adirondack Mountain Club all offer outing schedules for a variety of hikers. Each organization also fills a second role by providing opportunities for the hiker to return something to the land. With programs of trail maintenance, conservation, planning to prevent overuse, and education to promote wise use, these organizations help protect our wild lands.

Those who seek quiet in the forest preserve can also find that. Some of these routes are never heavily used. Others are, but early-spring and late-fall trips mix solitude with expanded vistas in ways sure to please any wilderness seeker.

The forests of the Catskills have been preserved as the Hudson Valley's water source and as part of the New York State Forest Preserve. Protection under the state constitution ensures these lands will remain "forever wild." Lands within the Blue Line of the Catskill Park contain all of the trails in this guide.

Almost all of the lands traversed by today's trails were once settled and used by farmers, miners, loggers, and romantics. Their presence is reflected in the lore that surrounds the trails. While this guide serves as an invitation to the Catskill Mountains, it cannot even begin to probe the vast history that enlivens each route. For further information, consult the bibliography at the end of this book.

BEFORE YOU START

There is an enormous range of trails in this guide, offering everything from easy strolls to strenuous climbs. The information about distance and time and the narrative contents of each chapter will help you gauge the difficulty of each trail and your level of preparedness. Read the material about your area of interest before you go! All of the trails in this guide are clearly marked, state-maintained trails, although this can change. Trail maintenance groups and outdoor organizations such as the Adirondack Mountain Club, the New York–New Jersey Trail Conference, and the Appalachian Mountain Club have undertaken to design, build, and maintain sections of trail in the Catskill forest preserve, and without these efforts, the trails would not be in the condition that we now enjoy.

The area surrounding the Catskills offers many more natural areas than are described in this book, and references to other excellent books are given in the bibliography. In order to discover other hikes or to become better prepared for outdoor adventures, you may wish to join one of the hiking groups listed at the end of the introduction.

Preparedness is key to your enjoyment, and you should be well equipped before you start. This includes knowing how to use a map and compass to complement the information in this guide. If you are new to hiking, it is definitely a good idea to join a hiking group and learn from those with experience. The more background you have on hiking in the woods, the greater will be your safety as well as enjoyment. Do not count on the following summary of what you need to know to prepare you for every situation you are likely to encounter. This introduction is not a primer for beginning hikers. Treat it instead as a checklist and a set of reminders.

The Weather

Whenever possible, wait for a sunny day—the pleasures are much greater and the problems more predictable. But even on sunny days you should be prepared for changes and extremes. It can be twelve or more degrees colder on the mountaintops of the Catskills than in the nearby Hudson Valley. Storms can appear on short warning.

It often can be too hot in summer for strenuous hikes. There are many that prefer hiking the Catskills in fall and spring, but these are the most changeable times. Extremes from heat waves to snowstorms can occur. But the rewards of fewer people and expanded distant vistas in the leafless season make it worthwhile.

Preparations

Even with the best of forecasts, your watchwords should be "plan for the unexpected." Possible changes in temperature mean you should take extra clothing, especially rain gear. Experiment with layers of light, waterproof gear. In the mountains you will want a layer of wool or polartec, even if in summer it is only a sweater or fleece in your day pack.

Many of the trails are as smooth as a sidewalk; some are as rubble filled as a rock pile. For most of these hikes a sturdy pair of well-broken-in, over-the-ankle boots is essential. Lightweight Gore-Tex or similar-material boots, in addition to being water-resistant, provide good traction and support, and usually they are all you need. More support is required when hiking on the higher mountain trails in early spring or winter, or when carrying a heavy backpack. An old piece of hiking advice that still holds true—especially for the tenderfoot—is to wear two pairs of socks, an inner lightweight pair and a heavy outer pair that is at least partially wool.

Carry a sturdy day pack, large enough to hold your lunch and a few necessities. These include a whistle, a waterproof case with dry matches, a knife, lip balm, and a space blanket. Bring a map and compass (and know how to use them), a flashlight in case you are delayed beyond dusk, and a watch so you do not panic if that happens. You also need a small first-aid kit containing a few bandages, first-aid cream, and moleskin for the unexpected blister.

Take along a small squeeze bottle of insect repellent—there are black flies in early spring. Fill a plastic bag with toilet paper and throw in a few towelettes to use before lunch on those dry mountaintops.

It is strongly recommended that you wear a pair of unbreakable glasses—light, tinted sunglasses—to protect your eyes, even if you require no prescription. It is all too easy to run into an overhanging branch or twig.

You may enjoy carrying a small, lightweight altimeter that works according to barometric pressure. On relatively steady days it is a good clue to progress on a mountain; on unstable days it can alert you to sudden changes in the weather—although a sudden drop in barometric pressure is not always a sign of impending bad weather.

Water

Of course, you should always carry water when you hike. The Catskills are dry much of the year, and few reliable springs exist. It is becoming increasingly dangerous to trust open water sources because of the spread of *Giardia* parasites. Remember to take enough water— 2 qts. per person per day seems enough in summer. Dehydration on summer days is a possibility; it can happen even on a sunny, leafless spring or winter day.

Personal Safety

Remember, hiking should be fun. If you are uncomfortable with the weather or are tired, turn back and make the complete hike another day. Do not create a situation where you risk yourself or your companions.

It is not always a good idea to walk alone, although many hikers will have no choice, and just as many prefer to do so. If you do, make sure someone knows your intended route and expected return time. Always sign in at the New York State Department of Environmental Conservation (DEC) trailhead registers where they are available. The unexpected can occur. Weather can change, trail markings can become obscured, you can fall, and you can get lost. But, you will minimize the danger if you anticipate the unexpected.

Lyme Disease

Lyme disease is caused by a tick-borne spirochete that may produce a rash, flulike symptoms, and joint pain. If untreated it may cause chronic arthritis and nervous-system disorders. It is difficult to diagnose but treatable if diagnosed early.

The deer ticks that transmit Lyme disease are found in the Catskills. Their range is expanding rapidly north and west, and users of this guide should take preventive measures.

There is no foolproof way to protect yourself from these minute ticks. Check yourself frequently; tuck pants into socks and boots; put insect repellent containing DEET on your pants, shoes, and socks (note that DEET does weaken elastics and is a suspected carcinogen); and wear tightly woven, light-colored clothing (making it easier to see the ticks). Above all else, shower and change clothes at the end of your hike; this is the best time to make a complete body check. Change out of your hiking clothes to prevent any ticks present from biting you. If you suspect you have contracted Lyme disease, call your physician right away—early detection is important.

Giardia Lamblia

Giardia, that renowned genus of single-celled intestinal parasite, is here to stay and should be heeded. The cysts are transmitted in the feces of animals and humans and are present in most water sources. They can survive for months in near-freezing water. Since they are rather small (16,500 can fit on the head of a pin) they are difficult to avoid without a quality filter of 2 microns or less, costing from $30 to $200. Other water-borne pathogens also require attention. Hepatitis virus, leptospira (from cattle urine), and cryptosporidium are smaller than *Giardia* cysts.

Boiling is the safest precaution against *Giardia, E.coli,* and other protozoa. *Giardias* parasites die at 176 degrees Fahrenheit, and all of these die after 10 minutes at 212 degrees Fahrenheit. Halazone, bleach and iodine will also work, but these disinfectants require a 30-

minute wait. Use four drops of bleach, five halazone tablets, or ten drops of 2 percent iodine per quart of water for safety, if you must drink from streams or lakes in the forest preserve. The colder the water, the longer the disinfecting process takes. Try to carry enough water for the trip. Piped springs and other subterranean sources at high elevation also require treatment. (It is important to realize that the official position of the NYSDEC forest rangers is that all water from natural sources should be filtered or treated.)

NOTES FOR USING THIS GUIDE

If you do not know how to read a map, you should learn to do so before hiking anywhere. Spend time walking with someone who does know how to read a map. The same holds true for using a compass. You may not need either on the easiest of this guide's trails, but walking the easier routes with map and compass will allow you to become comfortable with their use so you can extend your hikes beyond the trails described or to more difficult hikes.

DISTANCES AND TIMES

Mileages are given at the beginning of each trail in this book. These calculations are believed to be accurate. Within the text itself, state trail sign distances are sometimes given as a matter of reference and orientation only (with few exceptions) for the recommended direction of travel.

Because it is so difficult to establish absolute accuracy in distance over variable terrain the mileages given in this guidebook must be considered approximate. While every effort has been made to derive data that is very reliable, hikers must realize that there will be discrepancies. Distances shown on state trail signs will in a great many instances not match distances given in the text, and these differences are not always reconcilable. Typographic errors, errors in sign placement, errors in calculation, disagreements in calculation, different means of calculation, and other human effects all play their part in any computations. Hikers in the Catskills will very quickly discover that state trail signs do not always add up and that no two publications will always reflect identical distances to identical destinations. In consideration of this, hikers must take it upon themselves to judge book information against field observation with a degree of skepticism, and in doing so, make reasonable calculations and decisions. By becoming familiar with the map's scale—something that will become second nature after a few hikes—determining a reliable working sense for distance will become routine. Distance is a reference, not an absolute, and should be used accordingly. Rarely will conflicting distances between state trail signs and the text equal more than a few tenths of a mile.

The time estimates given for each trail in this book are based on a relaxed pace by hikers carrying day packs. Times will, of course, vary in accordance with several variables—a hiker's condition, experience, and goals; the amount of weight carried; the weather; and group size. One general rule of thumb that seems to work in the steep terrain of the Catskills is that backpackers will travel at 1–2 MPH, while day hikers will average 2–3 MPH. This takes into account the frequent short breaks that are inevitable (and recommended). Rarely will hikers average 3–4 MPH on backcountry trails and still have time to relax and enjoy themselves. Hourly estimates in this guide are calculated from an average of 2 MPH and are adjusted according to the terrain.

USE THE TRAIL REGISTERS

Use the registers that have been placed at important trail access points and junctions. Everyone using these trail systems is urged to sign the registers and give the information requested. This will enable the DEC to ascertain the number of people using a particular area and will assist field personnel in locating a party in the event of an emergency.

DEC RULES AND REGULATIONS FOR HIKERS AND CAMPERS USING STATE LANDS

The following are illegal and enforced by DEC:

- Defacing, mutilating, or destroying DEC signs, barriers, or other property.
- Throwing, dumping, or placing refuse, trash, garbage, litter, or any other offensive matter on DEC lands, waters, or structures.
- Staying in open camps (lean-tos) more than three successive nights or more than 10 nights in one calendar year; others may wish to use the lean-to.
- Using nails, screws, or other fasteners in lean-tos. Enclosing the fronts of lean-tos except by temporarily tying tarpaulins or building snow walls.
- Camping without a permit on undeveloped state lands for more than three successive nights or in groups of ten or more. Temporary permits may be obtained from DEC forest rangers. However, no permit will be issued to anyone under the age of eighteen. Remember that DEC may take down and remove any tent or other camping structure that is left alone for more than 48 hours.
- Camping above 3500 feet between March 22 and December 20, except in an emergency.
- Using motorized vehicles (cars, motorcycles, boats, aircraft, etc.) in wilderness areas or on other state lands where normal access to any state land is barricaded or otherwise prohibited unless a sign permitting their use has been posted.
- Leaving fires unattended. Clear all flammable materials from the perimeter of a fire to prevent its spread.
- Removing, destroying, or defacing plants, rocks, or minerals found on state land.
- Interfering with a DEC officer in the legal performance of his or her duty.
- Displays of unacceptable behavior.

- Camping within 150 feet of any road, trail, spring, stream, or other body of water except at camping areas designated by the DEC.

OTHER HELPFUL INFORMATION

The New York State Department of Environmental Conservation (DEC) Division of Lands and Forests
625 Broadway
Albany, NY 12233-5253
518-457-2500; 518-402-9405
www.dec.state.ny.us

The DEC, through its Division of Lands and Forests, manages the New York State Forest Preserve lands of the Catskills and detached parcels of state land outside the Catskills. The DEC is responsible for Search and Rescue, planning for management, supervision of campsites, and issuing of camping permits. The DEC also publishes regional trail maps. However, because each state region is run independently, it is easiest to obtain local information from one of the regional offices listed below.

DEC Region 3 Headquarters
21 South Putt Corners Road
New Paltz, NY 12561
845-256-3083 or 845-256-3082
Forest Rangers: 845-256-3026
Fishing: 845-256-3161
Hunting: 845-256-3098

DEC Region 4 Headquarters
Stamford Suboffice
65561 State Highway 10
Suite 1
Stamford, NY 12167
607-652-7365

State Campsites in the Catskills:

Beaverkill: 845-439-4281
Mongaup Pond: 845-439-4233
Kenneth L. Wilson: 845-679-7020
Bear Spring Mountain: 607-865-6989
Little Pond: 845-439-5480
Devil's Tombstone: 845-688-7160
North/South Lake: 518-589-5058
Woodland Valley: 845-688-7647

Camping reservations: 800-456-CAMP
Questions concerning camping reservation service: 800-777-9644
For information about camping discounts go to the DEC website:
www.dec.state.ny.us

Travel Information:
Ulster County: 800-342-5826
Sullivan County: 800-882-CATS; 914-794-3000
Greene County: 800-355-CATS
Delaware County: 800-642-4443

New York–New Jersey Trail Conference (NY–NJTC)

156 Ramapo Valley Road (Route 202)
Mahwah, NJ 07430
201-512-9348
E-mail: info@nynjtc.org
www.nynjtc.org

The NY–NJTC coordinates the construction and maintenance of some 1,500 miles of hiking trails, including the Appalachian Trail in New York and New Jersey and the Long Path, which connects the metropolitan area with the Catskills and beyond. They also publish regional maps of the Catskills, Northern New Jersey, West and East Hudson, Harriman State Park, the South Taconics, and the Shawangunks. Some 85 hiking clubs and conservation organizations belong to the conference, along with 8,000 individual members. Applications for individual membership are invited, and the annual fee includes, among other things, a subscription to the *Trail Walker.* This bimonthly publication describes the activities of the member clubs and features timely articles, book reviews, and trail updates. It is a reliable source of information on trail closings, relocations, and other potential problems associated with the hikes described in this book.

Appalachian Mountain Club (AMC)
New York–North Jersey Chapter
New York City office:
5 Tudor City Place
New York, NY 10017
212-986-1430
E-mail: Office@amc-ny.org
www.amc-ny.org

The Appalachian Mountain Club is America's oldest conservation and recreation organization. The AMC helps build and maintain trails in the Catskills. To find the chapter nearest you, go to www.outdoors.org.

The Adirondack Mountain Club (ADK Headquarters)
814 Goggins Road
Lake George, NY 12845
518-668-4447
E-mail: adkinfo@adk.org
www.adk.org

The Adirondack Mountain Club (ADK), and its chapters support an active program of hiking, backpacking, and trail maintenance in the Catskills. ADK is an effective advocate for protecting the Catskills. It publishes authoritative articles, books, and maps on the Catskills region.

The Sierra Club
Northeast Field Office
85 Washington Street
Saratoga Springs, NY 12866-4105
518-587-9166
E-mail: ne.field@sierraclub.org

The Sierra Club's grassroots advocacy has made it America's most influential environmental organization. Founded in 1892, the club has more than 700,000 members. The Catskills are included in the Mid-Hudson Chapter Area. The group conducts outings and speaker socials.

The Catskill 3500 Club
www.catskill-3500-club.org

The Catskill 3500 Club is primarily a hiking organization. Candidate members receive notices of trips and outings. A membership patch is given for completing climbs of 35 summits more than 3500 feet, 4 of which must be climbed a second time in winter.

The Catskill Center for Conservation and Development, Inc.
P.O. Box 504
Arkville, NY 12406-0504
914-586-2611
E-mail: cccd@catskill.net
www.catskillcenter.org

The Catskill Center for Conservation and Development is a regional advocate for land-use planning and environmental management, and it is active in natural-area and historic preservation, community revitalization, and public review of regionally significant projects. It publishes general-interest books and technical studies as well as a newsletter on conservation issues affecting the Catskills. Offices are in the Erpf House on Route 28 at Arkville, and applications for membership are welcome.

STATE AND LAND-USE CLASSIFICATION IN THE CATSKILLS

There are four basic land-use categories in place for the Catskill Park and Forest Preserve. These have been created because the preserve's wide variety of terrain, soil types, and forests have different capacities to support and recover from recreational use. Most of these classifications follow the same guidelines used for the Adirondack Forest Preserve. These management areas have been created and are being continuously developed based on physical land characteristics, biological considerations, established facilities, and both social and psychological factors. The New York State Department of Environmental Conservation describes these management units as follows:

Wilderness: The area (1) generally appears to have been affected primarily by the forces of nature, with the imprint of human's work substantially unnoticeable; (2) offers opportunities for solitude or a primitive and unconfined type of recreation; (3) has at least 10,000 acres of land (and/or water) or is of sufficient size and character as to make practicable its preservation and use in an unimpaired condition; and (4) may also contain ecological, geological, or other features of scientific, educational, scenic, or historic value.

Wild Forest: A wild-forest area is a section of forest preserve where the resource can sustain a somewhat higher degree of human use than a wilderness area. It may contain, within its bounds, smaller areas of land or water that are essentially wilderness in character, where the fragility of the resource or other factors require wilderness management. A wild-forest area is further defined as an area that lacks the sense of remoteness of wilderness areas and which permits a wider variety of outdoor recreation.

Intensive Use: An intensive-use area is a location where the state provides facilities for highly concentrated forms of outdoor recreation. These facilities include ones designed to accommodate significant numbers of visitors, such as campgrounds, ski centers, and visitor centers. These areas provide for congregations and/or accommodation of visitors to the park and sometimes function as a base for day use of wild-forest and wilderness areas.

Administrative: Administrative areas are locations within the Catskill Park under the jurisdiction of the Department of Environmental Conservation. They were acquired and are managed for nonforest preserve purposes.

LEAVE NO TRACE

With more people than ever using the Catskill Forest Preserve today, it is increasingly important that each of us know and practice the principles of leave-no-trace camping. User impact has become a serious issue everywhere, but especially here in the Catskills, a relatively small and fragile mountain range within a 4-hour drive of 60 million people. One of the most direct results of the high impact caused by both day and overnight hikers in the Catskills has been the prohibition of campfires above 3500 feet. Campfires continue to be one of the biggest impact issues in the Catskill Forest Preserve, even at lower, "legal" elevations, but that's just one example of impact. The DEC is grappling with a variety of impact issues, including both deliberate abuse (littering, vandalism) and "unconscious abuses" such as impacts on wildlife populations, plant communities, soil conditions, and water quality. The Catskill Park State Master Plan is designed to limit such environmental impacts, but the rest is up to us, the hikers and campers, the Catskills' largest user group.

An organization called the Leave No Trace Program (LNT) was formed to address these issues nationwide and to "promote and inspire responsible outdoor recreation through education, research, and partnerships." The educational component of Leave No Trace is maintained and supported by the National Outdoor Leadership School (NOLS). LNT is the leading philosophical force behind the practice of Leave No Trace, but it is more than simply a "clean campsite" campaign. LNT is a program "dedicated to building awareness, appreciation, and, most of all, respect for our public recreation places. LNT is about enjoying the great outdoors while traveling and camping with care." The LNT message has been endorsed and disseminated by the U.S. Forest Service, National Park Service, Bureau of Land Management, and the U.S. Fish and Wildlife Service.

Responsible campers not only will practice no-trace, low, or no-impact camping, but also will exercise what the Leave No Trace program calls "Negative Impact"—leaving a campsite in better shape than they found it.

These are the seven principles of Leave No Trace:

1. Plan ahead and prepare
2. Travel and camp on durable surfaces
3. Dispose of waste properly
4. Leave what you find
5. Minimize campfire impacts
6. Respect wildlife
7. Be considerate of other visitors

For more information about LNT, go to www.lnt.org.

TRAILESS PEAKS

It is not in keeping with the conservation ethic and practice of the Appalachian Mountain Club to identify suggested routes or trailheads to trailless peaks. There are several reasons for this restraint. First, the proliferation of recommended routes to these summits has caused the development of herd paths in some areas. Because hikers tend to climb a trailless peak by the most direct and logical means, no consideration is given to the potential design, carrying capacity, or terminal impact such trails can have on the environment. Professionally designed, DEC-designated trails take into account the most inoffensive routing of a trail as well as its proximity to sensitive or important ecozones; after its construction, a maintenance program is developed for its upkeep. Herd trails are not designed, designated, or maintained, and ultimately they produce undesirable patterns of erosion and impact.

Among the undesirable effects of herd trails is soil erosion, vegetative destruction, alterations in wildlife habitat and populations, and the deterioration of water resources. Trailless peaks are trailless for a reason, and discussing approaches to trailless peaks defeats the purpose of having them trailless to begin with.

User patterns reflect the popularity of climbing the trailless peaks, and many hikers join organized groups in order to do so, keeping tally cards and signing in at summit canisters. The establishment and maintenance of canisters on trailless peaks is a practice that has been called into question and debated in the public forums of the unit-management planning process. It should be noted that some public input to the Catskill Unit Management Plans has called for the removal of canisters on the Catskill summits. The Catskill Park Master Plan does not call for the construction of trails on any of the trailless peaks, nor have they called for the removal of the canisters. It is felt that the existing trails in the forest preserve are adequate at this time.

SAFE TRAVEL IN THE FOREST PRESERVE
Cell Phones

Cell phones will work from most mountain summits and many upper-elevation areas in the Catskills but seldom from valleys and hollows, and frequently they will not work from main roads in the interior Catskill Forest Preserve. They will work from slopes only if there is no significant geology between the phone and the tower. It can be difficult or impossible to reach 911 even from secondary roads that are surrounded by ridges. It is conceivable that a caller will be able to connect with and listen to a 911 operator, even when that operator can't hear the caller, because 911 transmitters are more powerful than cell phones. While the opposite is rarely the case, if you think your call may be being monitored by someone, it is helpful to be able to supply your exact location, ideally, using GPS coordinates if you are carrying one and can establish them.

If you are injured but still able to walk to a higher elevation or open area (sometimes even moving a short distance will help), your chances for getting through could improve. If you are confident in leaving an injured party, make sure to mark their location with a GPS if you have one. Also try calling local forest rangers' numbers or the number of the nearest state campsite. Under certain conditions it may be possible to reach information (555-1212) or any local land line that can relay a message for you. Hikers are advised never to rely on a cell phone for emergencies. The only "fail safe" wireless communications from any remote area are provided by expensive satellite telephones. Less-expensive satellite e-mail transceivers, such as the Magellan GSC100 (also a GPS unit), will work anywhere.

Global Positioning Sensors (GPS)

Some GPS coordinates are given in the text, primarily for difficult-to-spot trail junctions, or for the sake of orientation afield, but it is not necessary to carry a GPS in order to use this book, or even to travel safely and accurately in the Catskills.

However, with the introduction of AMC's Catskill Forest Preserve map, which was created by hikers carrying GPS units that recorded coordinates every five seconds, it is now possible to navigate the Catskills off-trail very accurately with your handheld GPS unit. While it has always been possible to mark your location, create legs, and navigate to known coordinates in the forest preserve using existing maps for reference points, the new AMC map makes it possible to program coordinates lifted from the map itself. With the introduction of this map, accurate map-to-land GPS navigation in the Catskills has been made possible.

Anyone can afford a GPS these days, and they are very useful tools. Proficiency comes with practice, and there is a good deal to learn about the GPS. Carry a compass to back up your unit. Carrying a set of spare batteries is advised.

Bring a Compass

Even if you plan to stay on marked trails in the Catskills, it is still advisable to carry a compass. Not only will a compass help you to verify directions you may question or help you find your way back to a trail you have wandered away from, a compass will aid in your identification of landmarks, which adds to the fun of hiking. The best compasses for the identification of unknown peaks is an orienteering compass, the kind with a flip-up sight that enables you to take bearings with about a two degree error or less. In using the book's bearings you will be able to identify points that are identified in the text. All bearings are given as magnetic. If you plan to navigate over land with your compass, be sure to correct for declination (13 degrees W).

Binoculars

A pair of binoculars will add significantly to the enjoyment of your trips to the mountains and to many other places as well. Chances are, the field glasses or monocular that you already own will suffice. Older generation hand-me-downs, typically porro prism designs (the ones with the two offset barrels) in those sturdy leather cases are very heavy while the newer, compact roof prism models (two single straight barrels) are both powerful and relatively inexpensive.

There are many advantages to owning a good pair of binoculars—from identifying the elusive hermit thrush on Slide Mountain to watching an eagle or a turkey vulture close-up. The ability to locate many of the landscape features identified in the text, especially those that are not visible with the naked eye, will give you a much better sense for regional geography than you will experience without magnification.

Binoculars can also be an enjoyable and frequently convenient addition to your multiuse pursuits, identifying wildlife and peaks on your cross-country, biking, and paddling trips. For hiking, you can see all you want with 8 x 21mm to 10 x 25mm magnification, still staying within the very light 6–10 oz. range.

Trekking Poles

Hikers have been catching on to the advantages that trekking poles have to offer. They help you to travel faster, easier, safer, and with less fatigue. In icy conditions, they increase your stability. Descending, they'll help save your knees. During ascents, they'll give you a little extra push and will contribute to upper-body tone during ascents, making a hike more of a "total body" form of exercise. For traversing across slopes, adjustable poles can be adapted to the angle of slope. Poles are a great advantage during slippery stream crossings. They can be used as tent and tarp poles.

Adjust your poles according to the slope and your comfort level. For climbing, use a shorter length. For descents, a longer adjustment will give you increased options for support points. For walking across a slope, make your downhill pole longer. For hiking on the level, adjust your poles so that your forearm is parallel to the ground when you're holding the grip. Once you get used to traveling with poles, you will want them on every hike, particularly in winter. A day pack with ski slits or compression straps will come in handy during times when you want your hands free. Bear in mind that trekking poles can at times contribute to environmental impact in sensitive areas.

Snowmobiles

On occasion you will encounter snowmobiles, although on most of the trails described here they are illegal. The state has designated carefully surveyed trails within the forest preserve, reforestation and wildlife management areas, and areas in state parks for snowmobile use. New laws and prohibitions set forth by the legislature have been designed to minimize the harmful effects of the snowmobile on the environment. Because the misuse or overuse of the snowmobile on public lands can lead to more restrictive regulations, it is important that as a forest-preserve user and citizen you report any violations.

Here are some regulations you should be aware of in regard to snowmobiles:

1. All snowmobiles used in New York State, with few exceptions, must be registered by the Department of Motor Vehicles, Bureau of Marine and Off-Highway Vehicles. In conjunction with the registration, it is necessary to have three-inch numbers displayed on each side of the cowling in a contrasting color.

2. Snowmobiles may be operated on forest preserve land only DEC-designated, marked snowmobile trails and on the frozen surface of lakes and ponds that can be reached by traveling over such trails or a public highway right-of-way that reaches or adjoins that body of water.

3. The harassment of wildlife is a misdemeanor, and violators are subject to fines of from $100 to $200 and/or a jail sentence.

4. Firearms may be carried on snowmobiles; however, rifles and shotguns must be unloaded and broken down or secured in their cases at all times.

Although the state provides that "snowmobile trails and appurtenances should be designed and located in a manner which will not adversely affect adjoining private landowners or the wild forest environment."

On the brighter side, existing snowmobile trails above 2700 feet will be closed, except for the High Peak, Roundtop Trail. However, new trails may be constructed to replace "any existing mileage of snowmobile trail or open roadway lost in the designation of wilderness or lost due to elevation limitations." This means that new-trail cutting "may occur where necessary to create desired loops."

Northeast Catskills

The Northeast Catskills are made up of six wild-forest areas (Windham High Peak, Blackhead Range, North Mountain, Kaaterskill, Hunter Mountain, and Phoenicia–Mount Tobias Wild Forest) and two wilderness areas (Indian Head and West Kill Wilderness Area). Travelers on the NYS Thruway will pass close to this region and marvel at the abrupt rise of the land from 500 ft. to 2500 ft. and then at the recessed peaks of nearly 4000 ft. These sudden, upper elevations are often established within a mile or two of the valley floor. This great, seemingly impenetrable wall of sandstone is the Escarpment, the edge of the great inland plateau that eroded into a peneplain 17,000 years ago, leaving a high, hilly region dissected by rugged cloves (clefts), ragged defiles, and the streams, hollows, and hemlock forests that mystified and delighted newly independent America's literary and artistic imagination—and in many important ways forged its new national identity. It was here in the Northeast Catskills that a unique American concept of wilderness was born, as well as the interest in its preservation that naturally followed.

The region is interesting to hikers in part because of those very same things that drew early visitors to the mountain houses—the forest scenery, "the sublime," and "the picturesque"—but more practically because of this sudden altitude gain. After only a short distance, hikers can reach relatively remote areas, devoid of the less errant public that walkers of the past delighted in. These altitude gains give way to the high plateau itself, where backpackers can enjoy long ambles over undulating terrain for days on end, reveling in far-reaching vistas amid the same lonely haunts that bewitched Rip Van Winkle and astonished Natty Bumppo.

The stories of the Catskill trails are the stories of early American civilization itself, and perhaps nowhere else in the range does this hold more true than in the northeastern mountains, the first of the Catskills to be visited by post-revolutionary leisure-class society, and the region that had the largest impact on the concept of wilderness in the American mind.

After the disappearance of the paleolithic hunters who followed large animal herds with the retreating ice age, the hunter-gatherers arrived, settling to the north and east of the Catskills, leaving evidence in the earth of their 7000-year occupation. These people—bands of Delaware Indians called the Lenne Lenape—were forced into the west after the initial contact period following a series of broken treaties and land grabs, while colonial expansion claimed the best of their riparian and agricultural lands.

After the British surrendered to the Colonists in 1781, valley settlers took a more confident attitude toward commercial investment, and many farmers and business people began to prosper. With the rise of economical river transportation, westward expansion began, roads penetrated the Escarpment, and bluestone-quarrying and tanning industries took hold in the Catskills. These early industries cut the first roads into the hills, and it is on many of these roads that hikers will travel today, oftentimes the roads passing the very quarries that made them. At one time this area was an unimaginable matrix of paths and skid trails, the vast majority now reclaimed by nature.

As the Catskills were denuded of their hemlocks and the quarries came to a sudden stop with the introduction of Portland cement, the Catskills enjoyed a welcome respite from ruin. By 1850 the tourism age was in full swing in the Northeast Catskills. The hotel industries created roads as well—and were the first to establish (unselfconsciously) leisure trails for walking—America's first true hiking trails, evolved from a simple love of nature. By 1840 there were more than a hundred steamships in service between New York and the Catskill Landing, providing round trips of under ten hours, a fact that suddenly—and for the first time—made weekend outings to the Catskills a reality for New Yorkers.

Innumerable foot and carriage trails emanating from the hotels survive today as marked state hiking trails. Scenic destinations in the northeast Catskills are the same places walkers visited as early as 1810. The Escarpment Trail was a marked trail for at least part of its present-day length as early as 1825. And it was the remarkable landscape scenery that drew visitors to the mountain houses. Figures such as Washington Irving, Thomas Cole, James Fennimore Cooper, and William Cullen Bryant drew enough attention to the Northeast Catskills that most of the visitors to the mountain house were being turned away as early as 1824—there weren't enough accommodations. The members of the Hudson River School of Landscape Painting set up easels on the ledges of the northeast mountains, immortalizing the views into a new romantic vision of wilderness.

But it is a romantic notion to suggest that the trails of the Northeast Catskills were formed in the footsteps of early laborers and artisans alone. An active policy of acquisition followed the state's creation and protection of the Catskill Forest Preserve when on May 15, 1885, Governor David B. Hill signed into law the requisite that "all the lands now owned or which may hereafter be acquired by the State of New York . . . shall be forever kept as wild forest lands . . ."

Hikes into most of the Northeast Catskills can be conveniently staged from the North/South Lake Public Campground in Haines Falls and from the Kenneth L. Wilson Public Campground east of Mt. Tremper. Camping opportunities in the forest preserve itself are plentiful. Two of the region's trails, the Devil's Path and the Escarpment Trail, provide the opportunity for multiday outings. The North/South Lake area has a handful of the best day hikes in the Catskills, all from the convenience of an established campsite. All of the trails in the region are hilly and wild. Services near trails are few, and water is scarce at upper elevations in all of the Catskills. Forest rangers are always willing to answer questions and provide advice on trip planning.

North Mountain Wild Forest

East

The North Mountain Wild Forest area (combined with what is now the North/South Lake Intensive Use Area), and the northern extremes of the Kaaterskill Wild Forest are two of the most popular hiking destinations in the Catskills, and has been for nearly two-hundred years. Scenic vistas here are among the best and most numerous in the Catskills. This area is the location of today's popular Escarpment Trail, which runs north and south through the forest and is one of the oldest continuously used recreational trails in the country (sections of this trail were marked as early as 1810 and used earlier by hunters, trappers, and surveyors). This area is the location of Kaaterskill Falls, postcolonial America's most famous landmark destination hike, and the Catskill Mountain House, America's first luxury resort hotel, which appeared on the wild ledges of Pine Orchard in 1824. The falls themselves received national attention with the publication of James Fennimore Cooper's *The Pioneers* in 1823—the same year the Catskill Mountain House was under construction. With the advent of Transcendentalism as espoused in the philosophies of William Ellery Channing, Ralph Waldo Emerson, and, later, Henry David Thoreau (Thoreau and Channing visited Kaaterskill Falls in the 1840s), the act of walking gained popular acceptance from its previously much lower status: only the poor were doomed to walk—the rich were meant to ride in carriages. The revolution in culture and the arts that followed had everything to do with what the Mountain House depended on for its success and survival—the world-class scenery that can still be enjoyed today not only in the classic artworks of the Hudson River School of Landscape Painting, but from the North Mountain area's historic trail complex.

None of the mountain hotels remain standing today, but much of the extensive matrix of garden paths, carriage roads, and famous lookouts survive to enchant modern hikers. The visitors of old left their marks here and there, many are still visible. As they languished over scenic outcroppings and read aloud from Cooper, Wordsworth, and Bryant, many chose to carve their names or even images into the precipice, and some of the results are astonishing for both their antiquity as well as their aesthetic refinement. Incredibly, some faded specimens at Kaaterskill Falls survive from 1810.

Hikers planning a thorough investigation of the North Mountain and North Lake Trail systems will find the public campground at North Lake ideal. Camping is legal and close at hand in the wild-forest area outside the posted recreational-area boundary, both north and south of the campground intensive-use area.

Escarpment Trail (ET)

Distances from Schutt Road (Escarpment Trail trailhead) to East Windham (terminus)

- *to* Sunset Rock: 1.7 mi., 40 min.
- *to* Inspiration Point: 1.9 mi., 50 min.
- *to* Boulder Rock: 4 mi., 1 hr. 45 min.
- *to* North/South Lake Campsite: 4.67 mi., 3 hr.
- *to* North Point: 7.13 mi., 2 hr. 20 min.
- *to* NY 23 East Windham 23.19 mi., 7–10 hr.

This popular, scenic, and fascinating 23-mile-long trail begins outside the entrance to the North/South Lake Public Campground. Many hiking parties use the ET for extended weekend backpacking trips, going as far north as the Windham High Peak and Blackhead Range Wild Forest areas. If a shuttle is arranged at the trail's northern terminus, the ET can be hiked in a weekend. Lean-tos and water are scarce. The section of trail between Schutt Road and North Point is very popular with day hikers, most of whom access the trail from the North/South Lake Public Campground. Day hikers seldom travel beyond North Point if they're entering the trail from the south; they seldom travel south of Blackhead Mountain if entering the trail from the north. In between is a long section of remote territory.

Parking for the ET is provided in the Schutt Road Corral parking area, 300 ft. south of CR 18 (North Lake Road) on Schutt Road (sometimes seen as "Scutt"). Forest Preserve Access Parking signs appear on the corner. A small corral located in the southwest corner of the parking lot is available to equestrians riding the Sleepy Hollow Horse Trail, which originates here as well. A signboard, maps, and camping/day-use information is posted (ticks, *Giardia,* bears, sanitation, etc.). The trail begins immediately opposite the parking area on the east side of Schutt Road, where it enters dense woods.

Mixed hardwood and hemlock shroud the heavily worn and often muddy trail. Descending easily, the trail is bordered by tall white pine, mixed hardwoods, and small spruce trees. The trail's surface improves, and at 0.4 mi. it crosses two old railroad beds. The first was the Catskill and Tannersville Railway, which discontinued service in 1915. The second, more established bed (ties are still visible), belonged to the Ulster & Delaware Railroad's Kaaterskill Branch, which remained in service until 1940.

At 0.45 mi., cross lively Spruce Creek (South Lake's outlet) on a footbridge, and ascend easily. Past the bridge 200 feet, an obvious but unmarked side trail leads left (north) away from the ET, and in a few moments arrives at the old bluestone laundry house and its barely detectable reservoir that once served the Catskill Mountain House. It appears as if there was a railroad siding and deck here, now in ruins and filled with 1940s vintage junk. Bits of coke can still be found on the trail. This is the oldest structure surviving from the heyday of the great hotels. Return to the Escarpment Trail.

The trail continues along a gentle uphill grade, crossing a small footbridge and rising to a four-way trail junction, 0.5 mi. from the ET's Schutt Road trailhead. The ski trail to the left (north) is marked with ski trail disks (yellow) but is unsigned. It gently ascends 0.5 mi. to South Lake Road. Straight ahead, the red Schutt Road Trail and yellow horse trail ascend. The blue Escarpment Trail continues to the right (south).

The trail turns right (west), descending through a barrier gate and over an eroded surface. A caboose, seen across Spruce Creek on a private parcel, once belonged to the Delaware and Hudson Railroad. This area at the south end of Schutt Road was also the site of the historic Glen Mary (boarding) Cottage, named for Mary Scribner (as was

Mary's Glen). A cottage and sawmill in this location (assumed to be the Scribners') were mentioned in the private journals of Henry David Thoreau, who visited the area in 1844.

Impact here has prompted the DEC to post no-camping signs. Beneath a hemlock-and-maple forest, the trail is road width and within audible range of Spruce Creek, which spills over Kaaterskill Falls 0.2 mi. to the west. Next to a narrow footbridge is the trail register. Registering here is strongly encouraged, because the country beyond becomes more remote and the trails are numerous. Be sure to describe your route accurately. The trail descends, reaching a T, where to the right can be seen the ramparts of a hand-laid, bluestone dam, all that remains of the Scribners' sawmill. Following left (southwest) and climbing, the trail soon flattens through white-birch woods. To the right (west) avoid the herd path (an unmarked trail sustained by hikers) that persists over the older route of the Escarpment Trail, which originated at the base of Bastion Falls on NY 23A and was closed due to intensive use and erosion in the 1980s (see Kaaterskill Falls Trail).

Mountain maple and aster, along with small oak and poplar line the trail as it descends toward Layman's monument, arriving at 1.2 mi. Mountain laurel is profuse at the monument, a significant bluestone obelisk commemorating Frank Layman, a firefighter who perished in the line of duty near this spot in 1900. A cut vista looks northwest into the clove with a view of Hunter Mountain (4050 ft.) and the Molly Smith Lookout on NY 23A, the trailhead parking area for the Kaaterskill Falls Trail. The trail ascends easily for a few hundred feet to a rock outcropping with extensive views. Dangerous vertical drops continue from this point, many very close to the trail. From this vantage the first sustained views of Kaaterskill Clove begin. Kaaterskill High Peak (3655 ft.) and Roundtop (3440 ft.) rise above the vast expanse of the northern Kaaterskill Wild Forest. The rugged, parallel ravines dissecting that slope—Hillyer, Wildcat, and Santa Cruz—are made obvious by their waterfalls, landslides, and deeply gouged channels. The precariously perched, cliff-edge homes in nearby Twilight Park (private) are visible to the west of the slide. Both Onteora Mountain (3230 ft.)

and Parker Mountain (2820 ft.) stand to the west. Raptors, mostly turkey vultures but sometimes a red-tailed hawk or bald eagle, can be seen along this stretch during warm weather, soaring the updrafts above Kaaterskill Clove. Even-aged oak and blueberry bushes populate the cliff zone. Isolated stands of large white pine dot the forest below. The trail ascends.

At 1.6 mi., the yellow connector trail to the Schutt Road Trail leaves to the left (north), while the Escarpment Trail continues straight, following the cliff edge. The trail levels, following the edge of Kaaterskill Clove, and reaches Sunset Rock at 1.7 mi. with its treacherous vertical drop. (There is another, more popular Sunset Rock on a spur off the Escarpment Trail beyond Artist's Rock at 5.1 mi.) The trail climbs a steep pitch to a large, open sandstone ledge covered in silt dust, projecting out over the clove above a vertical ledge at 1.9 mi. This is Inspiration Point. These ledges were popular spots for summer boarders, artists, and the literati of the nineteenth century. The trail continues, turning slightly left into the northeast as the view to the east improves. Hardwood forest follows, yielding to one last view from a small rock facing east, known historically as Bellevue. This lookout stands above Harding Road and the southern branch of the Sleepy Hollow Horse Trail. Kaaterskill Clove Lookout can be seen, as well as Indian Head (Point of Rocks). A few undesignated, illegal camping sites appear along the trail around Bellevue. At 2.5 mi. continue straight ahead where the Escarpment Trail joins a short section of the Sleepy Hollow Horse Trail, which comes in from the left (west). The horse trail represents the fastest, shortest route back to Schutt Road from this point. Coneflower grows here, blooming in mid- to late summer. Just 200 ft. ahead, the Escarpment Trail leaves the Sleepy Hollow Horse Trail (at this point a carriage road) and goes left (northwest), uphill, from the T.

At the T intersection with the Sleepy Hollow Horse Trail (and the Long Path), the Escarpment Trail becomes a narrow, rocky trail, covered in loose rubble and bedrock slabs, steadily ascending as it follows the original treadway of Harding Road toward the Hotel Kaaterskill site. At 2.9 mi. and 2250 ft. the trail flattens and assumes the character of the original stage road, and at 3.1 mi. it arrives at an intersection with the Schutt Road Trail.

The Hotel Kaaterskill site lies straight ahead, off the main trail to the north of the intersection. This large hotel, which was reputed at the time to be the largest wood-frame structure in the world, sat atop South Mountain (2460 ft.). A vague herd path leaves the intersection to the north and circles the site, where a few old foundations and dumps are all that remain. Completed in 1881, a kitchen fire burned the hotel to the ground in 1924.

The Escarpment Trail/Long Path continues to the right (northeast) toward Boulder Rock. A short distance beyond the junction, an unmarked trail departs to the left (north), leading downhill to the campground road. The Escarpment Trail is flat through this section. At 3.8 mi. signage is posted at a T where a red cutoff trail provides a shortcut north around Boulder Rock (this cutoff rejoins the Escarpment Trail in 0.2 mi.).

The Escarpment Trail bears right, descending among even-aged oak trees growing above mountain laurel, and passes a "balance rock" off to the right (south) of the trail. Passing Split Rock, a monolith that has fractured away from the bedrock, creating a deep fissure, the trail arrives very soon at a ledge and the large glacial erratic known as Boulder Rock. Old photographs depict the rock (then "Bowlder Rock") with a rustic gazebo perched on top. Good views up and down the Hudson River exist here, taking in a partial view of Overlook Mountain (3150 ft.) to the south. Here the carriage road originating from the Hotel Kaaterskill site ends. Continue uphill easily, at 4.1 mi. passing the red cutoff trail on the left (southwest). Continue straight ahead (north) along the Escarpment Trail.

A very short distance beyond the intersection a steep, unmarked herd trail drops off to the right (east). This is also an early route, once marked, which provided one of the few possible descents through the "Great Wall of Manitou" (the fanciful Native American name given the Escarpment during the American Romantic era). It joins the Sleepy

Hollow Horse Trail west of Palenville Overlook. The Escarpment Trail descends now, through rocky, terracing terrain with views east, as the forest becomes open and boreal. A distinctive rock (Eagle Rock) appears on the left, inscribed with carvings from 1850. The trail descends gradually through an area of moss-laden boulders and thick hemlock, passes the trail register and arrives at Pine Orchard (the pine is gone), the site of the Catskill Mountain House. The only thing that remains of the mountain house is the rear piazza steps, which lay concealed in a nearby thicket. Here there are exceptional views above the Hudson River Valley. Many interesting carvings dating from the early 1800s survive in the ledge stone near the dangerous precipice to the east. The derelict hotel eventually became a safety hazard and was burned by the DEC in 1963.

The Escarpment Trail crosses the clearing to the west, and marking becomes scarce. The old hotel service road (also the road to South Lake Beach) becomes prominent within 200 ft. Watch very carefully ahead as the dirt road forks to the right and turns north. (If you've reached the South Lake Beach parking area, you've gone too far.) Marking reappears at the fork, leading east, where the trail doubles back toward the Escarpment's edge, descending a short section of dirt road through a barrier gate. A trail sign is posted here, immediately south of the Otis Elevating Railway right-of-way, of which nothing remains but a wide scar in the earth. To the left, North Lake is visible and the bath houses, beach, and picnic area are located a moment's walk off the Escarpment Trail to the left (west; yellow markers may be present).

The trail continues north directly across the Otis right-of-way, following along next to the Escarpment. Watch carefully for markers. No trail signs exist on the north side of the Otis right-of-way, and marking is inconspicuous. Hikers using the beach, picnic area, or restrooms can return to the trail from the north end of the beach parking lot, where a yellow spur provides access to the Escarpment Trail. A large trail sign is prominent on the right (east) side of the main campsite road.

NOTE: Day hikers reaching the Escarpment Trail from North Lake Campground can most conveniently park at the public beach and day-use area (day-use fee; cars left overnight in this lot are also subject to cumulative day-use fees, which vary by season). The campground is open from the first weekend in May through the fall foliage season in late October. At all other times, access to the Escarpment Trail is available from outside the main gate (Schutt Road parking area). The North Mountain Trails trailhead is prominent at the North Lake beach and picnic parking area's north side along the campground road. This yellow spur goes east, joining the Escarpment Trail (blue markers) in 0.1 mi.

Follow blue markers as the Escarpment Trail goes north. Views to the east over the Hudson Valley are limited but improve dramatically ahead. The terrain terraces up through broken ledges and rocky flats. At 5.1 mi. the trail reaches Artist's Rock, a small ledge looking east over the Hudson Valley as far east as Mount Everett and its associated ridges in the southern Taconic region.

Continuing north and climbing gently the trail passes Prospect Rock and shortly beyond it the tilted, open crown of Sunrise Rock. The following ascent of Red Hill levels through hardwoods and passes by the western wall of a monolith, buttressed with vertical puddingstone (conglomerate). This was the site of Jacob's Ladder, which at one time scaled the wall to the top of Sunset Rock. The trail continues to the junction with the Sunset Rock Spur Trail, now the safest way to access this scenic landmark (see Sunset Rock Spur Trail).

The Escarpment Trail continues through hardwoods, climbing to Newman's Ledge at 5.8 mi. This exposed, vertical ledge at 2500 ft. is actually an overhang, largely unsupported from beneath. Old carvings on its face reflect its historic popularity. Views to the east are excellent, including the Hudson's two midregion bridges (Kingston-Rhinecliff and Rip Van Winkle); the Escarpment's eastern wild forests; bits of the cultivated lowlands of Ulster, Green, and Albany Counties; and on a clear day, Albany itself. The trail heads north over a rocky surface, climbing terraces through ledgy hardwood and spruce thickets. Circling to the north of a bog at 6.2 mi. and turning west, it reaches the junction with the Rock Shelter Trail, the site of Badman Cave at 6.4 mi.

The Escarpment Trail turns right (north), climbing up across a ledge and into a spruce woods. Another small ledge follows, when at 2700 ft. and 6.6 mi. the trail enters an open bald with views south, of Kaaterskill High Peak, Roundtop, Plateau, and Sugarloaf. Remaining level, the route retreats from its rocky ledges of spruce and pine and exposed rock to enter a shaded transition zone of striped maple, birch, and mountain laurel. The path turns to red clay silt. Flat stones have been placed on the trail in an effort to keep it from becoming too muddy. Following a section of level ground and open hardwoods, the Escarpment Trail meets the Mary's Glen Trail below North Point at 7.0 mi.

Climb steeply. Intensive use has necessitated rerouting and improvement of this section of trail on several occasions. Earlier routes are fenced off and recovering. Following a series of scrambles and ledges, the trail reaches North Point (3000 ft.) at 7.2 mi. This popular scenic destination is a large, open rock shelf 0.5 mi. east of (wooded, trailless) North Mountain itself. On summer days, it can be a busy spot, full of day hikers and, like many of the more accessible scenic locations in the Catskills, European visitors (the Hudson Valley is often referred to as "America's Rhineland"). The views are sensational, moving through the northwest to the southwest. A sliver of Overlook Mountain's summit appears (3150 ft., the firetower is barely visible at 211 degrees, above Plattekill Mountain). The northerly summit of Twin Mountain (3640 ft.) rises between Kaaterskill High Peak and Roundtop. The Shawangunk Ridge is obvious, and it is possible to see the Mohonk Mountain House, Sky Top, and the Hudson Highlands with binoculars. Sweeping views of the valley include several ranges in the tristate area around Mount Everett in Massachusetts. Hikers familiar with that region will be able to pick out Bash Bish, Washington, Alander, Brace, and Mount Everett. (The Appalachian Trail crosses Mount Everett's summit.)

To see the northerly views, move 300 ft. to the northeast of the point through low brush, to open rocks that provide intimate views of the Windham High Peak and Blackhead Range Wild Forests— Thomas Cole Mountain (3950 ft.), Black Dome (3990 ft.), Blackhead

(3950 ft.), Arizona (3400 ft.), Windham High Peak (3524 ft.), Burnt Knob (3190 ft.), and Acra Point (3110 ft.); the latter four destinations are traversed by the Escarpment Trail. Albany is visible with the naked eye on a clear day, as well as the mountains beyond it, in Vermont's Green Mountain State Forest.

Very few day hikers venture beyond North Point. Ahead, the land becomes remote, and there is no water for several miles (see Dutcher Notch Trail). A weathered signpost stands in the exposed rocks of North Point.

Proceeding straight ahead (west), with the North/South Lake viewshed to the left (south) the Escarpment Trail enters patches of woods, for the first 0.4 mi. keeping to the open southerly ledges of North Mountain, where blue-paint blazes guide hikers across bare, rocky flats. Within a short distance the trail crosses a bald of curiously eroded, pockmarked bedrock and arrives at an overlook that resembles a scaled-down, more private version of North Point, complete with the same southerly aspect (only higher) and similar views. From here the trail winds its way up and around low ledges, passing through woods and across open vistas. At 7.7 mi., and the site of a final clearing, approximating the summit of North Mountain (3180 ft.) the trail enters the woods and turns right (northwest) gradually, through mixed hardwoods and extensive red-spruce stands, ascending 240 vertical feet from North Mountain to Stoppel Point (3430 ft.). This diminutive lookout, while small, offers an attractive resting point and a legal camping area (stay back off the trail 150 ft.), with interesting views to the east from a small rock shelf in the spruce.

The trail continues straight, trending northwest, remaining generally level until swinging gradually to the north and passing a cut vista toward the Blackhead Range Wild Forest, and descends past a small plane wreck on the right (east) side of the trail at 9.7 mi. (3400 ft.). This somber visage is one among several aircraft that have fallen victim to not only the Escarpment's very sudden rise from near–sea level to 3950 ft. (Blackhead Mountain), but also to the severe downdrafts that can develop as air masses sweep across the Catskill plateau and into the Hudson Valley.

From the crash site, the trail descends through a forest of large birch and scattered spruce and levels along the Escarpment ridge to 3000 ft., coming upon Milt's Point Lookout, where Stoppel Point, North Mountain, the village of Catskill and the city of Hudson, and several mountain ranges can be seen. Cairo Roundtop is the small hill in the foreground. Albany is at 45 degrees. Bash Bish Falls gorge and Mount Everett can be seen on a clear day.

The trail soon descends and switches back over long, easy grades where the surface is worn to silt mineral soil. A flat ridgetop of cherry, beech, and birch trees follows. After a final, brief descent the trail arrives at the four-way intersection of Dutcher Notch at 11.0 mi., (named for Jim Dutcher, the "guardian spirit" of Slide Mountain and its best-known guide). For summer backpackers, the notch is important for its two nearby water sources. The closest is 0.4 mi. southeast on the Dutcher Notch Trail (yellow), a 10-minute walk downhill. The source is obvious on the right side of the trail, trickling from a ledge into a stone basin. This spring is ordinarily reliable but runs very slowly in hot weather. Groups are better off taking the Colgate Lake Trail southwest 1.0 mi. to the East Kill or one of several (seasonal) creeks that cross the trail in the East Kill watershed area. The nearest reliable source to the north is north of Lockwood Gap on the Black Dome Trail.

Because there are no views from this deep and relatively remote wooded notch, it is seldom visited as a day-hiking destination. The area has seen moderate but increasing use from backcountry skiers and, rarely, mountain bikers coming in from Colgate Lake. Opportunities for camping in the notch are limited, if not poor, but improve ahead on the (under 3500 ft.) flats of Arizona Mountain.

The Escarpment Trail continues straight ahead and rises very steeply to the northwest passing pure spruce stands, yielding to birch. This is about as steep as it gets in the Catskills—nearly 1000 ft. of vertical gain in slightly more than one mile. Most of the rise occurs immediately north of Dutcher Notch and eases as a lookout rock appears to the left (west) at the end of a short spur trail at 11.5 mi. (3100 ft., marked with yellow markers but easy to miss). Sweeping views, west to east include Hunter Mountain, Sugarloaf, Pecoy Notch, Twin, Indian Head, Roundtop, Kaaterskill High Peak, Stoppel Point, and North Mountain, with Parker and Onteora Mountains in the low foreground. The trail continues, offering only limited, seasonal views as the land rises and falls gently on the approach to Arizona's flat-ridge summit at 12.1 mi. Spruce and white birch give way to sparse vegetation across open blueberry balds with patches of goldenrod and reindeer moss. Although higher than many popular Catskill peaks, Arizona Mountain's (3400 ft.) relatively featureless summit and remote position has compromised its name recognition as well as its popularity as a destination hike. However, the mountain's all but viewless summit of flat rocks allows easterly views of the Hudson Valley as far north as Acra Point (3110 ft.). A vague, unmarked herd trail ahead at 12.2 mi. leads west to a view of the East Kill Valley. The trail remains flat along the summit ridge, climbing piecemeal to a viewpoint at 13.0 mi. where graffiti survives from 1902 and includes the etching of a small rising sun (looking east). Ascending, hikers will see a rock painted with the words "Camp Steel, 1936" marking the site where sustained impact from illegal camping becomes evident. From this point the Escarpment Trail ascends to the treed-in, thick balsam summit of Blackhead Mountain (3950 ft.) and the intersection with the Blackhead Mountain Trail at 13.6 mi.

From the junction the Escarpment Trail turns right (northeast) descending steeply and can be hazardous under icy conditions. As the trail turns into the north, a rock appears to the right (east) of the trail, offering views over the Hudson Valley (Cairo Roundtop is the small hill to the right). The trail terraces its way downhill, through birch, balsam, spruce, striped maple, and a ground cover of asters. After a short level stretch through a birch woods, the trail arrives at a well-marked, rocky intersection with the Batavia Kill Trail at 14.6 mi.

The trail continues north, descending slightly into a densely wooded area with a thick fern ground cover. In the middle to late spring, star flower, trillium, spring beauty, and Canada violet appear, and in some areas the trail is profuse with Canada mayflower. Climbing, the path becomes rocky and penetrates a spruce forest with limited views south toward the Blackhead Range. The trail crosses to the east side of the ridge, passing a campsite, closed due to overuse. Northern hardwoods appear and gain in maturity as you travel north and the trail flattens at 3000 ft. in an area where raven nest. Maple takes over becoming a pure stand as the terrain descends almost imperceptibly and the slopes of Burnt Knob Mountain at (3190 ft.) become apparent to the north-north-west. Descending slightly to the easterly side of the narrow ridge as the trail approaches Acra Point a small lookout point is seen. Ascending easily through an area where very thick grass appears in the woods, the trail descends gently to a small, flat-topped boulder on the right (north-east) of the trail at 16.4 mi. This (including the small blueberry bald just ahead) is Acra Point. "No Camping" signs are posted on the sum-mit itself. The interesting feature of Acra Point is that it faces Albany. On a clear day, the large mountain ranges of Vermont can be identified beyond the city. North of Acra Point a viewpoint looking southwest is reached within ten minutes, with views of Blackhead at 190 degrees, Elm Ridge, Burnt Knob, and Windham High Peak. The trail gradually descends 300 vertical feet into the saddle and the junction with the Black Dome Trail (red) at 17.2 mi.

The Escarpment Trail climbs straight ahead into the west, some-times steeply, making its way 350 vertical feet up the southwest-facing side of the ridge, offering only broken views of the Blackhead Range. As the trail levels onto Burnt Knob at 17.4 mi., a poorly marked spur trail leads left through a closed campsite to a ledge with excellent views southwest, including Acra Point, Blackhead, Black Dome, and Thomas Cole Mountains, and the long, flat ridge of Arizona Mountain. Views across the Hudson River include Mount Everett and Bash Bish Mountain. At the westerly edge of Burnt Knob, the trail curves left briefly to the southwest, dropping downhill between two shallow rock overhangs and making its way west again. Hikers will be expecting views to the north from this point (the trail draws close to the north edge of the ridge), which is heavily wooded. These views materialize ahead from a large, flat, rock vista at 18.5 mi. (2900 ft.). Albany and the mountains of the Taconic Range and Green Mountain National

Forest are plainly visible. The trail continues, shifting to the west side of the ridge through thick hardwoods, passing another lookout point on the left of the Hunter Mountain Wild Forest and West Kill Wilderness Area. A better view is soon encountered along the trail from a south-facing spur, with spectacular views of the Black Dome Valley and Windham High Peak.

At 19.1 mi., the trail begins its ascent of the southeast shoulder of Windham High Peak, passing a shallow rock overhang on the right before entering a small, pure stand of beech. Steepening for a short distance, a bald of blueberry bushes and stunted maple is crossed, and the trail continues level into dense hardwoods. Gaining elevation—never too strenuously—the 3500 ft. sign is reached, and within a moment beyond it, Windham's first significant viewpoint at 19.7 mi. From a rock that appears to hang in midair over the Hudson Valley, Albany and views north are again visible, along with the farms and open land of the Schoharie and Mohawk Valleys. To the north, the southern Adirondacks are seen. Large mountain ranges loom beyond Albany and stretch far south, from Mount Snow to Bash Bish. The rock itself is defaced with distasteful, low-grade etchings. At 19.8 mi. Windham's true summit is reached (3524 ft.), where bits of vintage graffiti appear on a stone that has broken away from the bedrock, dating from the mid- to late 1800s. Scattered balsam fir leads the way across the summit area to more isolated views, none of them as grand as the first.

Descending, the trail becomes grassy and worn over mineral soil at 20.7 mi. Wake Robins (purple trillium) appear, and the trail flattens below the 2700-ft. level where a seasonal creek marks the beginning of an extensive sugar-maple forest and grass carpets the ground. Soon the trail walks adjacent to large plantations of Norway spruce, which continue to 2100 ft. The trail penetrates these impressive conifer stands at several points ahead, making this the most attractive trail for day hiking Windham High Peak. Pass through an old stone wall and a settlement area, crossing a mossy bald into another large plantation area. (These forests can be identified from the summit of Blackhead Mountain.) At 22 mi. (2350 ft.), the Elm Ridge lean-to is seen on the left. It too is situated in very attractive evergreen forest and has an expansive, legal tent-camping area to the rear (south). A piped spring is located downhill (south) 0.2 mi. on the adjacent Elm Ridge Trail. Within hailing distance of the lean-to, the trail junction is reached.

The trail leaves the lean-to to the left (south) and within a hundred yards reaches the junction with the Elm Ridge Trail. The Escarpment Trail continues, bearing right (north). From the Elm Ridge saddle the Escarpment Trail follows an attractive, old dirt road to the north, which descends and switches back to the west at a point where an earlier road continues east again before settling into the northwest through hemlock woods. A signboard and trail register are located on the left side of the trail at 22.8 mi. Open fields and poplar appear as NY 23 comes into view. Cross a footbridge within sight of the road at 23.2 mi. Here the trail crosses the road to the trailhead parking area on the north side of NY 23 and at the corner of Cross Road (the Long Path continues northeast to Old Road). This is the northern terminus of the Escarpment Trail. From this point, the Long Path continues north.

Sunset Rock Spur Trail

to Sunset Rock from Escarpment Trail: 0.3 mi., 10 min.

This short (and level) side trip off of the Escarpment Trail to Sunset Rock is the most popular day-hiking destination between North/South Lake Public Campground and North Point, which by popular consensus is considered among the most appealing short hikes in the Catskill Mountains (and when combined with North Point, easily one of the best).

From the Escarpment Trail, 0.87 mi. from the North Mountain Trail's signboard at the north end of the North Lake beach parking area, the Sunset Rock Spur Trail goes right (east). Passing Lookout Rock to the left, the trail bends back to the south, the surroundings shifting from oak and mountain laurel to idyllic pitch-pine flats that approximate the appearance of Pine Orchard, the area where the Catskill Mountain House once stood. Sunset Rock is reached at 0.3 mi. This expansive lookout is fissured with dangerous, deep cracks (caution children against running!). The westernmost (and the deepest) is the

Bear's Den, one of several famous nineteenth-century landmarks. In reality the "den" is a series of labyrinthine, subterranean vaults, most likely harboring only porcupines. Exercise caution, particularly in icy conditions. The views immediately overlooking North and South Lakes, South Mountain (2460 ft.), the mountains to the south, and the Hudson River Valley are spectacular. Kaaterskill High Peak (3655 ft.) and Roundtop (3440 ft.) are most prominent to the southwest. The southerly views of the Shawangunk Ridge feature Sky Top Tower (the ridge juts out to the east of the southerly escarpment) and Overlook Mountain (3150 ft.), roughly 40 miles distant. North Mountain (3180 ft.) is the long ridge to the northwest.

Kaaterskill Falls Trail

to   Kaaterskill Falls: 0.4 mi., 25 min.

Kaaterskill Falls has proven to be one of the Catskills' most popular destinations—at one time this falls was more popular than Niagara Falls. Hikers will find the trail to the falls scenic, easy, and interesting. Recent improvements have made steeper sections of the trail more negotiable. Many people use this trail, especially on weekends, when hikers in search of solitude will chose to look elsewhere.

This trail originates next to Bastion Falls at the hairpin turn on NY 23A, 3.5 miles west of the intersection of NY 23A and NY 32A in Palenville. Parking is 0.2 mi. uphill beyond the trailhead. Exercise extreme caution walking from the parking area to the trailhead along NY 23A.

Locate the trailhead at the destination sign (Kaaterskill Falls, 0.4 mi.) in the deepest part of the hairpin turn on NY 23A. The trail is marked with yellow markers and travels northeast along the banks of Spruce Creek. The path ascends steeply at first, soon leveling through a virgin hemlock forest and arrives at the base of the falls, where large boulders provide excellent viewing of the two-tiered falls, both adding up to 260 ft. The first, higher tier is 175 ft; the lower tier is 85 ft. Behind the lower tier is an area long known as the Amphitheater—a spot that many people have died trying to reach, as they've fallen or slid 85 ft. off the icy, narrow herd trails onto the rocks beneath the second tier. It is also—according to some—the reputed resting place of Rip Van Winkle.

The Escarpment Trail once began at this trailhead on NY 23A and continued from here, climbing the southeastern wall of the gorge to join the present Escarpment Trail. This section of trail is closed due to severe erosion. Presently there is no marked trail access to the top of the falls, but they can be reached legally from the end of Laurel House Road off CR 18, 0.5 mi. west of the North/South Lake Public Campground and Day Use Area.

Rock Shelter Trail

Distances from CR 18 outside North/South Lake Campground main gate

   to Escarpment Trail at Badman Cave: 1.8 mi., 1 hr.

   to North Point: 2.6 mi., 1 hr. 30 min.

Skirting the campground to the northwest, the Rock Shelter Trail provides alternate access to the Escarpment Trail, as well as a quick route to Mary's Glen and North Point from outside the campground gate. It is used by those who wish to avoid paying the campground's day-use fees, or plan to be hiking for several days or more. In this case the Schutt Road Corral trailhead parking area should be used (the campground does offer a minimal "walk-in" fee). If the primary objective is to visit North Point, the Mary's Glen Trail provides the fastest access. This rocky, heavily wooded trail leaves from the north side of CR 18 immediately outside the North/South Lake Public Campground and Day Use Area opposite the trail sign near Schutt Road.

The Rock Shelter trailhead is inconspicuous, but a sign posted directly across the street near the corner of CR 18 and Schutt Road is the best means of locating the trailhead.

Heading north at its departure, the trail quickly turns northeast and continues on a nearly level grade through the boulder-strewn forest northeast toward Mary's Glen. Rocks and roots beneath dense foliage result in a slow pace with no views. At 1.4 mi., the trail arrives at the junction with the Mary's Glen Trail.

The trail continues through the junction, following yellow markers, and begins to ascend. During wet periods, water cascades over ledges to the left and large slabs of bedrock in the trail become slippery, so use caution. The state recreation facility boundary lies on the right (no camping permitted). As the trail gains elevation, hemlock appears as the path becomes a friendlier base of needles. The terrain ahead flattens, becoming amenable (and legal) to campers, and spruce thickets give way to the trail junction at Badman Cave, which can be found to the left of the junction. It is not really a cave, as the name implies, but a rock overhang, portions of which have collapsed next to the trail. This is the junction with the Escarpment Trail (blue), which at this point is also the Long Path.

Mary's Glen Trail

Distances from North/South Lake Campsite Road

- *to* Mary's Glen: 0.26 mi., 25 min.
- *to* Escarpment Trail: 1.3 mi., 45 min.
- *to* North Point: 1.5 mi., 1 hr.

A popular but very short hike to a small glen and waterfall (Ashley Falls), the Mary's Glen Trail is also commonly used as an alternate route or loop connection to North Point, although most hikers use the more scenic Escarpment Trail from the bathing-beach parking area. The trail begins inside the North/South Lake campground, 0.8 mi. from the main gate along the north side of the main campsite road. Park at the designated parking area, and walk back (west) approximately 100 yards along the road to the trailhead, just west of Ashley Creek, where signs are posted.

Following the western fringe of a small wetland and beaver meadow—filled with wildflowers by midsummer—the trail is sometimes overtaken by Ashley Creek. Within a few hundred feet, the trail passes the register in a mixed forest of hemlock and hardwoods, at 0.25 mi. reaching a yellow spur that branches right. The spur ends a few hundred feet ahead, at the base of Ashley Falls, where a huge pile of broken stones has fallen away from the streambed above. Small but vigorous in the spring, the falls dry up as warmer weather arrives. Return to the red trail, which bears right and climbs minimally into the glen itself, crossing above the falls to enter a birch-and-hemlock wood. The forest type shifts as the trail gains elevation, revealing the slow, partial recovery of an extensive red-spruce stand (once considered the finest in the state) that was clear-cut during WWI to manufacture aircraft. The trail remains rocky but footing becomes easier as the path approaches the junction with the yellow Rock Shelter Trail at 0.6 mi.

Bearing left (northwest), the trail continues through the junction (250 ft.), leaving the Rock Shelter Trail to the left slightly farther ahead. Wet ledges and lush forest characterize the area. The trail ascends gently, soon becoming level in a poorly drained area that sometimes remains wet for extended periods. Climbing again, the trail arrives at the junction with the Escarpment Trail. North Point is to the left (north); the North/South Lake campground is to the right.

Schutt Road Trail

Distance from Escarpment Trail

to Kaaterskill Hotel site: 1.1 mi., 30 min.

The Schutt Road Trail begins off the Escarpment Trail, 0.5 mi. from Schutt Road Corral at the four-way intersection of the Escarpment Trail and the nordic ski trail, just east of Spruce Creek. Part of the old carriage-road system dating from the hotel's heyday, it provides a short, uphill walk to the Kaaterskill Hotel site, where nothing remains but a few stone foundation ramparts. This is the shortest trail route to the Kaaterskill Hotel site, the Catskill Mountain House site, and the North Lake state campground beach and picnic area. Using the yellow spur trail, ahead 0.25 mi. on the Schutt Road Trail, it is also the shortest way to Sunset Rock and Inspiration Point.

Following red markers, the Schutt Road Trail heads uphill on a dirt carriage road. In some areas, the road is reinforced with original stonework, and the soft silt soil washes out occasionally. At 0.25 mi.

from the junction, a connector trail (yellow) turns to the right (south), joining the Escarpment Trail in 0.5 mi.

Following red markers, the trail continues through red oak that nearly tunnels overhead. State recreational facility boundary (SRFB) postings appear to the left (north). No camping is allowed within the SRFB. At 1.0 mi., the Schutt Road Trail ends at a four-way trail junction. Here, an unmarked trail going straight ahead circles the Kaaterskill Mountain House site. From the knoll (South Mountain, 2460 ft.) where the hotel stood, the view that made it famous no longer exists. At this intersection, the Schutt Road Trail joins the Escarpment Trail.

Sleepy Hollow Horse Trail

Distance from yellow connector trail joining Schutt Road Trail and Escarpment Trail

   to Escarpment Trail (Long Path): 0.7 mi., 20 min.

   to Shorey Point: 0.8 mi., 25 min.

   to Palenville Overlook: 2.8 mi., 1 hr.

   to Bogart Road (via Old Mountain Turnpike): 6.8 mi., 3 hr.

The Sleepy Hollow Horse Trail system begins at Schutt Road Corral (the Escarpment Trail trailhead), just outside the North/South Lake State Campground and Day Use Area's main gate, on CR 18. It provides the shortest route to scenic Palenville Overlook—and is the route of choice for backcountry skiers and experienced mountain bikers who are heading downhill to Palenville on either the Old Mountain Turnpike or Harding Road sections of the horse-trail system (both of these trails are very rocky at lower elevations).

The trail follows the Escarpment Trail to the Schutt Road Trail, reaching the latter at 0.5 mi. At 0.75 mi. the trail turns right (south) onto the yellow connector trail. At 0.95 mi., the horse trail leaves the connector trail to the left (east) and is from this point designated as a single-use trail (distance and time begin here). This initially flat and very attractive section of the Sleepy Hollow Horse Trail system is a multiuse trail used by hikers, skiers, and mountain bikers. The trail goes through an oak-and-laurel forest until, at 0.7 mi., it turns left (northeast) onto the Escarpment Trail for only a few hundred feet (also called the Harding Road Trail at this point). Signage is posted at the junction of the horse trail and Escarpment Trails.

The trail continues straight through this junction (northeast), arriving at Shorey Point (0.1 mi.), a one-time scenic location that has become heavily wooded. From this Y, the Harding Road, also part of the Sleepy Hollow Horse Trail system, descends to the southwest and is not signed. Trail markers are prolific, and the roadlike trail is wide and self-guiding. Aqua Long Path blazes appear here along with red trail markers.

Continue northeast on the horse trail, toward Palenville Overlook, then descend slightly, crossing a seasonal creek. At a boulder the trail splits—coming together again a short distance ahead. A few unmarked side trails appear as the trail narrows and flattens out. A descent follows and the trail switches back steeply over loose stone, arriving at a T at 2.3 mi. Snowmobile markers appear on the horse trail at this point.

The trail turns right (southeast) toward Palenville Overlook, remaining flat and narrow as it follows along the edge of a high, wooded ledge, arriving at the overlook at 2.8 mi. At this writing, a picnic table, fireplace, and designated campsite exist at Palenville Overlook, an area used on a fairly regular basis by pack-tripping parties from a nearby horse ranch. In spite of multiuse exposure, the level of impact at this site is surprisingly low, and few hikers visit the area. A short path south through a stand of pine reveals Palenville Overlook and excellent views over Kaaterskill Clove and the Hudson Valley. Vertical drops here are high and dangerous, so use caution. To the right at the same elevation is another lookout, known as Point of Rocks or Indian Head— the latter name for its profile as seen from Kaaterskill Clove. Shelving rocks, pitch pine, blueberry bushes, and dwarfed oak characterize the overlook. Kaaterskill High Peak (3655 ft.) and Roundtop (3440 ft.) command the southern skyline above the extensive forests on their northern slopes. A large piece of the Hudson Valley, from the lower Taconic region to the Hudson Highlands, sprawls across the southeast.

The trail hairpins back on itself in a tight loop, following markers to the left (east), downhill through a small pine grove. Within a few hundred feet the trail curves left, heading north. Marking is adequate. A small unmarked trail to the right leads to another ledge and an interesting old foundation—the former site of Halfway House, which at one time took in summer boarders. Hikers have assembled stone seats facing the sweeping valley views at the site where a small boarding cottage once stood.

The trail continues to the north on an even elevation along an oak-and-laurel-wooded terrace, heading north-northwest to a point north of the previous trail junction at 3.0 mi. Turn right (north). The terrain remains flat with only a minor descent as the trail approaches the Otis Elevating Railroad grade, where a cable railway (built 1892) climbed the Escarpment, bringing guests to the Catskill Mountain House and connecting with the Catskill and Tannersville Railway to points west. Nothing remains of the elevating railway but its abandoned right-of-way. The trail goes north beyond the railroad grade and climbs, switching back hard and steeply into the southwest, and quickly joins the Old Mountain Turnpike on the section known as the Long Level. To the left a 0.25-mi. section of the trail rises to the North Lake campground picnic area and beach. Turning right at 4.5 mi., the trail descends on the wide dirt road.

Descending to the first hairpin turn, winter views of Newman's Ledge appear to the left (west) and Rip's Rocks to the north. Continue the descent on Featherbed Hill, switching back to the south. At the next switchback at 5.5 mi., historically known as Cape Horn, is Little Pine Orchard, the site of a picnic area with a hitching post, fireplace, and picnic table as well as extensive valley views. From the towns of Hudson and Catskill, the panorama swings south across the Taconics, Mount Everett, the Hudson Highlands, and the Shawangunks. The turnpike descends again, over the section long known as Dead Ox Hill, which drops down to the head of Sleepy Hollow and the site of an old tavern ruin (the foundations can still be seen on the left before crossing the bridge). This tavern and rest stop, according to Catskill

Mountain House advertisements, was the fanciful home of Rip Van Winkle. The trail crosses the bridge spanning Stony Brook, turns right (east), passes the trail register, and descends along the brook and its deepening hollow, crossing Black Snake Bridge at 6.4 mi. A pine bluff on the north side of the trail precedes a northward curve in the turnpike, and the trail ends at the west end of Mountain Turnpike Road at 6.8 mi. At the turnpike trailhead, a sign is posted near the barrier gate.

Roadside parking is available to the east of a barn, within sight of the trailhead. Pelham Four Corners is 0.8 mi. east, at the corner of Mountain Turnpike Road and Bogart Road, where trail signs provide directions to the Sleepy Hollow Horse Trail. From the four corners, follow Pennsylvania Avenue right (south) to Bogart Road, and at 0.4 mi. find the horse-trail parking area. NY 23A is 2.0 mi. farther, at Palenville.

Harding Road Trail (Long Path)

to Kaaterskill Clove Lookout: 0.9 mi., 40 min.

to Escarpment Trail: 2.8mi., 1 hr. 20 min.

This trail follows the bed of an old carriage road. In the lower elevations, the old roadbed is still wide and well maintained, but as it rises to the escarpment's upper elevations, it assumes the character of a footpath.

The trail begins in Palenville, 0.2 mi. west of Whites Road on the north side of NY 23A (just before the "Entering Catskill Park" sign). Parking here is possible, but limited. Less-secure parking is available in the DEC-designated parking area on Whites Road, 0.6 mi. north off NY 23A. (Hikers using this lot will walk south through the woods 0.4 mi. to meet the Harding Road Trail and turn west at the junction). Signs at both trailheads are consistently poor in terms of distances and nonexistent for destinations at this writing, but the trails are easily followed, self-guiding, and well established. The trailhead on Whites Road is identified with forest-preserve access signs.

George W. Harding, a wealthy Philadelphia lawyer, built this road to deliver guests to Hotel Kaaterskill, and it remains in good condition today. Railroad engineers considered the project and refused to under-take it—the task was impossible, they said. So Harding hired local men who were familiar with the creation of tanning and quarry roads, and they completed the task in 1880.

From the NY 23A trailhead (watch for aqua Long Path blazes), ascend first northeast, then consistently to the west over a rocky, washout surface. At 0.5 mi., the trail passes the yellow spur trail to the Whites Road parking area and begins to climb. At 0.9 mi., arrive at a scenic bend in the trail known as Kaaterskill Clove Lookout with open views across the Clove of Kaaterskill High Peak (3655 ft.) and Roundtop (3440 ft.). A fireplace and hitching post are found here. At this point the trail is nearly directly beneath Point of Rocks (Indian Head) and Palenville Overlook and poised above Red Chasm. Curv-ing right (north) the trail follows a deep hemlock ravine that drops sharply downhill to the left, and at 1.2 mi. the trail swings left (south-west) through the Gulf, crossing a rugged tributary of Kaaterskill Creek. The ascent is continual but moderate. Above a bowl of terrain historically known as the Amphitheater, the trail turns sharply right (northeast), with ledgy terrain increasing as the road narrows and erodes. At 1.6 mi., water—in season—crosses the trail. The trail rises evenly to Shorey Point at 2.6 mi., meeting the Sleepy Hollow Horse Trail, then turns left, climbing 0.1 mi. to the Escarpment Trail. To the north, the Sleepy Hollow Horse Trail heads toward Palenville Over-look and Bogart Road. Except for Harding Road itself, signs are clear. The Harding Road Trail ends at this point, but the original imprint of Harding Road continues to the Hotel Kaaterskill site, following the Long Path and Escarpment Trails.

Section 2

Hunter Mountain Wild Forest

East

This rugged, steep, and scenic wild-forest area is slated to be joined with the West Kill Wilderness Area, pending approval of the Catskill Park State Master Plan. At just under 11,000 acres, it could qualify as a wilderness area itself, but for the presence of the Hunter Mountain ski area, which precludes this classification. Bounded by Stony Clove Notch and NY 214 on the east, the Hunter Mountain Wild Forest is contained by the northerly Schoharie Creek and the West Kill to the south. The West Kill Wilderness Area lies to the west and south. Due south and across NY 214, it is bordered by the Phoenicia–Mount Tobias Wild Forest, and to the east across Stony Clove lies the Indian Head Wilderness Area, which abuts the forest and is connected to it by the Devil's Path. There are three lean-tos and sixteen miles of trail in a total of six trails (including the Devil's Path).

Many hikers approach Hunter Mountain (4050 ft.), the Catskills' second highest peak, from the Hunter Mountain ski area, using the chairlift and the Colonel's Chair Trail to enjoy a significant distance and elevation advantage over other trailheads. This detail makes the trails around Hunter attractive to backcountry skiers and, on occasion, mountain bikers.

A fire tower is located on Hunter Mountain, north of the true summit. Recently renovated and reopened to the public, it provides an exceptional 360-degree panoramic view. The Department of Environmental Conservation (DEC) plans to staff the tower on weekends during the hiking season, at which times the public will have access to the tower's cab.

This forest area was the center of the Catskill tanning industry, which later gave way to furniture factories and their requisite sawmills. Quarrying, although present, has not been as ambitious here as in the east-lying northern Catskills. Hikers may see evidence of upper-elevation logging operations, especially in the area around Devil's Acre. Extractive resource enterprises in this area gave way to the tourism industry in the Hunter area, as the railroads made an increasing number of rooming houses and small hotels possible. The ski industry is "the mountain top's" largest industry and began with the 1960 construction of the Hunter Mountain Ski Bowl, which has been both an economic boost and an environmental challenge to the area.

Spruceton Trail

   to John Robb lean-to: 2.3 mi., 1 hr. 15 min.

   to Hunter summit: 3.35 mi., 2 hr. 30 min.

   to Becker Hollow Trail: 3.6 mi., 2 hr. 40 min.

The Spruceton Trail (blue markers) begins as a flat, wide thoroughfare, following the Old Hunter Road (originally Jones Gap Turnpike, circa 1880). This trail is a popular approach to Hunter summit (4050 ft.).

From the large trailhead parking area at the east end of Spruceton Road (CR 6), 6.5 mi. from the turnoff at Deep Notch (originally Deer Notch) and CR 42, trailhead signs are located on the left (north) side of the road at a large parking area. The trail begins here. (Another parking area, 0.2 mi. farther southeast, acts as the overflow parking for the smaller Diamond Notch trailhead parking at the extreme east end of Spruceton Road.

At the northeast corner of the parking area, the Spruceton Trail follows blue markers around a barrier gate and within moments Hunter Brook appears on the left (west). This is also a horse trail (yellow markers). Within a short distance, the trail crosses a bridge and begins to ascend. Cross a small stream, hiking uphill and traveling east. Several more stone culverts pass beneath this wide, grassy, well-constructed road. Restricted views open up to the right (southwest) of West Kill Ridge, North Dome, and Sherrill. At 1.5 mi. the trail reaches an intersection where Old Hunter Road continues straight ahead (north), descending into Taylor Hollow onto private lands in the Schoharie Valley. Avoid this unmarked trail. The blue Spruceton Trail turns right here.

Bearing right at the intersection, the trail begins to climb the steepest section of the Spruceton Trail. At 2.2 mi., two large, flat rocks and a hitching post to the right (south) mark a short spur off the main trail, leading one hundred yards to a spring.

Continue past the John Robb lean-to at 2.3 mi. on the left (north) at 3500 ft. Across the trail is a flat, open area with views of Rusk, Evergreen, West Kill, North Dome, and Sherrill. Located in an attractive setting, the lean-to is well positioned to take advantage of the prevailing southwesterly winds. At 2.4 mi., the Colonel's Chair spur trail departs to the left (north), descending to the Hunter Mountain Ski Area and summit lodge. The Spruceton Trail continues straight (east), ascending gently into a dense boreal (evergreen) forest zone.

Flattening out, the trail tends to retain standing water here for several days after periods of rain. A pure spruce forest yields to birch as the trail climbs, leveling again where standing, dead spruce snags loom over a lush and vigorous reproducing forest. The trail straightens, bearing right (south), soon revealing the shoulder of Hunter Mountain. On the left (northeast) a lookout frames the Blackhead Range. The trail crosses more rocky flats before it begins its final ascent to Hunter's summit, where it increases notably in angle and ascends over surfacing bedrock. Just before this incline (approximately 3.0 mi.) a spur leads left (east) 1500 ft. to a spring.

At 3.35 mi., the Spruceton Trail arrives at Hunter's open summit, the location of the fire tower and observer's cabin. Trail signs are obvious on the right (west). Just ahead on the right is the power-line right-of-way, heading downhill (this is not a view spur trail). Horses are not permitted beyond this point.

The panoramic view from Hunter's fire tower is among the most arresting and far-reaching in the Catskills. The western 180 degrees looks very similar to the view from the lookout near the old summit, a 10-minute stroll to the south on the Spruceton Trail (see Becker Hollow Trail for details). To the west are Rusk and Evergreen, Colonel's Chair, and the ski lifts of Hunter. To the north is Windham High Peak and the Blackhead Range. Continuing south is Stoppel Point, North Mountain, Pine Orchard, and South Mountain. North Lake and its beach area are visible, and slightly below and to the right, the great Amphitheater and double cascades of Kaaterskill Falls can just be seen with the naked eye. The Kaaterskill Wild Forest and Indian Head

Wilderness Area are visible. Far beyond on a good day it is possible to observe the Taconics, Berkshires, and Green Mountains. In the west, the mountains of the Big Indian–Beaver Kill Range and hundreds of lesser peaks—named and nameless, crowd the horizon. Although your compass will be rendered useless by the tower's steel frame, if you're fortunate to arrive while an observer is present (DEC plans to staff the tower on summer weekends), the original map and alidade will help to identify the landmarks.

The Spruceton Trail continues straight (south) along the western edge of the clearing, entering the woods through an enchanting section of spruce-fir forest, reaching the old fire-tower site and the junction of the Becker Hollow and Hunter Mountain trails at 3.6 mi. Trail signs are posted here at the end of the Spruceton Trail. Creative opportunities for backcountry ski touring are possible using this trail, possibly combining an ascent of Hunter's summit with a day's telemarking at the Hunter Mountain ski area. It is not uncommon (given a good base and, ideally, a fresh snowfall) for seasoned experts to follow the Hunter Mountain Trail to Devil's Acre, descending the Devil's Path west to Diamond Notch and a shuttle car.

Colonel's Chair Trail

   to Hunter Mountain ski area summit lodge: 1.2 mi., 35 min.

Beginning 2.4 mi. from the start of the Spruceton Trail, the Colonel's Chair spur trail descends from a point just uphill (east) from the John Robb lean-to. It's easy to miss the junction, because at present signs are not ideally placed for hikers coming uphill on the Spruceton Trail. The Colonel's Chair Trail itself is well marked with yellow trail markers, and signs are posted 20 ft. uphill and beyond (east) the junction. The views from "The Chair" (the northern spur of Hunter Mountain) itself are outstanding, offering an unusual contrast to those from Hunter's fire tower. If time allows, this interesting side trip will prove very worthwhile.

At the Colonel's Chair trailhead on the Spruceton Trail, the mileage (1.2 mi.) and elevation change (approximately 450 ft.) from both

Hunter's summit and the Colonel's Chair are nearly identical. A trail sign is located near the spur.

Descending north from the junction with the Spruceton Trail, within ten minutes the trail bears right at the trail register near the edge of a ski trail. Trail signs are scarce hereafter, but the trail is self-guiding until the (discontinued) summit cross-country ski-touring trails begin to confuse things somewhat. These trails are marked with numbers, and occasional signs point to the summit lodge. The trail goes straight (north) and is frequently traversed by multiterrain service vehicles. Tree cover is predominantly stunted hardwood. An easily missed trail arrow is accompanied by a tiny, weathered sign saying "Hunter Mountain, 1 mi." (the actual distance is 2.0 mi.). Descending, the trail approximates a woods road, passing a gravel pit on the left (west) at 1.0 mi., where Rusk's summit can be seen to the west. The trail levels, passing ski lifts on the left (west) side. Soon, the view opens up, and the other-worldly, concrete summit lodge appears, as the trail emerges from the woods near the top of an infamous ski trail. Known as K27, it boasts the steepest vertical drop (of any commercial ski area) in the east. From this ridge—the Colonel's Chair—are views of Hunter's summit and the fire tower. The best views from the Colonel's Chair are from this vicinity, from the picnic tables outside the lodge, from the lodge itself, and from the small gazebo near the top of the chairlift in front of the lodge (the Archer Winsten Monument). The views are far reaching. From the Winsten seat, the long, flat mountain straight ahead (northeast) is North Mountain. The hump to its left is Stoppel Point. Coming down off North Mountain is South Mountain, and the lowest point between the two is Pine Orchard, the location of the erstwhile Catskill Mountain House. Moving left (north) is Blackhead Range, Onteora Mountain, and Jewett Range. Kaaterskill High Peak and Roundtop are in the right (eastern) foreground. Colonel's Chair was named for Colonel William W. Edwards, a successful and influential tanlord who owned most of Hunter, then Edwardsville.

It's possible to take the Hunter Mountain chairlift, or Skyride, in either direction in order to "cheat" on this hike, an outing that would still require a moderately strenuous 4.0 mi. return hike with 1000 ft. of vertical rise (allow 4 hr.). The lift runs on Fridays and Saturdays from late June to September, and on Saturdays and Sundays in September and October from 10 A.M. to 5 P.M. (and times of adequate snow cover). The summit lodge is open for refreshments during these periods. Call in advance or check Hunter's Web page if you plan to rely on the lift (888-HunterMtn; www.huntermtn.com/Skyride.htm).

Becker Hollow Trail

   to Hunter Mountain Trail and lookouts: 2.05 mi., 1 hr. 15 min.

   to Hunter summit via Hunter Mountain Trail: 2.3 mi., 1 hr. 25 min.

Generally recognized as the fastest, steepest approach to Hunter Mountain (4050 ft., the Catskills' second highest), this 2.05-mi.-long trail rises out of Stony Clove, making a beeline for the (old) summit and climbing 2200 vertical feet.

The trailhead parking lot is well identified on the west side of NY 214, 1.2 mi. south of NY 23A, and 1.5 mi. north of the Devil's Tombstone public day-use and picnic area at Notch Lake. At this large forest-preserve access site, wild-forest signs and trail information is posted. This wooded route to Hunter summit enters Becker Hollow before rising steeply into the west. Some of the Catskills' best views lie ahead— the first are seen from the lookouts to the west of the true summit (2.05 mi.), and then from Hunter's fire tower, a short walk to the north of the true summit on the Hunter Mountain Trail.

The trail passes under a solitary, ruined stone archway at the entrance to the old Becker property, crosses open fields, and enters a hemlock woods. It then spans a footbridge, passing an unnamed (private) trail to the right (north). Ahead, off a short, unmarked path to the left (southeast) is an interesting, small concrete dam across Becker Hollow Brook. Following next to the creek, through small hemlock stands, the trail ascends into hardwoods, gradually at first over the rocky base of a tanbark road, and then very steeply. Pass through a small stand of very large spruce trees, with a deep ravine (Becker

Hollow) visible to the left (south). At 1.8 mi., pass the Fire Tower Spur Trail on the right (north).

The trail continues to ascend straight ahead (west) for about 10 minutes to the Hunter Mountain Trail junction. This trail intersection (the end of the Becker Hollow Trail) is where an observation tower and lean-to once stood. Straight (west) through the junction, an unmarked spur leads 300 ft. to a ledge providing a 180-degree westerly panorama, from north to south. Some hikers claim to prefer this lookout's views to the fire tower's. The lookout is the place to practice landmark identification using a map and compass (accurate bearings are not possible from the steel fire tower).

To the south, the Shawangunks are clearly visible, including Sky Top, Eagle Cliff, and Minnewaska State Park. Ashokan High Point is seen in the Sundown Wild Forest. The high peaks lie close to the southwest—Rocky, Lone, Wittenberg, Cornell, Table, Peekamoose, Slide (you can see the slide), Giant Ledge, and Panther Mountain. Diamond Notch and Southwest Hunter lie in the foreground. Mount Tremper's fire tower can be seen at 214 degrees. Balsam Lake Mountain's fire tower can be spotted with binoculars. Doubletop and Graham are also visible. In the foreground are the mountains and ridgeline of the Big Indian–Beaver Kill Range Wilderness Area. Directly in front of you is West Kill with its distinctive pyramidic crown.

Better views, although lacking the solitude of the lookout, are available from the fire tower. To reach it, return to the junction of the Hunter Mountain, Spruceton, and Becker Hollow Trails, and turn left (north), arriving within 10 minutes' time (see Hunter Mountain Trail, Spruceton Trail for details).

Hunter Mountain Trail

to Hunter summit: 1.6 mi., 50 min.

to Hunter Mountain lookouts: 1.35 mi., 40 min.

This upper-elevation connector trail joins the Devil's Path to Hunter Mountain summit and the Spruceton and Becker Hollow Trails. Hikers wishing quick access to the mountain from Stony Clove will find the Becker Hollow Trail (north of the Devil's Path) the fastest route (and also the steepest), unless they elect to take the Hunter Mountain ski lift to the Colonel's Chair Trail to climb Hunter from the Spruceton Trail. However, a loop hike can be taken by combining the Devil's Path, Hunter Mountain Trail, and Becker Hollow Trail if hikers are willing to walk the scenic 1.5-mi. road distance on NY 214 in order to close the loop. Begin from the trail junction of the Devil's Path and Hunter Mountain Trails and turn northeast onto the latter.

The trail is an old, rocky road, ascending easily through a forest of knee-high ferns under birch and spruce-fir. Star flower and Canada lily are common along the trail. Following a pair of switchbacks at 0.9 mi., the trail turns northwest and levels on the narrow summit ridge. At 1.4 mi. the trail arrives at the junction with the Becker Hollow Trail (right). Don't miss the lookout at the end of the spur to the left (west). See Becker Hollow Trail for details.

Fire Tower Spur Trail

to Becker Hollow Trail: 0.35 mi., 20 min.

Located to the north of the fire tower on Hunter Mountain, in the northeastern corner of the tower clearing, this spur trail provides a shortcut to the Becker Hollow Trail. The spur is marked with yellow disks, but is not signed and may take a moment to locate. The trail proceeds on the level through dense balsam, shortly switches back to the north, and drops steeply. Three stone steps are followed by another three, then more as the path swings back to the southeast, passing a large, flat boulder covered with trees. Sparse seasonal views are visible to the left across Stony Clove, as are a few old tin trail disks. Expansive birch woods characterize the trail. Large fir along the trail give way to groves of paper birch and fern, where a few small trickling streams are crossed before the junction with the Becker Hollow Trail is reached.

Diamond Notch Trail

to Diamond Notch: 2.4 mi., 1 hr.

to Diamond Notch lean-to: 2.9 mi., 1 hr. 15 min.

to Diamond Notch Falls: 3.6 mi., 1 hr. 30 min.

to Spruceton Road: 4. 5 mi., 2 hr.

This historic road climbs into the densely forested realms of Diamond Notch, passing scenic Diamond Notch Falls, crossing the Devil's Path Trail, and then joins Spruceton Road in the north.

This trail was developed in 1937 as a backcountry ski-touring trail, but due to slides and forest encroachment, it is a good deal narrower than it was originally, and casual skiers expecting even terrain—or anything resembling a tracked surface—will be sorely disappointed. This is the backcountry—rugged, rocky, unforgiving terrain—but hikers will have no problem following the established trail.

Five miles north of Phoenicia on NY 214, turn left onto Diamond Notch Road. The trailhead parking requires travel over a sometimes difficult rocky section, nearly impossible for two-wheel-drive vehicles, especially in winter conditions. Adding to the confusion, a landowner at the road's end has posted private "No Parking" signs. According to town and state police, Diamond Notch Road is a town road, and hikers are legally entitled to park anywhere along it provided they are not "obstructing movement" along the road. You cannot park off the side of the road on any private land. If conditions allow, drive into the woods at the end of Diamond Notch Road. An unposted lot appears to the left and another farther on, which is the designated trailhead parking area. Here you will find the trail register.

The trail, an old road, follows Hollow Tree Brook on the right. After crossing a wooden bridge, the trail ascends easily, soon crossing another bridge, followed by a steep flight of twenty stone steps that were placed here to avoid a washout. As the trail ascends, the creek is on the left. Ledges appear on the right as the trail gains elevation, and the sense of entering the notch increases dramatically as the trail crosses a relatively treeless slide. Acres of talus appear uphill and down, and the trail is reinforced on the downhill side, having been rebuilt time and again. At an open area midslide are views south-southwest of Slide (4190 ft.), Table (3847 ft.), Lone (3721 ft.), Peekamoose (3843 ft.), Cornell (3860 ft.), and Ashokan High Point (3080 ft.).

An old road descends sharply into the ravine on the trail's left (west) side. The trail approaches its highest point 1.7 miles into the notch, where West Kill (3890 ft.) and Southwest Hunter (3750 ft.) come so close together that you can touch them both simultaneously (in theory). In *The Catskills,* Alf Evers has joked that "a man who wants to make the effort can stand today with one foot on West Kill Mountain and the other on a supporting ridge of Hunter Mountain [Southwest Hunter was not yet recognized as such] so that he may boast ever afterward that he once stood on two mountains at the same time."

Across the notch, on the West Kill side, conifers appear, mostly red spruce. Now the trail crosses the notch, peaks, and begins to descend slightly. Diamond Notch disappears in the scabrous geology of Southwest Hunter Mountain, at a spot near the hemlock-shrouded Diamond Notch lean-to, on the right (east) at 2.9 mi. The shallow, upper elevations of the notch lie in front of the shelter. The trail descends and at 3.6 mi. arrives at Buttermilk Falls (Diamond Notch Falls) on Spruceton Brook. It passes the Devil's Path Trail to West Kill Mountain (3890 ft.) on the left (southwest) before the bridge, and passes it again on the right (northeast) after crossing the creek. In the past, this charming swimming and picnic spot has been overused, but the DEC's suspension of all camping has resulted in its recovery.

The Diamond Notch Trail continues beyond the notch itself, following the blue trail along a dirt road for 1.0 mi., with a creek to the left, arriving at the Spruceton Road trailhead to Hunter Mountain.

Section 3

Blackhead Range–Windham High Peak Wild Forests

East

The Blackhead Range–Windham High Peak Wild Forests will be combined into a single wilderness area with the approval of the Catskill Park State Master Plan, making the combined area in excess of 15,000 acres. What is presently defined as the Blackhead Range Wild Forest—to which the Black Dome Valley Wild Forest was previously annexed—consists of more than 11,000 acres, showcases rugged, steep terrain with a group of peaks that are the third, fourth, and fifth highest in the Catskills (Black Dome, 3990 ft; Blackhead, 3950 ft; Thomas Cole, 3950 ft.). Those with limited time are encouraged to hike Blackhead Mountain from the Black Dome Valley. It is perhaps the area's most popular and scenic day hike. These peaks are distinct landmarks from many of the Southern and Central Catskill trails, as well as from the northern part of the state and the surrounding states, forming the unmistakable skyline silhouette that has been likened to a camel's back. The two smaller peaks to the west on the Black Dome Range Trail are accordingly called the Camel's Hump and the Caudal (the tail). From these trails, hikers can see the Green Mountains, the Berkshires, and even the White Mountains of New Hampshire.

There is one lean-to in the Blackhead Range Wild Forest, west of the escarpment on the Batavia Kill Trail, and opportunities for camping below 3500 ft. are unlimited. Impact on the ridge's more scenic ledges has been a problem in the past, but increased management has resulted in their partial and continuing recovery. The area is very popular with day hikers, particularly the short (steep) hikes to Black Dome and Blackhead Mountains, and the relatively short outing to Burnt Knob (and less frequently, Acra Point) in the Windham High Peak Wild Forest is reached from the Black Dome Range Trail. The Escarpment Trail is very popular with college outing clubs and scout troops, and during the late summer months the hiker will encounter large groups of campers staging in the vicinity of Dutcher Notch and Colgate Lake, many of them having arranged shuttles at either end of the trail, or from its middle miles via the Colgate Lake and Dutcher Notch Trails.

The northern edge of the Catskill Forest Preserve is bounded by NY 23. This area—the Windham High Peak Wild Forest—is the terminus of the Escarpment Trail. Windham High Peak (3524 ft.) has long been a popular day hike and overnight trip, most often approached from the western Escarpment or Elm Ridge trailhead. The Elm Ridge lean-to and the dense, mature Norway-spruce plantations of the westerly approach make this route especially appealing.

Deer and bear reside in this area, as well as the mammals typically found in the northern hardwood forests and spruce-fir summits of the Catskills. Critical habitat identification for threatened or endangered plant and animal species is ongoing. With the possible exception of the Elm Ridge Trail, the unit is not suitable to mountain biking or cross-country skiing. Ridgetop hiking in both the Windham High Peak and Blackhead Range Wild Forest area is remote and dry. Hikers are advised to plan accordingly.

Dutcher Notch Trail

   to Dutcher Spring: 0.4 mi., 10 min.

   to Stork's Nest Road trailhead: 2.0 mi., 40 min.

This trail begins at the 11.0 mi. point off the Escarpment Trail. Part of the original turnpike from the site of old East Jewett to markets in Catskill, the Dutcher Notch Trail descends from Dutcher Notch into the east, providing the quickest egress from the Escarpment Trail's remote middle miles. It is also the fastest access (and one of few easterly approaches) to Dutcher Notch and the Escarpment Trail from the Hudson Valley. The eastern trailhead access point on Stork's Nest Road is seldom used by day hikers, but it does offer a vigorous hike to a scenic lookout point on the Escarpment Trail, 0.5 mi. north of Dutcher Notch (see Escarpment Trail for details). There are trail signs in Dutcher Notch.

From Dutcher Notch, the trail descends along the dirt roadbed, within 0.3 mi. passing the obvious Dutcher Spring on the right. The trail continues downhill, becoming washed out as it turns into the northeast, leaving state land and crossing directly in front of a private residence to the trailhead parking area (small, space is limited) on the right (south) side of Stork's Nest Road at 2.0 mi. Signs are present here.

Colgate Lake Trail

to site of old East Jewett: 3 mi., 1 hr. 30 min.

to Dutcher Notch: 4.25 mi., 2 hrs.

This historic trail, part of the old East Jewett–Catskill Turnpike, penetrates the dense wilderness of Blackhead Wild Forest, passing open fields, beaver ponds, and the site of an abandoned settlement. It provides unusually scenic vistas of the Blackhead Range. The trail is used frequently by cross-country skiers and occasionally by mountain bikers.

The Colgate Lake Trail is easily reached from Tannersville. Heading north on CR 23C, pass the elegant historic summer colony houses and gardens of Onteora Park, where Mark Twain summered at the height of his literary fame. At the intersection with CR 25 (by the stone Onteora Chapel), where there are good views of the Devil's Path mountains, bear left (northwest).

Turn right (east) 3.1 mi. from Tannersville, onto CR 78 in East Jewett. At 4.6 mi., pass Colgate Lake (public, state-owned), and a large white-pine forest to the right. At 5.0 mi., the forest-preserve-access parking area is on the left (north) of CR 78. Trail signs are prominent.

The trail heads north out of the parking lot through an open field with outstanding views of the Blackhead Range and the western slopes of the escarpment. Soon the East Jewett Range, Onteora, and Parker Mountain come into view. The trail enters the woods 1000 ft. from the parking area, passing the trail register and evidence of old farmsteads' stone walls and foundations. The trail becomes wide and flat, gradually turning to the east. White birch gives way to dense second-growth trees (which spring up after logging or fire), with stands of skinny hardwoods appearing throughout this logged-over tract. Watch yellow arrows closely as the trail turns left, skirting a private inholding (lands completely surrounded by state land) at 1.2 mi. and crossing the small inlet that feeds Lake Capra (private). After fording the creek, the trail rises out of a shallow ravine and crosses a woods road, turning left (north) as it joins another woods road at 2.4 mi. and a junction marked by a yellow trail arrow. The trail ascends slightly and swings 90 degrees to the right (east, trail arrow) at the edge of a small clearing. It then descends as it turns southeast to skirt a wet area before entering groves of large oak mixed with maturing hemlock.

Continuing level and well marked, the trail crosses a footbridge that drains a large beaver pond in dense hemlock over the East Kill. Following to the south of the wetland the trail again crosses the East Kill over a bridge, soon thereafter passing a ruined, disused stone arched bridge to the left of the trail. The trail bends to the right here, through a sugar-maple stand, passing the wreckage of a vintage auto-mobile. At 3.0 mi., at the edge of an open field and the reclaimed orchards of old East Jewett, the trail passes the site where a thriving farm community once existed. Views from the clearing are good, including Arizona Mountain, Dutcher Notch, Blackhead, Black Dome, and Thomas Cole.

The trail turns hard to the right (east), following the old road, and begins to climb through pine-and-maple woods, passing a little glen and mini-waterfall on the right (south). Scree slopes and mossy rock ledges follow as the trail climbs gradually up to the four-way inter-section with the Escarpment Trail and Dutcher Notch Trail in Dutcher Notch (2550 ft.) at 4.25 mi. This trail has proven popular with back-country skiers over the year, and is perhaps most attractive in winter, when it is possible to explore the beaver meadows and look for signs of bobcat, which are plentiful just west of the notch. (Hundreds of footprints can be seen after snowfalls.)

An 8.0 mi. round-trip, this is a serious day outing both for hikers and skiers. Enjoy the steep descent of this historic road as it continues along on the Dutcher Notch Trail, dropping 1300 ft. in 2.5 miles to provide a fast, narrow, and demanding ski tour. This requires expert-level ability, metal-edged backcountry skis, and the usual cautious winter preparations.

Blackhead Mountain Trail

to Blackhead Mountain lookout: 0.4 mi., 25 min.

to Blackhead summit: 0.6 mi., 45 min.

This short trail (yellow markers) begins in Lockwood Gap and rises to the east between Blackhead and Black Dome Mountains to the summit of Blackhead (3940 ft.). There are no destination signs for Blackhead Mountain in the gap at this time (see Black Dome Range Trail for additional information).

Heading east, the trail begins to ascend immediately out of Lockwood Gap, soon steepening through a section of scenic terraces, arriving at a popular lookout with broad views to the west that are considered among the Catskills' very best by knowledgeable hikers. West Kill Mountain (3880 ft.) is at 248 degrees, seen rising over the top of the Hunter Mountain ski slopes. Hunter's fire tower is visible. The high peaks, including Slide, Table, Cornell, and Wittenberg are seen. To the east of Hunter, the terrain drops steeply into Stony Clove Notch, rises to Plateau Mountain, drops again into Mink Hollow (where Mount Tobias rises in the distance), then Sugarloaf, Pecoy Notch, Twin, Indian Head, and Overlook. Roundtop and Kaaterskill High Peak and the mountains of the Indian Head Wilderness Area lie to the south. For those interested only in scenery, there is no use in proceeding any farther. The trail climbs steeply, relenting above the 3700-ft. mark where balsam becomes thick. Blueberry bushes and lilies gone to seed appear here in late summer, where red clusters of bunchberry give the trail a festive air. The summit is a viewless bald enclosed in a dense evergreen pocket about 20-ft. square. Here the Escarpment Trail goes north to the Batavia Kill and south to Dutcher Notch.

Batavia Kill Trail

to Batavia Kill lean-to: 1.3 mi., 35 min.

to Escarpment Trail: 1.6 mi., 50 min.

to Blackhead summit: 2.6 mi., 1 hr. 45 min.

The Batavia Kill Trail provides access to the Escarpment Trail and the Blackhead Range. It is most frequently used by hikers to complete a loop hike over Blackhead Mountain. The trail, like others in the vicinity, is characterized by steep climbs and deep forest cover. The area is very popular with backpackers and day hikers.

From CR 40 in the village of Maplecrest, turn right (east) onto Big Hollow Road (CR 56), passing farms and scattered orchards. At 2.2 mi., the road turns to dirt, soon after which a section of the Black Dome Range Trail leaves to the left (north). Continue another 100 ft. to the end of the public section of Big Hollow Road to the trailhead parking area. Trail signs are comprehensive and the trail system is very well marked. For the first 0.5 mi., the Batavia Kill Trail and Black Dome Range Trail share the same route. Signs are posted in the Batavia Kill trailhead parking area.

Red and yellow markers lead into the woods to the east. Pass the trail register on the right and cross the Batavia Kill. Ascend easily along the imprint of a dirt road through mixed hemlock and hardwood forest. Soon the trail ascends away from the kill, narrowing to the character of a footpath. Cross the kill again and shortly thereafter arrive at a junction and the confluence of creeks where the Black Dome Range Trail comes in from the southwest.

Cross the kill, bearing left on yellow markers. Maturing hardwoods, large maple, fern, and oxalis characterize the trail to the lean-to, positioned near the headwaters of the Batavia Kill. This kill frequently is running at this elevation (or slightly lower) late into the summer. Continuing above the lean-to the trail assumes a more alpine character, where spruce and painted trillium appear. The trail levels at its junction with the (blue) Escarpment Trail.

The Batavia Kill Trail is also used for its lean-to and for completing the popular loop hike over Blackhead Mountain. Both approaches (the Escarpment Trail from this point, and the Black Dome Range Trail via Lockwood Gap) are extremely steep in their upper elevations.

Elm Ridge Trail

to Elm Ridge lean-to: 1.05 mi., 35 min.

to Escarpment Trail: 1.1 mi., 30 min.

to Windham High Peak via Escarpment Trail: 3.3 mi., 2 h

The Elm Ridge Trail offers the shortest, most attractive route to Windham High Peak via the Escarpment Trail. From Maplecrest village, follow CR 40 to CR 56 (Big Hollow Road). Turn left (west) onto Peck Road and follow trail signs (posted at the intersection) 0.8 mi. to the trailhead parking area. Signs are posted here.

The trail leaves from the north side of the parking lot and passes the trail register. It enters the woods, follows yellow markers, and proceeds north on a dirt road, passing a residence off to the right. A spruce plantation to the right (east) has reclaimed the site of an early settlement area, a situation that continues as stone walls and a foundation appear. Ascending easily over bedrock and dirt, the trail gradually gains elevation and a piped spring is passed to the immediate right (east) of the trail. A vague, unmarked dirt road leaves the main trail to the left (west). The Elm Ridge Trail continues straight ahead and shortly arrives at the trail junction at 1.1 mi. (see Escarpment Trail for details). The lean-to is 500 ft. to the right. The Elm Ridge Trail ends here. Go right (east) to climb Windham High Peak on the Escarpment Trail.

Black Dome Range Trail

to Thomas Cole summit: 2.5 mi., 1 hr. 45 min.

to Black Dome summit: 3.2 mi., 2 hr.

to Lockwood Gap: 4.0 mi., 2 hr. 30 min.

to Big Hollow Road: 5.6 mi., 3 hr. 45 min.

to Escarpment Trail: 6.7 mi., 4 hr. 20 min.

Coming south from Maplecrest on CR 40 (or north from Tannersville on CR 23C to CR 40), turn east onto Barnum Road (aka Elmer Barnum Road) just south of Maplecrest village. The trailhead parking area is on the right (southwest) at 1.0 mi., at the end of Barnum Road. The trail begins adjacent to a private residence on the left (northeast) side of Barnum Road and heads southeast.

Following a washed-out dirt road uphill, the trail crosses several seasonal creeks in a hardwood forest. Marking is good. Within 0.2 mi., the trail turns northeast (left) at a poorly marked junction where an old dirt road continues east (don't follow it). In a stand of white birch, the trail register and signboard stand to the left at 0.2 mi. Aster appears in profusion as the trail begins to ascend over red silt soil, rising over ledges and gaining elevation, sometimes steeply. Nearing 3200 ft., the ascent relaxes considerably as you approach the Caudal (the Camel's Tail), soon flattening on the Caudal itself (viewless) at 0.1 mi. before descending briefly into a saddle at 3250 ft. The trail turns to the east now, through thick vegetation and a canopy of beech and sugar maple, where spotted touch-me-nots are common.

The trail climbs to the 3500-ft. mark (signed) and levels for a very short distance onto the Camel's Hump at 1.5 mi. (3550 ft.). As the trail attains level ground, avoid a short spur on the right (southeast) that leads to overgrown views, and watch for an unmarked spur just ahead, immediately to the left of a flat-topped, west-facing boulder. This short spur off the main trail leads to a rock with excellent views to the north and southwest, which include Albany, and to the right a few degrees, Equinox Mountain (3816 ft.) and the cluster of mountains around Emerald State Park, among them Woodlawn Mountain (3072 ft.). Farther to the south, in clear conditions it is possible to see Stratton Mountain (3936 ft.) and the associated peaks in the Green Mountain National Forest—Mount Snow, Glastenbury, Bald, and Haystack. Still farther south and closer to the west are Mounts Williams and Greylock in the Mount Greylock State Reservation, north of Pittsfield, Massachusetts—all views that are common to the north-facing Escarpment Trail lookouts during periods of clear weather. Windham High Peak and Burnt Knob sit in the northeast. The low-lying hills in the western foreground are Red Hill and Van Loan Mountain (the latter named for the early mapmaker and author).

The trail descends briefly to a spruce-fir-blueberry bald that characterizes the saddle between the Camel's Hump and Thomas Cole Mountain. As the trail ascends, a small lookout to the right offers good views to the south of the Jewett Range, West Kill, Hunter and its fire tower, Rusk, and Evergreen. Down through Stony Clove Notch over the back side of Carl Mountain, distant Samuel's Point juts eastward.

The trail steepens as viburnum, wood sorrel, bunchberry, and balsam suddenly appear. The grade then flattens onto the viewless summit of Thomas Cole Mountain at 2.5 mi. (3950 ft.), named for the founder of the Hudson River School of Landscape Painting. Ironically, it is viewless. Previously named Mount Kimball by Arnold Guyot, this peak appears on some old maps as "Black Tom"—for its profuse evergreen peak (which looks black from a distance), an affectation common to each of the three summits in the range. At or slightly beyond the actual summit a spur trail leaves to the right to a treed-in view. The tallest hikers may be able to see Kaaterskill High Peak, Roundtop, Indian Head, and Twin, but those continuing east can enjoy views from Black Dome (looking in the same direction) that more than compensate for Thomas Cole's. The trail follows flat over the remainder of the summit and descends into the high saddle on the approach to Black Dome, where views of the Devil's Path notches and peaks materialize to the south through the trees. Sparse seasonal views take shape to the left (northwest). The ascent barely levels as Black Dome's summit (3990 ft.) is achieved at 3.2 mi., offering spectacular views south from an idyllic, flat rock shelf.

Ugly graffiti surrounds a few interesting pieces from the mid-to-late 1800s, most notably the 1889 caricature by F. E. Elitt. Here are views of the interior high peaks in the Slide Mountain–Panther Mountain Wilderness Area beyond the Devil's Path Mountains, through Stony Clove Notch. Hunter, its fire tower, the ski slopes on Colonel's Chair, West Kill, and more peaks are seen to the west. In front of you are Onteora, Parker, and the Jewett Range. The long ridge running west from Stoppel Point is West Stoppel Point. The villages of Tannersville (best seen at night) and East Jewett lie below, with Colgate Lake east of Lake Capra (private).

The trail continues east, descending, turning south briefly to cross the top of a ledge where an obvious spur leads a few feet to excellent views east across Lockwood Gap. Blackhead Mountain commands the middle ground. Included here are views of North Mountain, Stoppel Point, the Hudson River, and the northeastern ranges and lowlands. The trail drops down sharply below the ledge and continues the descent to Lockwood Gap junction, arriving at 4.0 mi.

A poor, designated campsite exists to the northeast of the junction, a short distance beyond two closed sites. (The only tent site is on a slope.) Camping opportunities, especially for larger groups, improve at lower elevations. A reliable spring is located 0.3 mi. downhill from Lockwood Gap on the Black Dome Range Trail.

NOTE: Hikers wishing to take a short side trip in order to see one of the Catskills' best views should leave the Black Dome Range Trail here and go east following yellow markers toward Blackhead Mountain (see Blackhead Mountain Trail for details).

The Black Dome Range Trail continues left (north), descending very steeply. From this point (Lockwood Gap) the distance to the Batavia Kill Trail is 1.0 mi.; the Batavia Kill parking area in Black Dome Valley (Big Hollow Road) is an additional 0.5 mi. Continue descending to the junction with the Batavia Kill Trail, crossing a seasonal creek through maple-and-hemlock woods. Ordinarily there is water at this confluence, restricted to the main bed of the Batavia Kill itself during dry periods.

Bearing left (northwest), cross the kill on a footbridge. The trail improves, while descending an eroded roadbed. A few large spruce trees appear as the trail widens, again crossing the kill on a footbridge. The trail passes the register and trail signs, arriving at the trailhead parking area at 5.6 mi.

The Black Dome Range Trail continues from a point 100 ft. west of the trailhead parking area at the east end of Big Hollow Road. From this access point it provides the shortest and fastest access to the Escarpment Trail and the scenic destinations of Burnt Knob and Acra Point. Hikers with limited time will appreciate the fact that Burnt Knob Mountain (3190 ft.) is both closer and considerably more scenic than Acra Point. Signs are posted here.

Locate the red markers and trailhead signage that mark the continuation of the Black Dome Range Trail. Within 200 ft. of the road, the trail passes the register and crosses the Batavia Kill on a footbridge at 5.7 mi., heading north. The trail climbs next over mineral soil to a tributary into a hemlock woods, ascending through a stand of spruce on the left (west) side of the trail. Hemlock increases as the trail follows alongside the creek and then crosses it (this is the nearest water to the junction and the most reliable water in proximity to the long stretch of the Escarpment Trail between the Batavia Kill and Elm Ridge). The trail passes through a flat, grassy area ideal for camping, shortly thereafter arriving at the ridge and the Escarpment Trail at 6.7 mi. Go left (northwest) to reach Burnt Knob (see Escarpment Trail for details).

Section 4

Indian Head
Wilderness Area

East

The scenic Indian Head Wilderness Area lies between the Hudson River Valley on the east, where the escarpment rises suddenly from 750 ft. elevation to 2500 ft. (the average altitude of the escarpment), and extends westward to Stony Clove, crossing five major peaks—Plattekill (3110 ft.), Indian Head (3573 ft.), Twin (3640 ft.), Sugarloaf (3810 ft.), and Plateau (3840 ft.).

Collectively known as the Devil's Path Range, these mountains and notches of the Indian Head Wilderness Area are host to one of the Catskills' most renowned and difficult hiking trails—the Devil's Path. It is an area of steep ascents and descents of varying and rugged terrain. Its notches deepen as the hikers travel west, leading to increasing vertical rises through steep terrain. Although day hikers frequently climb these summits from the feeder trails that primarily enter the range from the north (the Mink Hollow, Pecoy Notch, Jimmy Dolan Notch, and Catskill Center for Conservation and Development Trails), and less often from the longer southerly approaches on the Overlook Mountain and Southern Mink Hollow Trails, few but the most serious backpackers travel the entire Devil's Path from east to west or vice versa. For hikers, the result of this user pattern is a good deal of wilderness solitude and the opportunity to experience extended periods of isolation.

Many old roads, primitive paths, bluestone quarries, and dugways (trenches made in slopes that acted as log or stone chutes) exist in the area. Hikers will see the remnants of early industry and will often notice hand-tooled stones on the trails that have fallen from ox-drawn quarry wagons in the early 1800s. Although decimated by the tanning industry, the Indian Head Wilderness Area is still densely populated with hemlocks, sometimes in isolated virgin stands. Extensive northern hardwood forest covers the lower elevations, and summits are often clad in dense, nearly impenetrable fir called "cripplebrush." Quarrying, tanning, glassmaking, sawmilling, the charcoal industry, and the ensuing tourist development have left their mark on this now silent and lonely wilderness. Much of the preserve lands were acquired in the early twentieth century, with trails being constructed by the state and

55

the Civilian Conservation Corps. Today the trails are maintained largely by volunteer organizations such as the New York–New Jersey Trail Conference, the Adirondack Mountain Club, and the Appalachian Mountain Club.

It is believed that fishers populate this area along with the typical big-game species found in the Catskill ecozone. During the 1800s, wolves were common in the area, and today campers will often hear packs of howling coyotes that can sound chilling to the uninitiated, although these animals have not been known to approach humans. Packs of a dozen or more animals may "sing" for periods of several minutes at a time. They are wary and rarely seen.

The only natural lake in this wilderness area is the twelve-acre Echo Lake, a glacially dammed, shallow pond with a population of brook trout. Other ponds in the area are seasonal beaver impoundments, existing primarily at middle elevations and often seen from trails. There are three lean-tos in this wilderness area as well as more than twenty-five miles of trails.

Devil's Path (Indian Head–Hunter–West Kill Range Trail)

Distances from Prediger Road trailhead

   to Old Overlook Road (Overlook Trail): 1.85 mi., 40 min.

   to Indian Head summit: 4.2 mi., 2 hrs.

   to Twin summit: 5.7 mi., 3 hrs.

   to Sugarloaf summit: 7.6 mi., 4 hrs.

   to Plateau summit: 9.85 mi., 5 hrs.

   to Stony Clove Notch (NY 214): 13.0 mi., 6 hr. 30 min.

   to Devil's Acre lean-to: 15.6 mi., 7 hr. 45 min.

   to Diamond Notch Falls: 17.2 mi., 9 hr.

   to West Kill summit: 19.4 mi., 10 hr.

   to Spruceton Road: 24.2 mi., 12 hr.

The Devil's Path is named not only for the Devil, whom Dutch settlers believed lived in the deep, wild hollows and jagged cloves of the Catskills—it is known even more by hikers for its demonic and unforgiving ascents, its rugged and punishing peaks, and particularly in the summer, its fiendish lack of water. Next to the Escarpment Trail, the Devil's Path is perhaps the most popular and challenging trail for extended backpacking and day hiking in the Catskills, offering several peaks and loop hikes in beautiful forests with sensational mountaintop scenery. All hikers are advised to take things easy on this difficult trail, planning cautiously and keeping daily mileage quotas reasonable (a ten-mile day on the Devil's Path is like a twenty-mile day elsewhere). Backpackers will average little more than 1.0 MPH over such highly variable terrain. Even day hikers traveling light will find the vertical rises and rocky ledges daunting and should plan for sudden changes of weather with corresponding drops in temperature and possible high winds and wind chill along exposed ridges.

The Prediger Road trailhead marks the "official" beginning of the Devil's Path. Located on CR 16 (Platte Clove Road), the trailhead is best reached from NY 23A in Tannersville. From the light in the center of town, travel 0.25 mi. east on NY 23A, turning right (south) on Spring Street (CR 16), which becomes Platte Clove Road. At 5.7 mi., find Prediger Road on the right (south) side of CR 16, marked with state trail signs. Follow Prediger Road 0.4 mi. south to the trailhead parking area. Parking is limited to the right (west) side of the road.

The trail begins at the right (west) side of the road and crosses a small bridge through a private easement into the forest preserve. The trail is a level woods road, leading in 0.5 mi. to a lively creek and the intersection with the Jimmy Dolan Notch trail.

The trail bears left to the east over level ground through hardwood forests and narrows into a footpath. This section of the trail is a designated ski trail, but it receives little or no use by skiers. The trail is suitable (though not very interesting) for accomplished backcountry skiers, but it is by no means diagonal striding terrain.

Considerable base is necessary to cover the trail's many rocks, blow-downs, and short, steep pitches.

The path leads east over hillocks and across small seasonal rills, one of which has a very well-made stone step bridge. Many locations along the trail are flat and convenient for camping, and those headed for the popular Devil's Kitchen lean-to (which is located on the Overlook Trail) on a busy weekend might consider this option.

The Devil's Path joins the Overlook Trail at 1.85 mi. This junction is not well identified. Turn right (south) and within 200 ft. turn right (west) again to continue toward Indian Head Mountain.

This trail leaves the Overlook Trail from the right (west) side of the Old Overlook Road, turning back into the southwest and climbing gently but steadily uphill. Initially the trail climbs and levels through a grove of hemlocks, some of them very large. Through the years, these groves have proven to be popular bivouacs, and far off the trail it is not uncommon to find old fire rings. An open forest follows as the trail gains elevation in small doses amid moss-cloaked boulders and large, exposed roots. This pattern of climbing and leveling continues as views appear to the north (provided there are few leaves). Views improve dramatically ahead. A northern hardwood forest predominates until the trail narrows and steepens, becomes grassy, turns east, and descends slightly to an expansive lookout at 3.15 mi. An exposed rock, it faces northeast. This is Sherman's Lookout, named for Civil War hero General William Tecumseh Sherman, an 1890 visitor to the Catskill Mountain House. With this last bit of elevation gain, small balsam fir marks the beginnings of a nearly contiguous Canadian boreal forest. This is a dangerous ledge with substantial vertical drop—stay ahead of your children now.

On a clear day, the views from Sherman's Lookout are extensive. The monolithic mountainside close on your right is the western face of Plattekill (3100 ft., trailless; just on the other side of that ridge running north-south at 2600 ft. is the Overlook Trail). Roundtop (3440 ft.) and Kaaterskill High Peak (3655 ft.) are the two closest mountains to the north, directly in front of you. On the right, sloping downhill and to the southeast from the long shoulder of Kaaterskill, above Platte Clove on the rocky ramparts of the escarpment, is Huckleberry Point (84 degrees). Continuing to the right is a piece of the Hudson River (North Germantown Reach) where several cement plants, stacks, and industrial silos around Duck Cove and Inbocht Bay impose upon the otherwise pastoral valley landscape. Across the Hudson, hikers can identify Bash Bish Gorge. The falls themselves are not visible.

The most impressive view of all is heavily dissected Platte Clove itself and the adjacent deeply eroded streambeds that join it from the north. These clefts run parallel to the direct line of descent and are accordingly labeled parallel drainage by geologists. Platte Clove was formed by the retreating Wisconsin Ice Sheet about 15,000 years ago; the difference in what we see today is merely cosmetic. The most notable difference is perhaps the loss of the hemlock trees. In the days before the tanbark period, stands were thick and covered much of the landscape.

The trail curves to the south; be cautious near another vertical drop on the left, very close to the trail. Swinging away from the ledge the trail climbs easily, nearly tunneling over with balsam as it curves around to the northwest. A limited view appears on the left, just before the trail's best southerly vantage. At 3.4 mi., the trail is now level and narrow as thick stands of spruce-fir suddenly give way to phenomenal views of the central high peaks area and the lowlands between, from the Hudson River to the Ashokan Reservoir, and west across the high summit skyline, taking in most of the major peaks from Ashokan High Point to Slide and beyond, toward the Delaware Valley.

The Devil's Path now approaches boreal summit on the Indian's long, oblate chin. Off the trail the dense, scrubby evergreen cover is nearly impenetrable cripplebrush. The trail descends gently. Ahead and uphill, the Indian's "eyebrow" (as it appears from the north) looms directly overhead. A short scramble follows through a steep, heavily impacted and eroded crevice beneath the high rock overhang of the eyebrow. Roots and rocks provide handholds, but the pitch requires careful footing, especially in icy conditions. At 3.8 mi., the trail reaches an open view from a small, dangerously exposed flat outcropping over a substantial vertical drop. Keep your children behind you as you approach the rock, and use extreme caution!

There are minimal views upriver to the north from this point. More imposing are those to the south, most immediately of Overlook Mountain and the Sawkill Valley. Overlook's cellular tower caused a large but unsuccessful public-resistance effort, and for those of us who do not use cellular phones, it serves only as a convenient marker for the surrounding, somber gray ruins of the ill-fated Overlook Hotel. Equidistant between the eyebrow and the long ridge of Overlook and Plattekill Mountains are the thickly oak-forested, south-facing slopes and headwaters of the Sawkill, which drain through unnamed tributaries to the southwest, filling Cooper Lake, the City of Kingston's water supply. The strip of water to the right and beyond the cell tower is the Ashokan Reservoir (often it is mistaken for the Hudson, which flows farther to the east), and to its westerly extreme the first big peak is Ashokan High Point. Following into the west are the Catskills' high peaks. The Tibetan Buddhist monastery appears at 208 degrees in the saddle between Overlook and Guardian Mountains in Meads. Finally, off to the south-southwest at 219 degrees and nearly as far as the eye can see even with good binoculars is High Point, New Jersey's highest point at 1803 ft., with its distinctive war monument. The Appalachian Trail goes through that section of High Point State Park and turns east toward Harriman State Park and the Hudson Highlands, which can be seen to the southeast.

A series of short, steep climbs follows through ledgy, virgin spruce-fir terrain that becomes a nearly homogeneous and impenetrable fir canopy, tunneling over flat, mossy rock. At 4.2 mi. an overstory of large, dead and dying red spruce characterize the balsam summit, and the trail is sparsely decorated with mountain ash and paper birch. The remaining red spruce, which were originally damaged in a 1950 hurricane, are suffering the effects of exposure and drought. There are no views until the westerly descent to Jimmy Dolan Notch begins, and these are of neighboring Twin Mountain and the Blackhead Range to the north.

Like most of the saddles between the Devil's Path summits, the descent into Jimmy Dolan Notch is moderately steep, although short (elevation drop, 470 ft. from summit). At 4.7 mi., the trail intersects with the (blue) Jimmy Dolan Notch Trail in the notch itself.

From Jimmy Dolan Notch, the trail rises steeply to the west on the approach to Twin Mountain, quickly gaining 500 ft. in elevation. The trail relaxes, heading southwest briefly. A cut view appears east of the trail, providing views of Indian Head Mountain (3573 ft.), Overlook Mountain (3150 ft.), Kaaterskill High Peak (3655 ft.), and Roundtop Mountain (3440 ft.). A beautiful stone trail follows, lined with blueberry bushes, spruce, and fir.

At 5.1 mi., the trail reaches the south peak of Twin Mountain (3650 ft.) and an expansive view southward, one of the Devil's Path's finest. From the eastern side of this open area Overlook Mountain and its fire tower can be seen. Most of the Ashokan Reservoir is seen, as well as Cooper Lake in the foreground. To the left of Ashokan High Point is Sky Top and Eagle Cliff in the Shawangunks' Mohonk Preserve and the Mohonk Mountain House. In the Slide Mountain–Panther Mountain Wilderness Area are the Catskill high peaks, showing Slide Mountain (4190 ft.), Cornell (3870 ft.), and Wittenberg (3790 ft.), with Terrace Mountain (2360 ft.) tapering down to the right. Over the top of Giant Ledge the landscape blurs into the vaporous peaks of the Big Indian–Beaverkill Range Wilderness Area. Panther Mountain (3730 ft.) appears to the right of Giant Ledge. Mount Tremper (2740 ft.) can be spotted in the middle ground—with binoculars you can see the fire tower. The north shoulder of Twin is immediately to the west, as well as Sugarloaf (3810 ft.) at 320 degrees, and to the left, Plateau Mountain's long ridge (3850 ft.), from which Olderbark Mountain (3440 ft.) projects south.

The trail proceeds west, descending easily, and varies in composition from sandy loam and moss-margined rock to densely foliated spruce-fir as it rises to Twin's summit (3650 ft.) at 5.7 mi. Slightly below this point is a rock outcropping and a view that provides a more northerly vantage than the last, including the previously unseen Hunter Mountain (4050 ft.) and its fire tower, and a good look at Table (3847 ft.) and Peekamoose (3843 ft.). The trail drops downhill through a crack to the left of an overhanging rock that has been abused by careless campers. This is the 3500-ft. mark. The trail's surface is covered in broken slabs over roots as it descends through ledges, passing a conspicuous boulder on the right. An extensive boulder field covers the well-marked trail and provides for open views to the north of the Blackhead Range and of Sugarloaf Mountain, immediately west. This rocky terrain continues through scrubby hardwood forest and nearly into Pecoy Notch, where the terrain relaxes in the saddle at 6.4 mi. (2800 ft.). There are no views. Opportunities for camping in the tangled, dense underbrush are limited; one overused site is closed. The Pecoy Notch Trail leads north and downhill to the Roaring Brook trailhead parking area (this is the fastest egress). The Devil's Path continues straight ahead (west) toward Sugarloaf Mountain.

The Devil's Path swings north for a short distance before switching back to the southwest and climbing steeply into an 850-ft. vertical rise to the summit of Sugarloaf. Increasingly clear views of Twin and its terraced, sedimentary geology are visible to the east across Pecoy Notch. A few ledges require light hands-on work. As higher elevations are achieved, natural vantage points appear, each of them looking easterly. The trail begins to level, passing the 3500-ft. mark, and long, flat, boreal ridge follows, nearly tunneled over in thick spruce and fir trees. At 7.6 mi., the trail reaches the summit of Sugarloaf, which lies in the vicinity of a short spur trail that leaves left (south) a few hundred feet to a lookout featuring the Catskills' high peaks, (those of the Burroughs Range), Giant Ledge and Panther, the Ashokan Reservoir, and the Hudson Highlands, way to the south. The Shawangunks are clearly visible, and to the west are the hills and peaks of the Big Indian–Beaverkill Range Wilderness Area (more in-depth details of southerly landmarks visible from the Devil's Path are described in the Twin and Indian Head summits sections).

The trail descends over a grassy treadway, passing a lookout facing Plateau Mountain, and thereafter views to the north of the Blackhead Range appear. The hulking spires of large, dead spruce trees loom overhead as the trail descends over broken ledges with some steep drop-offs that are potentially dangerous, at one point passing beneath an unstable-looking precipice of loose, overhanging rock. The trail passes beneath a natural rock bridge at one point and continues its descent into hardwoods when at 8.5 mi. the Mink Hollow Trail to the Roaring Kill parking area appears on the right (northeast) at 2500 ft. in elevation. (Don't confuse this trail with the abandoned Mink Hollow Trail that leaves to the north from the intersection straight ahead. The trail shortly arrives at the junction with the southern section of the Mink Hollow Trail at 8.6 mi.)

The abandoned Mink Hollow Trail descends on a woods road to the north. It is the fastest egress from the Devil's Path in case of emergency. To the left (south) is the lean-to. Thru-hikers should be aware that the nearest provisions are in Tannersville. There are no provisions or services in Lake Hill to the south—only a post office.

The Devil's Path continues straight ahead (northwest) to climb Plateau Mountain. Plateau is the westernmost peak of the Indian Head Wilderness Area, from which the Devil's Path drops steeply into Stony Clove. Once called Stony Mountain, its boreal summit ridge is long and flat, averaging 3800 ft. This section of the Devil's Path was built by the Civilian Conservation Corps in 1935. Plateau is a remote and attractive peak, offering solitude and far-reaching scenery.

The trail heads northwest and flattens through hardwoods, providing sparse views of Mink Hollow and Sugarloaf Mountain to the east. Climbing steeply, through rocky, ledgy terrain, the trail passes through a stand of very large red-spruce trees and continues to ascend until leveling out near 3700 ft., where views to the north reveal Kaaterskill High Peak (3655 ft.), Roundtop (3440 ft.), and neighboring Sugarloaf Mountain (3810 ft.) to the east. Soon afterwards the trail arrives at the (viewless) true summit at 9.85 mi. The ridge narrows, the trail becomes soft duff, and hikers will sense the abyss on either side of the mountain as they travel west.

A long, nearly level hike along the summit ridgeline follows the actual summit on the southeast side of the mountain. Thick, often impenetrable stands of large spruce trees thin as the trail heads west. To the north (right) a nameless lookout shows Roundtop and Kaaterskill High Peak sloping down into Platte Clove. Use caution at this fairly steep drop. The trail wanders along the flat ridge, where it has been worn into the soft soil. At 11.8 mi., the trail passes a more significant lookout on the right (east), where a large boulder is etched with the image of a rising sun. This rock has long been known as Danny's Lookout. Visible far (80 mi.) to the northeast at 58 degrees is the Green Mountain National Forest. Although the individual peaks are difficult to isolate, among them are Bald Mountain (2865 ft.), Glastenbury Mountain (3748 ft.), and beyond it, Stratton Mountain (3936 ft.), with Mount Snow to the east of Glastenbury. Moving south is the Taconic Range and Mount Greylock State Reservation. Roundtop, Kaaterskill High Peak, and Sugarloaf are still with you—beyond them are far-reaching views of the eastern Hudson Valley. Thomas Cole (3950 ft.), Black Dome (3990 ft.), and Blackhead (3950 ft.) are easily identified to the north-northeast, along with Arizona Mountain (3400 ft.) southeast of Blackhead, where the escarpment drops down into Dutcher Notch.

The trail continues north along the flat ridge, dense with trout lilies, until reaching Orchid Point at 12.05 mi. (aka Orchard Point, Plateau Mountain Lookout), where another startling gulf of valleys, ridges, and mountains presents itself. Stony Clove is carved into the landscape below. Across it stands Hunter Mountain (4050 ft.) and its fire tower, with West Kill and Southwest Hunter to the south. Slide is obvious at 220 degrees, and, interestingly, its namesake landslide can be seen, especially when residual snow cover sticks in the surrounding forest. Many other peaks in the Slide Mountain–Panther Mountain Wilderness Area are prominent.

The trail descends, leaving spruce-fir for stunted birch, passing a shallow rock overhang, and, at 3400 ft., swinging into the south across a flat, wet area with large, flat stones, before switching back and descending again. Spring beauty, Dutchman's britches, and purple trillium (Burroughs' wake-robin) appear among the now isolated spruces. A stand of pure white birch signals the final steep descent, as the trail drops into Stony Clove. The tree type changes to beech as the trail makes a sharp turn from south to west. Ahead to the southwest you can see Slide and Wittenberg. A nameless tributary of Edgewood Stream runs down the clove to the left (south). Finally reaching Stony Clove, the trail crosses the footprint of the old Stony Clove & Catskill Mountain Railroad, which brought tourists from as far as Philadelphia to the Catskill Mountain House and the Hotel Kaaterskill. A short walk on to the south of the trail will reveal remaining railroad ties. The trail continues straight ahead, descends a flight of wooden stairs, and, at 13.0 mi., crosses NY 214 at Notch Lake, a point 0.3 mi. north of the Devil's Tombstone Public Campground. Here there is a parking area, trail signs, picnic tables, and fireplaces. (No swimming is permitted in Notch Lake.) This steep and attractive trail penetrates the Hunter Mountain Wild Forest to the northeast shoulder of Southwest Hunter Mountain before descending into Diamond Notch. Thru-hikers should note that there are no showers at the Devil's Tombstone Public Campground. The nearest provisions are in Hunter or Tannersville to the north, or in Phoenicia to the south.

At the south end of Notch Lake, the Devil's Path continues, crossing a wooden bridge and rising to the trail register. The rocky trail ascends steeply, switching back and forth through a dense sugar-maple forest. Within 15 minutes it passes a moss-covered ledge on the right of the trail, at the corner of which is a shallow rock overhang. The trail continues steeply through ash-and-maple stands, and up a short flight of rock steps, switching back into a hemlock grove and turning north for a moment, ascending at a more relaxed pace.

Beech appears as the trail levels, the forest type changing to include birch and cherry trees, with a ground cover of oxalis and moss. Soon the trail assumes a course along a southeastern slope of Southwest Hunter Mountain (3740 ft.), allowing obscure summer views across Stony Clove and beyond. Bright, white birch appears and the trail turns from rock to dirt, becoming flat. Striped-maple saplings hang into the narrow trail, and little stands of red spruce dot the woods. This is the headwater slope of Myrtle Brook, which the trail crosses. The trail remains level for some time as it turns west, at 15.2 mi. arriving at the junction with the Hunter Mountain Trail (yellow).

The Devil's Path bears left (west) following red markers, within moments coming upon the lean-to. Because it has been ravaged by porcupines, the privy is fully encased in hardware cloth. The lean-to, although very old, is in good condition, with a broken concrete fire ring campers have improved upon with piled-up rocks.

Just beyond the lean-to the trail crosses a brook. At a point just beyond this, the trail makes a right-angle turn across the same shallow brook, while prior to this turn, an unmarked trail (easy to mistake for the mail trail) goes left a few hundred feet to an appealing, established, and legal campsite. Birch trees tower above a vast understory of fir as the main trail follows a slope heading west, climbing easily. As the terrain flattens an unmarked but obvious path leaves to the left (south) and is cairned with small rocks to alert the hikers of the Catskill 3500 Club that this is the bushwhack route to Southwest Hunter Mountain. This interesting trail follows a reinforced, graded bed that most likely served as a horse-drawn log railway in the early 1900s.

The trail descends, becoming rocky as it turns north and relaxes, remaining generally flat as it follows along a ridge amphitheater above Diamond Notch. At 15.6 mi., a short spur trail to the left of the main trail leads a few feet to views of Southwest Hunter (3750 ft.) and West Kill (3890 ft.) Mountains and into Diamond Notch. This is an extremely dangerous ledge—a fact that is not apparent until its edge is reached. Return to the Devil's Path, which passes a few overused and discontinued campsites. The trail becomes somewhat muddy, catching runoff from the steep westerly slopes of Hunter Mountain, only 0.5 mi. uphill to the east (not visible). A long, steady downhill follows through dark, majestic stands of tall sugar maple, with an attending undergrowth of stinging nettle crowding the trail. The trail crosses several runoff trickles and a larger tributary of the West Kill before it arrives at the grassy, open field adjacent to West Kill Falls (aka Buttermilk Falls, Diamond Notch Falls) and the energetic West Kill Creek at 17.2 mi.

At the trail register (presently contained in a section of PVC pipe to protect it from porcupines) at the intersection of the Diamond Notch Trail (blue) and the Devil's Path (red), sign in. Diamond Notch itself is a short distance to the south along the blue Diamond Notch Trail. The

Devil's Path continues to the left, crosses the bridge, and immediately turns right (west), heading into the West Kill Wilderness Area.

The trail passes beside the falls initially. The large pool at their base is a popular swimming spot. Following the West Kill Creek for a few hundred feet, the trail turns uphill to the southeast, ascends over a varied surface from mineral soil to rock, and turns to the southwest, passing a spring to the left of the trail at 17.9 mi. (2900 ft.). The path turns rooty, offering only wintertime views of Rusk Mountain (3690 ft.) and Evergreen Mountain (3360 ft.) to the right (north). Broad sheets of bunchberry and oxalis (wood sorrel) cover the forest floor. At 3420 ft., the forest assumes a more alpine character, and the trail levels and turns to the west, becoming muddy in spots. At 18.6 mi., the trail passes a shallow rock overhang midtrail at 3490 ft., where illegal fires have scarred the rock. Just above this ledge, the 3500-ft. sign appears. Birches become gnarly and stunted now, then there begins a long level stretch with an understory of small balsam fir beneath even-aged stands of larger fir.

At 3700 ft., open space is visible to left and right, but no views appear. Descending slightly to 3600 ft., the trail passes a spur trail that drops downhill to the left (south) to a treed-in view. (This once cut vista has recovered, but the trail's sensitive vegetation hasn't.) Don't be distracted by these tantalizing spurs that lead nowhere—there are several—the scenic reward is at Buck Ridge Lookout. After a brief ascent the trail flattens and without warning arrives at Buck Ridge at 19.4 mi. (3740 ft.). The view is beyond expectation—one of the eastern Catskills' best.

Hunter Mountain (4050 ft.) and its fire tower are at 94 degrees. Across Diamond Notch is Southwest Hunter (3750 ft.); across Stony Clove is Plateau Mountain (3850 ft.), with Olderbark jutting south. Just over the lowest point between Plateau and Olderbark Mountains (3440 ft.) is Overlook (3150 ft.) and its fire tower. Conspicuous in the east-northeast is the entire Blackhead Range, as well as Windham High Peak (3524 ft.) and Burnt Knob (3190 ft.). The open ski slopes of Hunter Mountain West are obvious to your left. The enormous easterly ridge of West Kill lies directly to the east. On a good day you can see sailboats in the Hudson River. Moving to the right (south) across the Rondout Valley is Sky Top, Eagle Cliff, and the Trapps.

Then, the Shawangunk Ridge in Minnewaska State Park cuts west. The large pointy mountain to the left of Sky Top and in the foreground is Mount Tobias (2550 ft.), and to its left, back in the Shawangunks again, is Bonticou Crag. Mount Tremper's (2740 ft.) fire tower can be seen at 190 degrees. Wagon Wheel Gap in Sundown Wild Forest can be seen directly over the top of the tower. The central high peaks are visible, including Slide and Wittenberg.

The trail continues west. A spur immediately to the right (north) leads to a rock with northerly views of Huntersfield, Tower, Cave, the Blackhead Mountains, and the townships of Lexington, Halcott, Roxbury, Conesville, Prattsville, Ashland, Windham, and Durham. You can see a piece of the Schoharie Reservoir in the north-northwest. The trail continues to the flat summit at 19.4 mi. (3890 ft., signed), which is enclosed in balsam fir, and passes through a wet area dense with cow parsnips and Solomon's seal. The westerly shoulder of the mountain provides only curious hikers with additional lookouts to the west, toward North Dome (3610 ft.) and Sherrill (3550 ft.). The trail descends from the boreal zone and walks level through hardwoods. At 3300 ft., the trail climbs steeply again, through a short stretch of tilted slabs. Although self-guiding and adequately marked, the trail is faint in places, showing considerably less use than the much-shorter easterly approach. At 3400 ft., from a false summit at 21.45 mi., are seasonal westerly views across Mink Hollow of the easterly slopes of North Dome. Descending steadily, at 22.8 mi. the trail arrives at the margin of a wetland in Mink Hollow, where the trail turns sharply to the right (north).

The trail descends through Mink Hollow. Nettle and sugar maple lead to a dense hemlock forest where a private parcel is posted to the right. A trail arrow alerts hikers to a sharp left turn. As the Devil's Path begins its final descent to Spruceton Road, the trail register is reached on the right among large white pine. State-land wilderness-area signs are posted here. At 24.2 mi. the trail ends at the parking area and the western Devil's Path trailhead. Signs are posted here, just across Spruceton Road. Some distances are misleading and need revision at this time (distances for Prediger Road and Hunter Mountain fire tower are reversed on opposite sides of the sign). Revised distances are as follows:

red (east)

West Kill Mountain (ascent, 2030 ft.):	4.7 mi.
Diamond Notch lean-to:	7.7 mi.
Spruceton Road:	8.7 mi.
Devil's Acre lean-to:	9.4 mi.
Hunter Mountain fire tower:	11.2 mi.
Devil's Tombstone campground:	11.7 mi.
Prediger Road:	24.3 mi.

Jimmy Dolan Notch Trail

Distance from junction with Devil's Path

   to   Jimmy Dolan Notch: 1.6 mi., 1 hr.

The Jimmy Dolan Notch Trail is a popular route, used often for loop hikes of Indian Head Mountain (3573 ft.) in concert with the Devil's Path, or as an out-and-back ascent of Twin Mountain (3650 ft.), also employing the Devil's Path. While the notch itself provides little in the way of scenery, its proximity to these two neighboring peaks in the Indian Head Wilderness Area makes it a useful and attractive alternate route for scenic day outings.

This trail begins at the 0.5 mi. point on the Devil's Path (which begins at the Prediger Road trailhead). At the junction of the Devil's Path and Jimmy Dolan Notch Trail, signs are posted.

The Jimmy Dolan Notch Trail turns right (west) here, passing through stands of hemlock and soon a pure beech forest. Several seasonal capillaries of the Schoharie will be encountered, but they are unlikely to be evident in summer or early autumn. The trail is rocky, even, and often grassy as it follows the abandoned road. Storybook hemlock forests occupy the middle realms of the trail at 0.5 mi., yielding to sparse hardwood cover as the terrain steepens into the south, with a lively creek to the right (west) through the woods some distance. Late-arriving parties will find many attractive places to camp along this section of trail (there are no established sites), in proximity to the upper Schoharie Creek, an area that is preferable to camping near the notch, which is difficult to do legally.

The trail climbs steeply but briefly beyond the hemlock stands and into the notch (3100 ft.) at the junction of the Devil's Path Trail. The notch is named for Jimmy Dolan, who kept a tavern here in the late nineteenth century.

Roaring Kill Trail

Distances from Roaring Kill parking area

> *to* Pecoy Notch Trail: 0.25 mi., 10 min.
>
> *to* Mink Hollow Trail: 0.25 mi., 10 min.

Locate the Roaring Kill parking area and trailhead off CR 16, roughly 3 mi. from Tannersville where the yellow-marked Roaring Kill Trail goes south. From NY 23A, take Spring Street (CR 16, at the east end of the village), bearing right onto Elka Park Road at roughly 2.0 mi; the trailhead can also be reached from Platte Clove Road (also CR 16) via Dale Lane, 1.0 mi. west of Prediger Road (the Devil's Path trailhead). A signboard is located at the trailhead. The Roaring Kill, lying in view a short distance to the west of the parking area, makes for a worthwhile visit. It flows north and joins the Schoharie Creek headwaters. The area is heavily wooded. Elka Park Road is dirt here, and is not maintained by the town during the winter, although it is generally passable. Across Elka Park Road is a section of wild forest that could be used for late-arrival, low-impact camping (legal, undesignated, unestablished). Camping is also possible and close at hand in the flat areas above the trail's initial ascent, in the wilderness area itself. Observe the 150-ft. law.

The trail enters the woods, briefly ascends, and then continues level through mixed hardwood and hemlock over roots and duff soil. Within 5 or 10 minutes (0.25 mi.), arrive at the junction of the Mink

Hollow (blue) and Pecoy Notch (blue) trails at elevation 2150 ft. The Roaring Kill Trail ends here.

Pecoy Notch Trail

to Dibble's Quarry: 0.7 mi., 30 min.

to Pecoy Notch: 1.7 mi., 1 hr.

From the junction of the Roaring Kill and Mink Hollow (northern section) trails, the Pecoy Notch Trail leaves to the south to join the Devil's Path between Sugarloaf (3810 ft.) and Twin (3650 ft.) Mountains.

The trail ascends, moving across slope through open hardwoods until reaching an obvious quarry pit where it levels. A few large stone "flags" are leaning against the mined face just inside the quarry. The trail remains level through sugar-maple-and-ash woods and is self-guiding, providing minimal summer views to the east. Uphill to the right (west) is a steep and rugged talus field of fragmented rock and tangled vegetation. Increasingly dense, maple shades the ground cover of spring beauty and trout lily.

The trail enters a shady hemlock stand, at the eastern edge of which is a closed campsite. Additional, legal sites exist on this fairly flat plateau, farther to the south. The trail turns immediately to the left (northeast) after entering the hemlock (this 90-degree turn is not obvious) and turns east again as it descends to a large, open talus field at 0.7 mi. Excavated from an extensive quarry, it provides open views to the north and east at 2300 ft. This is Dibble's Quarry. Hikers have assembled a variety of stone art here in fascinating druidic configurations, including a pair of comfortable seats surrounding an arch Druid's throne. Such seats are traditional among the better-known quarries of the Catskills, but this is the representative example of the art form, established to take advantage of the view over Platte Clove and Huckleberry Point. As a general rule of thumb, always keep in mind that rattlesnakes like quarries too, although they are found primarily in oak woods.

Twin Mountain is across Pecoy Notch on the right. The building with the terra-cotta roof is the Hutterian Bruderhof. Kaaterskill High Peak and Roundtop are in the upper-elevation foreground. The trail turns to the right, into the south. Slightly below the trail on the quarry's left (east) side is a large rock overhang, sufficient to shelter several people, but technically illegal (nonconforming) for camping. Hikers will see more tables and chairs of stone in the inner quarry, surrounded by overgrown tailing hillocks and crumbling hut foundations. Standing water near the quarry faces sometimes encroaches upon the trail. The trail continues straight ahead (south) until once again entering hardwoods, at 1.0 mi. crossing a footbridge over a nameless tributary of the Schoharie Creek. The trail ascends thereafter, turning left (east) along the edge of an open marsh and beaver pond/meadow at 1.3 mi., with views of the northern face of Sugarloaf Mountain (3810 ft.) to the right (south).

Turning south and steepening, the trail penetrates the heavily wooded notch. There are no views, except for the shoulder of Sugarloaf to the right (west) and sparse winter vistas to the north and south. Camping possibilities are poor in the rugged terrain, improving both east and west along the Devil's Path, ahead. The trail reaches the notch at 1.7 mi. The only suitable campsite within the notch itself is closed permanently (impacted, nonconforming). Pecoy Notch was named for a glassmaker named Pecor who operated in the Plains (called the "Glass Plains," because the broken, discarded glass reflected in the sunlight and appeared as a plain from the mountain) of the upper Sawkill Valley on the south side of the Devil's Path range. The word's transformation to Pecoy was a typographic error.

Mink Hollow Trail (south of the Devil's Path)

to Mink Hollow, 3.0 mi., 1hr. 30 min.

This trail is popular with day hikers, cross-country skiers, and backpackers who are headed for the craggy Devil's Path. It is not scenic with vistas, but it is extremely attractive forest, imparting the rugged, deep-woods motif of the Indian Head Wilderness Area with its steep, rocky scree and ledge slopes.

The trail begins at the top of Mink Hollow Road in the hamlet of Lake Hill, a few miles west of Woodstock off NY 212. From NY 212, drive 2.9 miles to the end of Mink Hollow Road. Parking is good at the trailhead, where a kiosk displays forest-preserve information. Be careful to avoid private property, access to which is shared briefly by the trail. The distance from the parking lot to the lean-to is 3 mi., with 1180 ft. of elevation gain. The trail leaves the parking lot to the north and passes around a barrier gate by the trail register, in moments crossing a brook, and continues along the stream's edge. Ascending, the trail crosses the stream again near a small, crumbling abutment, which could date back to the road's construction in the late 1700s.

The trail steepens. Hemlock pockets and large, isolated hardwoods lead to extensive stands of beech as elevation is gained. The ledgy terrain makes excellent habitat for bear and bobcat, which are sometimes seen (or heard). Most of the hollow is a deer winter-concentration area owing to its protected, south-facing slope; it has also been identified as important habitat for the northern water shrew, which likes good ground cover near cold water. Birds and other wildlife abound, and the hollow is a good place to listen for them. It is possible that you might see the hairy woodpecker, which is on the National Audubon Society's Blue List (of special concern).

As the trail approaches the saddle, it steepens dramatically before leveling again on its final approach to the height-of-land where the lean-to is located. You'll wonder how oxen could have pulled their heavy burdens of passengers and uncured hides over the mountain to the tanneries in Hunter.

The area surrounding the Mink Hollow lean-to (2680 ft.) is marked with "No Camping" signs as the result of previous, heavy impact. There is little in the way of suitable tent space nearby. The setting is forested with stocky beech, birch, and maple trees. There is a small colony of common burdock (sunflower family) in front of the lean-to. The lean-to is in good condition, except for the primitive fire ring. Within view of the lean-to to the north is the Devil's Path intersection. The hollow's southerly aspect provides sunlight until late afternoon, dramatically illuminating the western slopes of Sugarloaf. Strong winds will tunnel through the hollow noisily, lending to the remote atmosphere—and the wind-chill factor.

Mink Hollow Trail (north of the Devil's Path)

Distance from Roaring Kill Trail

   to Mink Hollow: 2.6 mi., 1 hr. 30 min.

Enter the Mink Hollow Trail from the Roaring Kill Trail, which begins at the Roaring Brook parking area on Elka Park Road (seasonally maintained). Locate the Roaring Kill parking area and trailhead off CR 16 roughly 3 mi. from Tannersville, where the yellow-marked Roaring Kill Trail goes south. From NY 23A, take Spring Street (CR 16, at the east end of the village), bearing right onto Elka Park Road at roughly 2.0 mi., and look for the trailhead on the right (south) side of the road. The trailhead can also be reached from Platte Clove Road (also CR 16) via Dale Lane, 1.0 mi. west of Prediger Road (the Devil's Path trailhead). A signboard is located at the trailhead. This is the longer of the two options for climbing Sugarloaf Mountain from the north (the other is the Pecoy Notch Trail). Each trail is interesting and many hike Sugarloaf as a loop, using both. At the trail junctions of the Roaring Brook, Pecoy Notch, and Mink Hollow Trails, bear right (west).

   The trail is flat through a maple woods with ledges and scree along the northerly slopes. The forest type shifts to mixed hardwood as off to the northeast Roundtop Mountain (3440 ft.) and the Blackhead Range can be seen (seasonally). The trail follows an early quarry road that washes out occasionally. Talus piles are seen, heaped with forest litter, along with quarry pits and a few identifiable hut foundations. The high ridges of Sugarloaf Mountain come into view during the leafless months. Hemlock pockets take hold in the mossy, ledgy terrain as a larger, well-preserved quarry is encountered at 0.6 mi. (2500 ft.) at a bend in the trail. Here an old dirt road leaves to the right (west) onto private property, over which the original quarry road descended through the Roaring Kill Valley to Mink Hollow Road. Turning left (east) here, the trail rises through wind-ravaged terrain where blowdowns are common and swings into the south as the long ridge of Plateau Mountain (3850 ft.) and Spruce Top (3380 ft.) appear immediately to the northwest. A shallow rock overhang appears along the trail at 2800 ft., where yellow-paint blazes denote the state-land boundary, and a lookout point appears on the right (northwest) looking beyond Mink Hollow, directly at the eastern ramparts of Plateau Mountain and beyond into the Schoharie Valley. The route turns back on itself nearly 180 degrees here. Descending, in continuous view of Plateau Mountain, you turn to witness Sugarloaf's western ridge, looming ahead as the trail flattens. At 2.2 mi., in a bowl formed by the head of Roaring Kill Hollow, cross a rustic handmade footbridge, the stringers of which were (illegally) cut from a solitary grove of virgin, standing hemlock (you can still see the flat-sawn stump in the streambed downhill) that would have outlived the bridge itself by decades. Sadly, this shallow creek does not require such an elaborate—and, in terms of labor, costly—construction. The original bridge with its still-visible bluestone abutments was necessary only for wagons carrying heavy loads.

Ascending now, you approach the hollow. Arrive at the junction with the Devil's Path in dense hardwoods at 2.6 mi. Bear right (west) on the Devil's Path (red), 0.2 mi. to the junction with the southern section of the Mink Hollow Trail and the Mink Hollow lean-to (see Mink Hollow Trail, south of the Devil's Path).

Catskill Center for Conservation and Development (CCCD) Trail, Platte Clove Section (Platte Clove Nature Preserve)

Distance from Platte Clove Road

   to Devil's Path junction with Overlook Trail: 1.0 mi., 30 min.

This trail begins at the CCCD's Platte Clove Nature Preserve on Platte Clove Road, a few hundred feet west of the small cabin that the CCCD uses for its artist-in-residence program. The preserve is located on Platte Clove Road (CR 16). Travel southwest off NY 23A onto Spring Street from the east end of the village in Tannersville, 0.25 mi. east of the light. At 1.9 mi.,CR 16 turns into Platte Clove Road, bearing left (southeast). The CCCD Preserve is identified with signs on the right (south) side of Platte Clove Road at 6.4 mi.

This trail is the shortest, prettiest trail in the Indian Head Wilderness Area. It is perhaps the most popular approach to Indian Head summit. Find the Platte Clove Nature Preserve Trail a few hundred feet west of the residence on the south side of CR 16 (Platte Clove Road, seasonally unmaintained from November 15 to April 15). Parking is poor and often limited on the road's widened south shoulder, but additional space is available in the Kaaterskill High Peak Wild Forest parking area 0.25 mi. southeast of the preserve off Platte Clove Road (see Kaaterskill Wild Forest).

The trailhead is identified and marked with the CCCD's diamond-shaped green markers. You may also see some of the older markers, green arrows on rectangular silver backgrounds. There is no destination signage at this time. Trail markers are infrequent, and because this is not a state-marked or state-maintained trail, there is no trail register at this time.

The trail descends slightly to the headwaters of the Plattekill Creek, crossing a beautifully crafted, handmade timber-framed bridge. Just across the creek, the trail ascends gently, following to the right of the old road, which is for some distance a deeply eroded drainage ditch, worn several feet deep into the duff and soft silt subsoils. The area is densely foliated with a predominance of hemlock and assorted hardwood cover. Soon the trail assumes the original roadbed, in a very pretty setting where smooth surface bedrock has resisted erosion. A nameless tributary of the Plattekill crosses the stone trail, rarely exceeding a depth of several inches.

Within 20 minutes or so of the trailhead, the trail passes a quarry close on the left (east). Much of the talus has been reclaimed by nature, buried in moss and duff. These tailing piles can be explored easily, but this particular site is inferior (as quarries go) and less accessible than the highly attractive (and scenic) Codfish Point quarry, just ahead off the Overlook Trail. Use caution—footing is poor, the ledge pools are often deep and flooded, there are a few substantial pits (as in most quarries), and although they are seldom reported and this is not an identified denning site, rattlesnakes prefer this kind of ledgy (but typically more remote) habitat amid the forest.

At 1.0 mi., and a very short distance beyond the quarry, on state land, the Plattte Cove Nature Preserve Trail ends where the Devil's Path (red) comes in from the right (west) from its Prediger Road trailhead (this junction is poorly marked). The Devil's Path turns right (southwest) to Indian Head only a 2-minute walk farther (south) at the junction of the Overlook Trail (which is a continuation of the Old Overlook Road).

Devil's Kitchen lean-to is 0.2 mile ahead on the Overlook Trail, situated alongside the Cold Kill (see Overlook Trail for details).

CCCD Trail, Plattekill Falls Section (Platte Clove Nature Preserve)

to Plattekill Falls: 0.2 mi., 15 min.

The short path leads to a picturesque waterfall at the head of Platte Clove. The Platte Clove Preserve, located at the top of precipitious Platte Clove on CR 16, is owned and maintained by the Catskill Center for Conservation and Development (CCCD), a nonprofit, member-supported conservation advocacy organization (see CCCD Trail, Platte Clove Nature Preseve Trail; Platte Clove Section). The preserve is posted and well identified. Hikers are permitted to visit the property year-round. The center maintains a cottage on Platte Clove Road that is used seasonally by their artist-in-residence program (it is believed that Jack London spent time here during one of several extended visits to New York). There are two trails on the preserve. One goes south from a point just west of the cottage (see CCCD Trail, Platte Clove Nature Preserve Trail; Platte Clove Section); the other leaves from the cottage grounds and is accessible at the end of the driveway (please don't block the driveway).

Follow the old roadbed east, keeping an eye out for the green diamond Platte Clove nature Preserve Trail markers and even some of the older CCCD arrow markers. Bear right at the first fork (unmarked) and descend into a hemlock forest. As the trail drops steeply, it turns back to the right (the west). Avoid the unmarked spur to the left, particularly in winter, because it comes dangerously close to the vertical wall of the clove (it is possible to slide on the steep, icy surface with no means of arrest). The trail follows a slope above the Plattekill, soon arriving a the picturesque falls, which are about 50 feet high and normally run year-round. This is the end of the footpath.

Echo Lake Spur Trail

to Echo Lake lean-to: 0.6 mi., 25 min.

Echo Lake is a secluded pond lying to the north of Overlook Mountain at 2100-ft. elevation. Its lean-to has made it a popular spot for both backpackers heading for the Devil's Path and day hikers coming in from Meads on the Overlook Summit Trail.

From the Overlook Trail (1.4 mi. north of the intersection with the Overlook Summit Trail) the Echo Lake Trail drops downhill into the west (yellow markers). A descent of 600 ft. follows over the next 0.6 mi. The lean-to is situated on the north shore and is sometimes subject to noisy weekend visitors. Additional (legal) campsites exist to the east, where the trail follows the lakeshore for some distance.

Echo Lake is a fragile and popular spot, which is subjected to high-use quotas—staying within the legal parameters of camping will help to preserve this area. Echoes are good and were touted as a tourist attraction here during the heyday of the Overlook Mountain House.

Codfish Point Quarry Spur Trail

to lookout, 0.1 mi., 5 min.

This spur off of the Overlook Trail provides the only summer views along the approach to Overlook Mountain from the north. It is identified by a single yellow trail disk and is barely noticeable from the Overlook Trail.

At a point 0.6 mi. above (southeast) Devil's Kitchen lean-to, just as the trail levels and turns south to follow the eastern edge of Plattekill Mountain, the Codfish Point spur goes east. It is a vague but established footpath. Two large, flat puddingstones on the west side of the Overlook Trail, in the woods just opposite the spur, act as convenient markers (GPS N42.06.776/W074.04.656).

The spur trail begins level and descends slightly along the edge of the quarry, ending above a large, treeless talus field with an open easterly view of the Hudson Valley. The Saugerties lighthouse can be seen (with the naked eye) at 125 degrees. Tivoli Marsh is visible on the east side of the river behind Cruger and Magdalen Islands. Far into the east are farms—silos, barns cultivated hillsides—in Columbia and Dutchess Counties. Overlook Mountain and the fire tower can be seen at 218 degrees; the rock outcropping on the eastern slope is the Minister's Face. The Hudson Highlands (loosely defined by the definitive cut in the river between Storm King Mountain and Breakneck Point, just north of West Point) appear at 190 degrees. In the Shawangunks you see Guyot Hill and Bonticou Crag.

"No Camping" signs are posted in the quarry itself, which extends hundreds of feet south. Bits of old crockery, parlor stoves, and hut foundations conjure up images of quarrying days. As in many bluestone quarries, abandoned stones show evidence of manual tool work and lay among the piles. Against the vertical, working face of the pits, water gathers into shallow pools. Jim Morton (now eighty-seven), a lifelong resident of Platte Clove, tells the story of his grandfather, a quarryman who together with his coworkers was snowed in at the quarry for several days in the winter of 1890. Having finished all the tinned food available, they were reduced to the last few crates of salt cod, which they detested. In protest, and to identify the snowed-in quarry road to their "rescue" party, they nailed a piece of codfish crate to a tree. This marker remained in place for years, giving the point its name.

Stones from this quarry and others were used to pave the sidewalks of New York City and other Hudson River towns and were shipped in sailing vessels. Some may have ended up as far away as Havana, Cuba.

Section 5

Kaaterskill Wild Forest

East

The classification of this forest area as simply a wild forest can be deceiving—its 8,000 acres have the feel and nearly the size of a true wilderness area. It is also not heavily used, a feature that adds to its appeal, and is attracting an increasing number of visitors. Its two peaks, Kaaterskill High Peak (3655 ft.) and Roundtop (3440 ft.), get some attention from bushwhackers, and High Peak itself, although informally marked by a private user group, is classified as "trailless" by the DEC. The Long Path cuts through this area and is often used by thru-hikers as well as day hikers. Over the past twenty years, Huckleberry Point has gained in popularity, resulting in the trail's designation and marking with state trail markers. It is perhaps one of the most scenic and appealing destinations in the Northeast Catskills. The snowmobile trail that encircles Kaaterskill High Peak and Roundtop is both long and seldom used by hikers, but it remains popular with snowmobilers and has become a fairly popular backcountry ski route—one of the few practical routes in the eastern Catskills. An early trail emanating from Twilight Park in the northwestern extremes of the forest was once popular with Twilight Park residents and area hotel guests and crossed the northerly ridgeline above Wildcat and Hillyer Ravine to Poet's Ledge and Red Gravel Hill Road in the mid-nineteenth century. Abandoned for years, the trail was resurrected by the New York–New Jersey Trail Conference under permit by the DEC and formed the "missing link" of the Long Path, finally connecting to the northern Catskills in the 1980s. During the process, conference members led by Cap Field rediscovered and flagged a route to Poet's Ledge, and this early destination once again became a marked hiking trail. It is evident from the field sketches and finished works of Sanford R. Gifford that he used this vantage to render scenes of Kaaterskill Clove. Today, Poet's Ledge makes a practical and scenic day hike from Palenville. Hikers visiting the ledge should plan to take the extra time to see Wildcat Ravine and Buttermilk Falls, just to the west.

Kaaterskill Wild Forest Trail (Long Path)

   to Buttermilk Falls: 5.0 mi., 2 hr. 15 min.

   to Wildcat Falls: 5.5 mi., 2 hr. 30 min.

   to Poet's Ledge: 7.4 mi., 3 hr. 30 min.

   to Palenville: 9.0 mi., 4 hr. 30 min.

This remote and wildly scenic, upper-elevation trail provides exciting opportunities for extended day hiking, backpacking, and backcountry ski touring. It is also marked as a snowmobile trail for the first 3.5 mi., after which the foot trail descends into Kaaterskill Clove, passing a pair of vertical waterfalls and the historic Poet's Ledge.

   The trailhead can be reached from the east via precipitous Platte Clove, using Platte Clove Mountain Road (closed in winter), which is identified as CR 33 in West Saugerties (Ulster County), and as CR 16 "on the mountain" in the town of Hunter (Greene County), where the trailhead is located. Those electing to use this road should either be traveling in periods of dry weather or have a four-wheel-drive vehicle, as it is seasonally unmaintained. The safest route to the trailhead is from NY 23A in Tannersville, turning south onto Spring Street (CR 16), 0.25 mi. east of the only light in town. CR 16 becomes Platte Clove Road and heads east approximately 6.4 miles to the Kaaterskill Wild Forest trailhead parking lot.

   Turn left (north) on the dirt access road and go a short distance into the parking lot. Locate the trail sign adjacent to the barrier gate, where the trail departs to the north.

   The trail begins on deeply embedded Steenbergh Road (named after an early quarryman and landowner) uphill through a mixed forest of hemlock and hardwood, with a private parcel on the right (east). Marking is thorough, with snowmobile-trail signs and blue Long Path trail disks. At a fork (0.7 mi), the trail levels and trail signs appear. To the left (west), the road branches off onto private property. At this time the present trail signs are in error and should instead have been placed at the intersection with the snowmobile loop trail, 3.0 miles ahead.

Bear right and ascend steadily but easily. The trailbed, made of soft, red shale, tends to wash out. At 0.95 mi. (2300 ft.), at a fork, the trail turns right (east) off the more-established route and onto a foot trail (an old, abandoned road), following trail arrows, blue Long Path disks, and snowmobile-trail markers. Within 5 minutes or less of this intersection, at 1.05 mi., the Nature Friends Trail goes right (southeast) to Huckleberry Point (signed, yellow markers). The Kaaterskill Wild Forest Trail goes straight ahead here (northeast), ascending slightly. The terrain flattens through a hemlock forest, at 1.4 mi. crossing a footbridge over a sluggish creek where bear tracks often appear in the mud. It very soon crosses a plank gangway and another footbridge before ascending, beneath ash and maple trees. Touch-me-nots bloom profusely along here, where yellow blazes and cairns define the forest-preserve boundary to the left (west).

Stately hemlock emerges as the trail gains altitude over rocky, rooty footing, relaxing and climbing again into a beech woods before leveling out at 2.25 mi. (3000 ft). This picturesque section of the forest, where the trail is covered in bedrock and moss and lined with blueberry and an increasing density of spruce-fir, is called the Pine Plains. Water tends to pool here in the spring and winter. The area is densely foliated; tangled blowdowns and rotting snags lie off the trail, and slender green and white saplings of striped maple along with viburnum lean into the trail here and there. Also visible are some of the old-fashioned, yellow steel snowmobile markers. The trail continues flat and boreal until descending gently to the northwest under a sugar-maple canopy, arriving at an unsigned junction at 3.5 miles. The snowmobile loop trail around Kaaterskill High Peak (distance, 7.64 mi.) leaves to the left (southwest), where a short spur trail goes uphill to the loop itself. The Kaaterskill Wild Forest Trail continues straight ahead but is not signed and shows only unofficial, plain-blue trail disks at this time (for directions to the unmarked Kaaterskill High Peak foot trail, see Kaaterskill High Peak Snowmobile Trail).

The trail turns to the north at 3.7 mi. and begins to descend gradually through a mixed hemlock forest, arriving at the edge of a ridge where at 2200 ft. a large, conspicuous boulder is blazed with yellow forest-preserve-boundary paint. This marks the edge of the private Twilight Park's lands and the extension, from Twilight Park, of the old Kaaterskill High Peak Trail (unofficial). Bear right, dropping downhill through a ledge at this point, as the trail switches back, trending north, continuing its descent. As the terrain flattens, the trail heads briefly northwest before making a sharp turn into the east. Marking is poor here, and for a short distance the trail is not self-guiding. Watch carefully. Heading east, the trail draws close to Kaaterskill Clove, the heavy foliage providing only hints of South Mountain and the abyss to your left. Beginning from the snowmobile loop trail, this hundred-plus-year-old foot trail that was for so long marked with rusting tin-can tops, remained unmarked until volunteers from the New York–New Jersey Trail Conference revived it as a section of the Long Path. It is a part of the old Red Gravel Hill Road.

At 5.0 mi., the trail crosses the top of Buttermilk Falls, an unimaginative name for this spectacular falls that looks out across Kaaterskill Clove into North Mountain Wild Forest. Be especially aware of the steep drop here—the precipice is spotted with slippery moss and the bare, wet stone is slick. Although there may have been no water on the trail (and there may be none at all here in John Case Brook), there is almost always a barely audible stream of water flowing from the headwall under the falls themselves, even in very dry periods. Across Kaaterskill Clove, Stoppel Point (3420 ft.) appears as the highest landmark at 60 degrees. The deep ravine between Buttermilk Falls and Stoppel Point is the location of Kaaterskill Falls, which is not visible. North Mountain is to the right of Stoppel Point. With binoculars you can see North Point to the immediate right as a series of open ledges, where the Escarpment Trail works its way north. Below, serpentine NY 23A can be seen winding its way through Kaaterskill Clove.

The trail continues straight into the southeast on level, duffy ground, spotted with remote colonies of Indian pipes. At 5.5 mi., hemlock-shrouded Wildcat Falls is seen 50 ft. to the north of the trail and is a higher, more dangerous fall than Buttermilk Falls. The two open rock ledges at the eastern extreme of South Mountain are Indian Head Lookout (a historic profile rock) and Palenville Overlook, or High Rock. Stoppel Point and North Mountain are still visible, along with an open expanse of Hudson Valley flatland to the northeast.

Mountain laurel and colorful bunchberry decorate the trail as it continues east now, into an extensive hardwood grove that cuts across the dual streambeds above Hillyer Ravine at 6.0 mi., below which (and not visible from the trail) is Viola Falls. The trail curves into the north now, through an area of gravelly washouts that drain into Hillyer Ravine. The forest type changes to spruce and red pine, with increasing mountain laurel as the spur trail to Poet's Ledge is reached at 6.8 mi. (see Poet's Ledge Spur Trail for details). The Kaaterskill Wild Forest Trail terraces its way downhill steeply at times, through hardwoods, flattening amid laurel, and descending through deciduous forest. A level stretch over a narrow red sandy loam path follows, heading south, and the trail turns into the northeast to join the now-graded, road-width Red Gravel Hill Road at 8.5 mi., thereafter descending to a barrier gate. The trail turns left (north) after the gate, where a trail sign indicates the "Hiking Trail," and follows a private easement 100 ft. to Malden Avenue at 9.0 mi. A very popular local swimming hole in Kaaterskill Creek is just across the street and to the left here. Those continuing on the Long Path should turn left, passing through the guardrail at the dead end of Malden Avenue, turn right on NY 23A, and left again into the forest preserve at 0.3 mi., where a small parking area, state wild-forest signs, and aqua Long Path blazes are seen on the north (left) side of NY 23A. Food and services are available in Palenville, a few minutes' walk east of the trailhead.

Huckleberry Point Trail (The Nature Friends Trail)

Distance from Kaaterskill Wild Forest Trail (Long Path)

   to Huckleberry Point: 1.4 mi., 1 hr. 15 min.

This increasingly popular trail is a fascinating day hike, leading to a sweeping view of the Hudson Valley beyond Platte Clove. From the

Kaaterskill Wild Forest Trail (snowmobile and foot trail), 1.0 mi. north of the Kaaterskill Wild Forest parking area on Platte Clove Road, the Huckleberry Point Trail (aka Nature Friends Trail) goes east. A sign and trail arrow mark the junction. Old foundation stones and rock piles cleared for pasturelands by early settlers may be seen along the trail off in the woods. This junction marks the former residence of the Steenbergh family, who worked a quarry northeast of here at the end of Steenbergh Quarry Road. This trail was established by a group of German expatriates, escaping from their inflation-ridden, war-torn country in the 1920s. They established the trail and marked it with tin-can lids, which until recent state marking were maintained in white with a red center dot. They called themselves the Vanderverder—the wandering birds.

The trail is level but soon descends gently to cross Mossy Brook, which is easily forded under normal conditions. On the brook's north side, a reclaimed (by nature) road goes to Dunker's Clove and the site of an old quarry. The Huckleberry Point Trail continues south-southwest, soon climbing amid mountain laurel, oak, and hemlock. At 1.6 mi. (3000 ft.), the trail levels and it is possible to see Indian Head Mountain (3573 ft.) to the southwest, along with bits of the eastern Devil's Path, as well as Kaaterskill High Peak (3655 ft.) to the northwest. Even Overlook Mountain (3150 ft.) can be seen. The trail soon descends, passing a small, vague quarry on the right (south) side of the trail. A pure pitch-pine stand covers a knoll to the north as the point is approached. Suddenly the trail ends at the top of a series of vertical ledges overlooking the valley, with uncommonly good views of Platte Clove and the Devil's Path Mountains. There's a shallow quarry at this location also. The near precipice is covered in blueberry bushes.

Overlook Mountain and its fire tower is seen at 218 degrees. The crag on the eastern slope of Overlook is the Minister's Face, known for its famous rattlesnake den (folklore holds that the oil of these particular snakes has medicinal properties). Beyond, Sky Top and Eagle Cliff are visible. An arm of the Ashokan Reservoir is visible. Far south in a widening of the Hudson River, the Esopus Meadows lighthouse can be seen with binoculars. Plattekill Mountain (3110 ft.) is in the foreground, east of Indian Head. The rest of the Devil's Path range (with the exception of West Kill Mountain) is visible, including Twin (3650 ft.), Sugarloaf (3810 ft.), Plateau (3850 ft.), and Hunter (4050 ft.) Mountains.

Aside from its appeal to view-seekers, the strong thermal updrafts of warm air from the Hudson Valley lowlands make Huckleberry Point a popular spot for observing soaring raptors—most of them turkey vultures.

Poet's Ledge Spur Trail

to Poet's Ledge: 0.47 mi., 20 min.

From its junction at 6.8 mi. on the Kaaterskill Wild Forest Trail northeast of Hillyer Ravine, the Poet's Ledge Spur Trail drops 0.47 mi. to the west. At this time it ranks as the best-marked trail in the Catskills. The trail drops downhill to an open, flat rock with a makeshift fire ring (illegal) and a much older, more thoughtfully constructed fireplace, its foundation stones gathering moss. The trail bears left (southwest), following a low vertical ledge, and turns to the west at a flat ledge. Bearing left again (southeast), the trail ends at Poet's Ledge (1800 ft.), a west-facing platform divided by a narrow crevice that can be hazardous, especially when concealed by snow. This early hiking destination was known to many, possibly even to the "Kindred Spirits"—William Cullen Bryant and Thomas Cole—and it was more than likely the vantage used for composite sketches in several of Sanford R. Gifford's other well-known works including *Twilight in the Catskills* (1861), *Kauterskill Clove* (1862), and *October in the Catskills* (1880).

This view looking west into Kaaterskill Clove includes South Mountain (2460 ft.), with North Mountain (3180 ft.) above it, and Stoppel Point (3430 ft.) to the left. Blackhead (3950 ft.) and Black Dome Mountain (3990 ft.) stand over the top of West Stoppel Point

(3100 ft.). The solitary bump at 324 degrees is Parker Mountain (2820 ft.), and the large mountain sloping into it on the left is Onteora (3230 ft.). Kaaterskill High Peak (3655 ft.) and Hurricane Ridge and Hurricane Ledge are up high to your left. The various parallel drainages on the left (south) wall of Kaaterskill Clove are Hillyer, Wildcat, Buttermilk Falls, and Santa Cruz ravines, each of them joining Kaaterskill Creek. This is a spur trail and does not continue. The only way out is back the way you came. In the future the Long Path may be rerouted from the end of Poet's ledge Spur Trail through Kaaterskill Clove.

Kaaterskill High Peak Snowmobile Trail

around loop: 7.64 mi., 3 hr.

The Kaaterskill High Peak Snowmobile Trail loop begins at the 3.5-mi. point of the Kaaterskill Wild Forest Trail. In addition to being only slightly popular with hikers and very popular with snowmobilers, this trail has gained some popularity with backcountry skiers. The latter should be well aware that the loop is easily underrated in terms of its remoteness, difficulty, and distance, as it requires a fairly strenuous 3.7 mile uphill skinning or snowshoeing effort (which, depending on conditions, might be walkable), the 7.64-mi. loop itself, and the 3.7 mi. backtrack to the trailhead—a total of more than 15 miles. In addition, the track is often irregular, rocky, muddy, and icy after snowmobiles have compacted it, leaving little if any smooth diagonal striding terrain, notwithstanding fresh snowfall. Skiers should carry scrapers, skins or snowshoes, extra tips, and adequate provisions for exposed, upper-elevation travel. Steel edges and mountaineering outfits are advised.

The Kaaterskill High Peak Snowmobile Trail loop begins 3.5 mi. from the Kaaterskill Wild Forest Trail trailhead parking area in Platte Clove. The loop actually begins 300 yd. uphill (south) from this junction. Once on the loop, which circles both Kaaterskill High Peak (3655 ft.) and Roundtop (3440 ft.), at a mean elevation of 2800 ft., a sign indicates the total loop distance of 7.64 mi. The trail goes left (southeast), and slightly uphill. The first few hundred yards are grassy and thick with nettles before entering the shade of a northern hardwood forest. Turtleheads appear frequently, and do in fact resemble turtles' heads. (The genus name, *Chelone,* is Greek, for "tortoise.") In periods void of snowcover, hikers will see pieces of a shredded airplane that crashed here in 1989. Kaaterskill High Peak is close to the flatlands and subject to high winds and downdrafts. Like the rest of the escarpment area, it has claimed several aircraft. From this somber spot, stinging nettle becomes the worst anywhere, growing typically among sugar maple. A scree slope appears to the north amid pockets of fern and solitary stalks of meadow rue. Within 25 minutes of the crash site, and 1.7 mi. from the loop's beginning, the trail reaches a cairned, four-way intersection at 2900 ft., where the unmarked, unmaintained trail to Kaaterskill High Peak departs to the right (north). To the south the trail is marked with unofficial blue trail disks and descends to cross private lands. This is not a well-identified intersection, and without the cairn, it could be missed all together (GPS N42.09. 473/W074.04.942).

Continuing straight (west), the trail descends gradually to the 2700-ft. mark before turning northwest, where hemlock and very large ash trees appear. The trail ascends shortly, heading northeast and leveling. Hardwood shifts to intermittent hemlock as the trail moves farther east, at 4.4 mi. arriving at a three-way intersection. To the left (northwest), the trail is not immediately marked and descends to Clum Hill Road (in fact, snowmobile markers appear farther down this trail, which provides the fastest emergency egress onto private Cortina Valley ski area). A trail sign here reads "Around Loop and Return to This Point, 7.64 mi.," just as it does at the loop's beginning. The trail bears right (northeast), heading uphill. Traveling on the level through hardwoods and muddy swales, pass the northerly (unmarked, unofficial) Kaaterskill High Peak trailhead (GPS N42.10.057/W074.04.888), which leaves to the right (south) and over High Peak itself. This is a difficult spot to identify for hikers coming from the west, but it is just a 3-or 4-minute walk west of the next intersection, which is the starting point of the loop trail. Go left to return to the Long Path (Kaaterskill Wild Forest Trail).

Section 6

Overlook Wild Forest

East

This small (560 acre) parcel of wild forest is joined to the Indian Head Wilderness Area and lies within the Ulster County town of Woodstock. Overlook's summit (3150 ft.) and fire tower are the forest's main attraction for hikers, who often continue north to camp at Echo Lake or access the Devil's Path Trail. The Overlook Wild Forest is also the location of the Overlook Mountain House ruins, which still stand beneath the mountain's summit along the hiking trail.

Overlook Mountain, the large cornerstone peak seen from the NYS Thruway and from areas to the east, forms the southeasternmost limits of the escarpment. The mountain often figured in the works of Thomas Cole and other members of the Hudson River School of Landscape Painting, and it is believed that Cole himself gave the mountain its name in 1847 (it was previously called South Peak). Later artists were drawn to the scenic Saw Kill Valley, among them Ralph Whitehead and Hervey White, who founded the Brydcliffe Summer School of Art in Woodstock.

Overlook's fire tower attracts thousands of day hikers each year. Views from the summit are among the best in the Hudson Valley, including the interior Catskills and Shawangunks, the Hudson Highlands, Taconics, Berkshires, and beyond. Just as many hikers are drawn to the hotel ruins, a hazard the state has considered dismantling. The existing ruin is that of the third and last mountain house. The first mountain house was built in 1871 and burned in 1874. The second (1878) burned in 1924, at which time it was rebuilt with concrete. The depression slowed the building's construction, and during the Second World War the building was boarded up. The Department of Environmental Conservation (DEC) advises hikers to stay out of the ruin, parts of which are collapsed.

Overlook Mountain (3140 ft.) Summit Trail

to Overlook Trail: 2.0 mi., 1 hr.

to Overlook Summit: 2.5 mi., 1 hr. 20 min.

Overlook Mountain provides a simple, moderately strenuous, and very popular day hike to the mountain-house ruins and fire tower, with one of the best Catskill Mountain views available. From the Woodstock village green in the colorful heart of town, turn north off Tinker Street onto Rock City Road. (This spot is 2.8 miles from the forest-preserve-access parking area at the Overlook Mountain trailhead.) Within moments the associated ridges of Overlook Mountain and the Indian Head Wilderness Area appear; Woodstock was settled by artists on account of this landscape. Soon Overlook Summit and the fire tower are seen toward the eastern (right) edge of the ridge. At 0.6 mi. from the green, go straight through the four-way intersection of Glasco (glass company) Turnpike, where Rock City Road becomes Meads Mountain Road. Continue steeply uphill to the trailhead. The trail begins at the apex of Meads Mountain Road, opposite the Tibetan Buddhist monastery, Karma Triyana Dharmachakra. At the trailhead, there are close-up views of several mountains—most notably Indian Head—and hikers have a considerable elevation gain already behind them. Now at 1800 ft. there are only 1300 ft. remaining to climb Overlook, making this perhaps the easiest hike with such a remarkable scenic payoff in all the Catskills.

Signs and a map kiosk are located here. Follow red markers. The trail climbs, following the fire- and radio-tower maintenance road, a road originally pioneered by tanners and quarrymen and improved by the builders of the Overlook Mountain House (1871). Mountain laurel, hemlock, and oak characterize the foliage of this consistent and moderately strenuous ascent (the total elevation gain of 1300 ft. translates into a 520 ft. per mile rise (1000 ft. per mile and above is considered steep for the Catskills). Hikers may encounter skiers, sledders, walkers, other hikers and backpackers, joggers, mountain bikers, artists, photographers, birders, picnickers, families, forest rangers, tie-dyed members of the Rainbow Tribe—even the Dali Lama. This trailhead is often used by thru-hikers headed for the Devil's Path and points west, a trip that allows for more than 30 miles of continuous hiking.

Views of the Ashokan Reservoir appear in the southwest as elevation is gained, and Indian Head, among other ridgelines in the neighboring wilderness area, can be seen to the north (all views from the road are dwarfed by those from the fire tower). At 2900 ft., the trail passes the drab and haunting skeletal remains of the Overlook Mountain House. Adjacent to it is the new transmission tower, which local residents and environmentalists fought against desperately. The open, roofless ruins (and the nearby annex) are in certain areas unsafe, and unit management plans have called for their removal at some point. Inside the main hall, trees reaching 8 inches in diameter are growing vigorously. Intent upon demonstrating the hotel's visual history, local artists have decoupaged the walls with fascinating printed information and photos. These biodegradable artworks are presently dissolving (the posters are ingeniously made with fertilizer that will foster tree growth). The last attempt to rebuild the hotel was abandoned in 1928, a result of the Depression. Just a few minutes' walk uphill from the hotel site, at 2.0 mi., the trail arrives at the junction with the Overlook Trail.

The Overlook Summit Trail bears right (east) at the junction and ascends, passing a number of unmarked spur trails that the DEC has placed off-limits, then passes a small, strip-mined red-shale pit (it was used for road improvement and paint in the early days). Continuing the easy ascent, the trail wraps around the mountain through ledges, approaching the summit from the southeast. The trail becomes a footpath as it goes past the observer's cabin on the right and continues to the tower. On summer weekends the tower is open and staffed, and the cab can be entered. (For safety, only six people at a time should climb the tower, according to the DEC.) If the cab is closed, visitors can still climb to the highest flight of steps and survey the stunning scenery—easily ranking among the best Catskill views. (There are some views to the west here, which can be enjoyed by disabled hikers. The state is reviewing extending access plans with the aid of the New York State Office of Advocacy for Persons with Disabilities. Handicapped access, according to the DEC, may include the use, under permit, of four-wheel-drive vehicles or ATVs.) A compass won't work here because of the steel superstructure, and there are so many mountains that identifying individuals is difficult.

A piece of the mountain blocks a small easterly valley view. Observers can see bridges spanning the Hudson River from both Kingston and Rhinecliff. The Esopus Meadows lighthouse can be seen with binoculars in a widening of the river south of Kingston. Mills Mansion can be identified to the left of the lighthouse on the east shore. In the Shawangunks, you see the Trapps, Eagle Cliff, Sky Top tower, Guyot Hill (named for Arnold Guyot, the Princeton geologist and founder of the National Weather Service—he measured all the major Catskill peaks), and Bonticou Crag. Moving west into the high-peaks area Slide Mountain dominates a knuckly congregation of peaks, above and beyond Cooper Lake. The peak just above Cooper Lake and to the right is Mount Tobias (2550 ft.). Left of Cooper Lake is Mount Guardian (two-peaked). To the right of the cellular tower is Carl Mountain (2880 ft.) and next to it, Mount Tremper (2740 ft.). Beyond Tremper and to the right is the West Kill Wilderness Area. To the north are close-ups of the Indian Head Wilderness Area, including all of its mountains—Plattekill (3110 ft.), Indian Head (3573 ft.), Twin (3650 ft.), Sugarloaf (3810 ft.), and Plateau (3850 ft.). Kaaterskill High Peak (3655 ft.) and Roundtop (3440 ft.) in the Kaaterskill Wild Forest are plainly visible in the north, and beyond them are the Blackhead Mountains.

In addition to these views, another scenic area is located at the end of a trail that goes to the right of the observer's cabin and past the outhouse to a ledge looking south. The landscape painter Charles Lanman named this the Eagle's Cliff (vertical drops here are very dangerous). Mount Everett, at the Massachusetts–New York–Connecticut border can be seen from here, as can the Slide Mountain–Panther Mountain Wilderness Area, so this vantage offers sensational, sweeping views even to those who are reluctant to climb the tower. The large beige strip of wetland on the Hudson's east shore at 130 degrees is Tivoli Marsh. You can see the main dam on the Ashokan Reservoir (the last of the handmade dams, circa 1914) and the dividing weir at 228 degrees, with Ashokan High Point rising beyond the west basin.

Overlook Trail

to Devil's Path: 3.7 mi., 1 hr. 20 min.

This popular trail connects the Overlook Wild Forest to the trail system of the Indian Head Wilderness Area, in particular, the Devil's Path. Combining the two will provide hikers with extended outings up to 30 mi. in length.

The trail begins at the 2.0-mi. point of the Overlook Mountain Summit Trail, 0.5 mi. below Overlook's summit, and descends gently, passing around a barrier gate onto what is sometimes still referred to as the Old Overlook Road (blue markers), which goes north to Platte Clove Road. Various remains of the Overlook Mountain House's barns and support structures lie in the general vicinity, slowly disappearing into the underbrush. Water, flowing across the trail and out of a spring on the right side of the trail at 0.4 mi., is absent by early summer. Views of the Indian Head Wilderness Area develop to the northwest as the trail descends and slowly curves around to the east in a northern hardwood forest of sugar maple, beech, and yellow birch. The trail's surface is gravel and stone. Mountain laurel appears and the terrain flattens as the trail turns slowly left to the northeast. At 1.4 mi., the Echo Lake Trail heads downhill to the left (west). Continue straight as the trail heads due north and levels along the eastern slope of Plattekill Mountain. Limited views of the Hudson Valley improve with winter. At 1.2 mi., the trail swings farthest west (directly beneath Plattekill Mountain) and passes Skunk Spring on the left. The trail soon climbs gently, leveling out again as it passes a vague but established spur trail on the right. A solitary yellow marker exists at this time, indicating the short path to now forgotten Codfish Point, the only uninterrupted view available from the Overlook Trail (see Codfish Point Quarry Spur Trail).

Hereafter the trail descends, turning northwest, at 3.5 mi. reaching the footbridge spanning the Cold Kill, and shortly afterward (in view) the Devil's Kitchen lean-to. The stone remains of a charcoal kiln exist on the left of the trail near the lean-to and was the creek's original namesake (Coal Kill). A large quarry lies against the western slope above the trail as it descends, where remnant foundation corners and moss-laden talus slopes are evident. Below the lean-to and off the trail, the Cold Kill flows northeast into precipitous Platte Clove, first dropping over 100-ft. Black Chasm Falls, a fall used by ice climbers and considered dangerous on account of its remote location and steep terrain (it has claimed lives in recent years). At 3.6 mi., the Devil's Path is reached at the point where it leaves to the west to ascend Indian Head Mountain. This is the "official" end of the Overlook Trail, but the Old Overlook Road continues north 1.0 mi. to Platte Clove Road over the CCCD Trail (Catskill Center for Conservation and Development). That trail can be found another few hundred feet north, at a point where the Devil's Path joins the Overlook Trail, coming in from the east from Prediger Road trailhead parking area and the beginning of the Devil's Path. To identify the junction, pay close attention—marking is poor.

Section 7

Phoenicia–Mount Tobias Wild Forest

East

There are six mountains more than 2500 ft. in this wild forest, of which Tremper Mountain (2740 ft.) is the most prominent and most often hiked. The recent rerouting of the Long Path through Silver Hollow (to save hikers from walking the road miles to Mink Hollow) has made Silver Hollow Mountain (3000 ft.) accessible from Tremper's summit, also providing more direct access to the Indian Head Wilderness Area and the Devil's Path. Mount Tremper's fire tower provides a 360-degree panoramic view that attracts the public year-round, often bringing large numbers of hikers to this relatively low and otherwise viewless summit.

The mountain's two attractively situated lean-tos shelter many backpackers and provide respite for an increasing number of Long Path hikers. The Silver Hollow Trail (Long Path reroute) provides visitors to this area with one of the few north-south links between the southern and northeastern Catskills and crosses a high valley in a remote setting where pristine Warner's Creek spans the hollow. Additional trails are planned for the Mount Tobias and Toren Hoek parcels in the near future. An unmarked but increasingly popular old woods road, referred to as the Tanbark Trail by the Department of Environmental Conservation (DEC), follows the Mount Tremper ridge above Phoenicia and may be maintained for use under permit by several users.

Mount Tremper's appeal is enhanced by its position in the center of a vast bowl formed by much higher mountains and considerably larger forests and wilderness areas. Slopes in the unit are generally very steep, but the trails follow old tanbark, quarry, and fire-tower maintenance roads that switchback frequently and allow easy but steady climbing through the transitional hemlock-and-white-pine northern hardwood forests.

Mount Tremper Corners, situated at the southeastern extreme of the wild forest area at the crossroads of NY 212 and CR 40, was the site of an early fortification of the Continental Army (Great Fort Shandaken, 1779). Placed at a strategic location in the narrow flats of the upper Esopus Valley between Mount Tremper and Romer Mountain, the fortification guarded against surprise raiding parties of British soldiers, Tories, and their Mohawk allies who used such easily traveled lowland routes to raid the Hudson Valley settlements from the north and west. After the Revolutionary War, the area followed development patterns typical of Catskill Mountains, giving rise to sawmills, tanneries, bluestone quarries, and, later, furniture factories and railroads.

Hikers can examine the remnants and scars left by the quarry mines of yesteryear but are advised to use caution while exploring Mount Tremper's quarries, one of which lies close to the trail. According to the DEC, this quarry has one of the largest documented timber-rattlesnake concentrations on the southern slopes of the Catskills. These otherwise shy and reclusive creatures are most active on sunny and warm spring days, when they can be found lying among the warm rocks and slabs in the quarries. Hikers are more likely to see deer, bear, wild turkeys, ground squirrels, snowshoe and cottontail rabbits, and—with any luck—bobcats. Hikers who enjoy fishing are advised to come prepared—the Mount Tremper trailhead is located next to the Esopus Creek in an area of easy public access. Supplies are available in Phoenicia, 1.7 mi. west on CR 40.

Phoenicia Trail

to Mount Tremper summit: 2.8 mi., 1 hr. 30 min.

Mount Tremper (2740 ft.) has consistently proved a popular climb due to its fire tower and easy access from the nearby tourist towns of Phoenicia and Woodstock. As a result of its increasing use, the trailhead has been moved farther east along CR 40 (between Phoenicia and Mt. Tremper Corners), where a large parking area is located. The addition of a Long Path link accessible from the summit, running from Carl Mountain through Silver Hollow (created so hikers could avoid walking the road miles along NY 212), is an attractive hike in itself and will host a growing number of thru-hikers.

Mt. Tremper has the "feel" of a large mountain, as many hikers have noted of its stiff southwestern approach, long known as the

Phoenicia Trail. The mountain can also be climbed "the back way," up the path less taken from Jessup Road in the town of Willow, a hike involving less vertical rise but more distance (see Willow Trail). Hikers often arrange for shuttles to enable a loop hike of both trails, although parking is problematic at the Willow Trail trailhead. The Phoenicia Trail provides the most direct and practical route for the visiting day hiker. The fire tower, without which there are only limited easterly views from Mt. Tremper, assures its popularity for day hikers, and two lean-tos and a spring contribute to the mountain's practical appeal as an overnight destination.

Enter the trail from CR 40, a mile or so southeast of Phoenicia and 2 mi. northwest of Tremper Corners. Romer Mountain (2240 ft.) can be seen to the southwest from the parking lot. The trail begins next to the road and sign kiosk, where two wooden bridges lead to a string of stone steps. There is no distance signage at this time. The path levels as it heads north-northwest to join the truck trail at 0.5 mi. The trail then turns right (northeast) at the trail register, following along a flat section through hardwood forest, where rocks have been laid across the road to check seasonal runoff, a system that appears to be working well at this time. Large isolated hemlocks and a few giant oaks break the overstory of sugar maples as the trail climbs steadily to the first of a series of switchbacks, turning a long gradual arc into the south. Ledges appear uphill, and the large talus pile of an early quarry is evident on the left (north), its original roadbed visible. This side path can be followed to a high, right-angled rock face where the slabs were removed. The DEC has documented the existence of rattlesnake dens in this quarry, something hikers might want to consider before exploring it.

The Phoenicia Trail continues to ascend, switches back again and relaxes somewhat, becoming grassy as it travels through beautiful, open hardwood forest and winds its way past the Baldwin Memorial lean-to on the right (southeast) at 2.0 mi. (2000 ft.). There are no summer views from here. A short distance uphill on the left at 2.1 mi. is a piped spring, after which the trail bears slowly around into the northeast, maintaining its bearing uphill as the downslope forest cover turns to a welcome stand of evergreens. At 2.7 mi., the Mount Tremper lean-to is reached, and at 2.75 is the summit, where the tower stands in a small open patch of grass and rock enclosed by red-oak trees. At the tower's base is the original cornerstone of the long-gone observer's cabin, bearing the initials AA and CB, and the number 27—denoting the builders and the year of its construction, 1927.

The tower has been rebuilt using materials carried up the truck trail by ATV. The cab, the tower's enclosure, is sometimes staffed by volunteers on weekends and is only open during those times. But the top flight of stairs will provide the same promised views, a bit of wind, and respite from the black flies in late spring.

From the higher stages of the tower it is possible to look out over the canopy at dozens of peaks. Plattekill, Indian Head, both summits of Twin, and Plateau Mountains in the Indian Head Wilderness Area lie to the northeast (Olderbark is blocking your view of Sugarloaf). Continuing left (westerly) are Black Head and Black Dome in the far distance, and (closer) Hunter (looking carefully, you can find Hunter's fire tower with binoculars), Southwest Hunter, West Kill, and the seemingly endless array of peaks in the central Catskills, including Belleayre and Balsam among a chaos of hills (remember, the Catskills have 100 peaks more than 3000 ft. in elevation). To the south are Ashokan High Point, bits and pieces of the Ashokan Reservoir, and several high peaks including Wittenberg and Slide. To the right of Slide are Giant Ledge and Panther. To the east is Cooper Lake (Kingston's water supply), as well as Overlook Mountain. Sky Top and Eagle Cliff are seen in the Shawangunks to the south, with the Hudson Highlands beyond.

At this point, the Phoenicia Trail ends, but the trail itself continues northeast as the Willow Trail and the Long Path.

Silver Hollow Trail (Long Path)

Distances from Willow Trail/Phoenicia Trail junction

   to Warner's Creek: 2.0 mi., 1 hr. 15 min.

to Silver Hollow Notch: 5.4 mi., 2 hrs. 30 min.

Completed in 2000, the Silver Hollow Trail provides a Long Path link that was designed to eliminate the need for thru-hikers to walk additional road miles between Willow and Lake Hill. Because it is so recent, the trail is not yet entirely self-guiding, and hikers are advised to pay close attention to trail markers. This is a well-designed, interesting trail that explores Warner's Creek and Silver Hollow, some of the quietest country in the Catskills.

Beginning at its junction with the Willow Trail and the Phoenicia Trail, 2.1 mi. northeast of Mount Tremper, the trail heads north, descending 400 ft. along the imprint of an old roadway before leveling out at 0.5 mi. on the western slopes of Carl Mountain (2880 ft.) at 2000 ft. The trail descends, switching back into the northeast through the long, steady drop into Silver Hollow. During leafless months, views of West Kill Mountain (3890 ft.) open up to the left (northwest) across Stony Clove. The ridge slopes away steeply to the left as ledgy terrain rises to the right (east) and the grade relents. From a small flat rock with a northerly exposure at 2100 ft., views across Silver Hollow reveal both West Kill and, now, Plateau Mountain (3850 ft.) to the northeast. At 1.4 mi. the trail descends very steeply into the hollow, approaching an eroded streambed while switching back along its left (west) bank. Marking becomes scarce at times, but the trail remains within audible distance of the creek, soon crossing it above the site of two small bluestone quarries on the right (east) of the stream. Tailings strewn into the creek bed mark the excavations, which can be explored east of the trail, and bits of tooled stone can be seen in the trail as it descends straight ahead (northeast). The trail now follows the treadway of the original quarry road, and the grade relaxes as it arrives in Silver Hollow, passing the foundation ruins of a house and barn on the right (east). The trail turns right (east) here, following picturesque Warner's Creek, where several ideal camping locations present themselves in the hemlock woods beyond the 150-ft. legal camping distance from the creek. Drawing close to Warner's Creek, at 2.0 mi. the trail switches back

180 degrees to ford it (there is no bridge at this time; watch your step) and follows east (right) again on the north side, on an old road. Within a few minutes' walk, cross a small tributary and watch to the left for the point at which the trail turns left into the north, following an eroded and sometimes vague path as it ascends through a sugar-maple forest over rocky footing. Large oak follow, and hemlock appear as the trail cuts across slope, rising briefly into the northwest through boulder-strewn forest. Leveling at 3.10 mi. (2700 ft.), onto a ridge where small wet areas flood flat pockets of woods, hemlock appear in isolation, and many blowdowns (black cherry) appear. At 4.0 mi., the trail descends, following next to a low ledge on the left (northwest) before rising slightly onto the northerly corner of the ridge at 2700 ft. A small, very old fire ring that significantly predates the trail sits near an open ledge among tufts of reindeer moss. Limited views exist to the northeast of Olderbark and Plateau Mountains. Skirting ledges to the right (north) and descending, the trail enters the Silver Hollow Notch at 5.4 mi., joining a disused section of Silver Hollow Road at 2350 ft. Members of the NY–NJTC have thoughtfully placed small, unobtrusive signs here. Watch carefully for them.

Hikers wishing to park at this (north) end of the trail can best do so from NY 214 north of Phoenicia and coming south onto Silver Hollow Road north of Phoenicia, where it is possible to park legally along the roadside 0.5 mi. north of the trailhead. Limited roadside parking is also available on the section of Silver Hollow Road south of the trailhead (the middle 1.5 mi. of Silver Hollow Road is not drivable). Designated parking is both unavailable and unlikely to be established on either side of the notch, and pullover parking on both sides requires some walking to the trailhead. This area is heavily hunted, and like many places where state and private lands abut, boundaries may be inaccurately posted to discourage otherwise legal public access. This practice is especially true of the southern approach, which although easily followed, is not marked.

Willow Trail

to Mount Tremper: 3.2 mi., 2 hr.

This is the less popular of the two traditional approaches to Mount Tremper (2740 ft.). It follows the route of an old road, penetrating Hoyt Hollow into a remote section of the Phoenicia–Mount Tobias Wild Forest.

From NY 212 in Willow, take Van Wagner Road north 0.3 mi. to Jessup Road, turn left, and find the trailhead at 1.5 mi. There is no trailhead parking area provided, and a private party has posted the road access. It is legal to park on the side of the road before this point, and to walk on the public easement to the trailhead, 0.3 mi. ahead.

The trail begins on the left (southwest) side of the road in a small clearing and immediately gains elevation, turning to the northwest at 1550 ft. Here it climbs against the steep northeast wall of Hoyt Hollow, allowing only seasonal views of Olderbark and Little Rocky. Leveling briefly and again climbing, the trail makes its way to the shallow saddle at 1.5 mi. (1900 ft.) between Carl Mountain and Mount Tremper, where it joins the Long Path, which departs north toward Silver Hollow. The Willow Trail turns left (southwest) toward Mt. Tremper.

The trail follows blue markers along the heavily wooded and remote northwest ridge of Mt. Tremper. There is little steady elevation gain. Oak provides the dominant forest type here as the trail steadily and easily climbs to the summit ridge beyond 2400 ft. Sparse winter views open up as the trail hugs the eastern ridge, which narrows as hemlocks and low ledges appear. This exposed section of the ridge is often ravaged by high winds, and cherry trees, especially, are often blown down from their tenuous grasp in the shallow soils. One last rise remains and the hiker's elevation debt is paid in full as the fire tower shows itself at 3.6 mi. (2740 ft.). The lean-to is just beyond the summit (see Phoenicia Trail).

Southern Catskills

The Southern Catskills include the region bounded by NY 28 and NY 28A in the north and northeast, by Big Head Indian Hollow (CR 47) to the west, and CR 3 and NY 55 in the south. Because of the concentration of high peaks in such a vast and scenic wilderness setting, the Southern Catskills, comprised of the Slide Mountain Wilderness Area, the Sundown Wild Forest, and the Willowemoc–Long Pond Wild Forest are the Catskills' most popular hiking destination, and claim the Catskills' highest mountain (Slide, 4190). There are many marked trails, lean-tos, designated campsites, trout streams, rugged peaks, and expansive scenery here. Opportunities for extended backpacking trips are plentiful. Several rigorous day hikes can be arranged from most of the trailheads.

The wild-forest areas to the south and west of the central high-peaks wilderness area offer hikers another kind of experience, one with far fewer hikers and deeper, quieter forests of less challenging terrain. Together these areas (the Willowemoc–Long Pond and Sundown Wild Forests) offer the best backcountry ski-touring trails and the best mountain-biking trails the Catskills have to offer. The rest of the terrain in the southern region is self-limiting to these sports.

The Southern Catskills are also the headwaters of important streams such as the Neversink, the Esopus, and the Rondout, each of which contributes to New York City's water system. The southern watersheds themselves have drawn a great deal of tourism to the area, mostly fly fishers. A good deal of championship-level kayak racing has been conducted on the Esopus as well. Born on the slopes of Slide Mountain, the Esopus is well known for its spring run of rainbow trout. The fish winter in the Ashokan Reservoir and run upstream to spawn in the early spring, often becoming record catches. Hikers are advised that swelling spring waters produce good upper-elevation fishing for wild strains of native trout.

The Southern Catskills have been important to the proliferation of the state's most harvested big-game animal—the white-tailed deer. Hikers are advised to take precautions when traveling afield during hunting season. Check with the forest ranger in the area you expect to travel and, when possible, wear brightly colored clothing (ideally blaze orange).

Section 8

Sundown
Wild Forest

East

The most interesting areas to hikers of this 30,000-acre wild forest are the 4100-acre Kanape section's trail to Ashokan High Point and the 8600-acre Vernooy Kill Falls section with its matrix of snow-mobile, hiking, skiing, and bike trails. The forest is comprised of low mountains and ridges, with ten mountains more than 2000 ft. This wild forest has a wilderness feel as the result of the neighboring Slide Mountain Wilderness Area to the north and the 14,900-acre Willowemoc–Long Pond Wild Forest to the west. To the northwest, along the section of Peekamoose Road at Bull Run, it is bordered by Peekamoose Wild Forest, which is popular for its primitive camping areas.

The geologic centerpiece of this lonely, mostly trailless group of quiet hills, collectively known as the Ashokan Catskills, is the huddle of crowns around High Point itself. The area's lower elevations once supported bluestone quarrying and water-powered milling. Berry harvesting as well as the gathering of wintergreen (for oil) were confined to upper elevations.

The floral diversity of the forest is perhaps the most fascinating feature of this wild-forest area, which is in many ways typical of the rest of the Catskills. Although there are no threatened or endangered floral communities in the Sundown Wild Forest, it is interesting to note the presence of the globally rare small-whorled pogonia, an orchid that was identified by the botanist Herbert Denslow in the 1920s. It has not been rediscovered since, notes the Olive Natural Heritage Society. The three birds orchid, another of Denslow's finds, was rediscovered here by Henry Dunbar in the 1950s.

Among the most fanciful references to this area is the account of a lost, secret hideaway near Ashokan High Point's summit. Outlined in Dewitt Clinton Overbaugh's *Hermit of the Catskills* (1900), this hermit cave was lavishly appointed with animal skins, rustic furniture, and lamps fueled by bear fat. The hermit and his mate, a beautiful Indian princess, had played host to such dignitaries as George Washington and the murderous Mohawk chieftain, Joseph Brant (presumably not at the same time—Brant's military efforts were on behalf of the British). Still, both their portraits hung on the cavern's walls.

Hikers will also find the Vernooy Kill Falls area of interest. A high plateau, hemlock forests, and extensive wetlands surround a matrix of roads connected by hiking trails that are suitable for mountain biking and backcountry skiing. The most popular destination is Vernooy Kill Falls, a series of low cascades and shallow pools.

Several excellent primitive campsites can be found off the Vernooy Kill Falls–Bangle Hill trailhead. Located in four distinct areas— the Upper, Middle, Lower, and Trailer fields—these sites are managed by forest rangers. Permits are required for trailer camping, and for stays of more than three nights (tent campers included).

Ashokan High Point Trail

around loop, return to trailhead: 8 mi., 5 hr. 30 min.

to Ashokan summit: 3.6 mi., 1 hr. 45 min.

This peak (alternately called High Point, Shokan High Point), while smaller than many trailed summits in the Southern Catskills, is unusually scenic. It is also more easily accessible from NY 28 than the neighboring Catskill high peaks, and although a rigorous climb, is easier than most of them. The mountain is within a wild forest, but it conveys a true wilderness feeling because it is joined physically to the Slide Mountain Wilderness Area, of which hikers will enjoy intimate and spectacular views. Ashokan High Point is an ideal destination for a satisfying overnighter, especially for the small family new to backpacking, or for the inexperienced hiker seeking a moderately challenging route. It is also a popular trek among day-hiking parties interested in the kind of close-up, big-mountain scenery that is typically a feature limited to the interior Catskills' highest (and busiest) peaks, and for those who want to pick over one of the few former commercially viable blueberry crops in the Catskills.

The trail begins deep in the rugged, densely wooded valley of Peekamoose Clove. The recommended (road) route from the east is from Winchells Corners in Shokan on NY 28, then coming south across the Ashokan Reservoir's dividing weir (0.3 mile). The view from the weir is possibly the best available view of the Catskill peaks and Ashokan High Point from anywhere in the eastern Esopus lowlands, a spectacle that ranks easily among the most impressive views in the Hudson Valley. This particular vantage of High Point inspired the pre-impoundment landscape *High Point,* by the Hudson River School of Landscape Painting's cofounder (with Thomas Cole), Asher B. Durand (1853).

Those using this particular route will cross the weir dividing the reservoir's western and eastern basins and turn right at the T onto Monument Road, crossing the original Ashokan Dam on its narrow causeway. At this point, Ashokan High Point is ahead and slightly to the left (south). Bear right onto NY 28A toward Olivebridge, skirting the edge of the posted buffer zone's extensive evergreen forests. Five miles beyond the T, bear left onto Watson Hollow Road (CR 42) toward Sundown, and follow gradually uphill along the winding Bush Kill into Peekamoose Clove.

Four miles uphill into the Clove on CR 42, turn right (north) into the Kanape Brook trailhead parking area. A map kiosk and outhouse are present at this time. On the south side of the road and downhill 200 ft., enter the trailhead (red markers) on a wooden bridge spanning Kanape Brook. The trail is self-guiding, an old road used by early settlement farmers to reduce travel time between here and the Rondout Valley. In 1930 the road was improved by the Civilian Conservation Corps and remains in excellent condition with the help of a local scout troop. The surrounding forest is primarily a second-growth mix of birch, maple, and ash, but the Kanape itself is thick with hemlock.

The trail passes the register on the left and climbs slightly. Stone heaps, wall remnants, culverts, and the ramparts of a small bluestone dam (perhaps used to power a mill) appear along the trail and in the surrounding woods (these were part of the Watson's farm, for whom Watson Hollow is named). Little Rocky (3015 ft.) emerges through the forest canopy to the right (south), and neighboring Mombaccus

(2840 ft.) soon appears. Laurel hems the trail and Norway spruce is evident singly and in isolated stands.

The trail levels as a designated campsite is reached at 1.5 mi., where a broken fire ring stands in an open clearing of grass adjacent to the Kanape and a dense, boreal glen of Norway spruce. Aside from the summit balds, this is the optimal campsite. Backpackers can expect to reach this site in under an hour from the trailhead. Should the campsite be in use, many more legal (though undesignated) camping opportunities exist in the extensive Norway-spruce plantation in proximity to the brook (observe the 150-ft. rule and use the designated site, if possible, to limit impact). It is also possible to camp near the saddle ahead.

The trail erodes and ascends, steepening through a hardwood forest with a few very large oak, ash, and hemlock trees. A hemlock understory develops as the saddle is approached, where the terrain levels into a grassy, open woods. Note the trail arrow at the T and the obvious summit trail to the left (north) at 2.5 mi., before resting at the saddle 300 ft. beyond, where a large, open campsite (legal, undesignated) and fire ring exist adjacent to private land at 2100 ft. At this point the old road descends into Samsonville (Marbletown), becoming Freeman Avery Road. There is no legal access from the south at this time.

At the previous T, the trail turns northeast toward Ashokan High Point, within 150 ft. passing the vague and poorly marked loop trail on the left (northwest), which is the longer approach to the summit. Continue straight ahead (northeast) as the trail turns from road to footpath, quickly gaining elevation into an oak-and-laurel forest. Water bars are frequent as the trail terraces, rising in sometimes steep shelves between easier pitches. An obvious but unmarked, short spur to the right (south) leads to poor southerly views. The trail continues to ascend at a 30-degree incline, while views to the southwest open up. The summit is attained at 3.6 mi., with its restricted scenery to the south. Other peaks in the area showcase views to the south in a much grander fashion (in particular, Wittenberg) but the views from High Point of the southeast-facing slopes of the Burroughs Range to the northwest are among the most striking to be found anywhere, and these will be encountered a very short distance farther along the trail.

From High Point summit, several significant landmarks are visible, however. Sky Top tower of the Mohonk Preserve, Eagle Cliff, and the Mohonk Mountain House itself are visible at 165 degrees magnetic, across the Rondout Valley. The Hudson Highlands (to the right of Sky Top and far south) are roughly 45 miles away (between Storm King and Breakneck Mountain a small section of the Hudson can be identified). The city of Kingston and the seemingly unbroken woodlands of Hurley, Rochester, Marbletown, and Wawarsing lie below. The ridge horizons to the south (following right from Sky Top) are the lands of Minnewaska State Park. Given a clear day, you can see into the ridges of New Jersey's Kittatinny Mountains to the thin tower on the state's highest point, High Point. Views of the Ashokan Reservoir, to the east, are very limited.

The Samson No. 1 and No. 2 benchmarks are imbedded in the summit, as well as the anchor bolts for a dismantled triangulation tower. There are several poorly scribed graffiti, dating to 1878. Just beneath the summit is a rock overhang that might shelter a hiker or two from the rain and a flat area that has been significantly damaged by (illegal) camping. The trail continues to the north. It is marked, but not immediately obvious, and leads a short distance to several southwesterly vantage points, the first of which again shows the Kittatinny's High Point tower at 220 degrees and Little Rocky in the immediate foreground. In the west, fine views begin to take shape, first of Peekamoose and Table Mountains. This north-facing area of the summit is a nearly continuous bald of late lowbush blueberry *(Vaccinium angustifolium),* the best blueberry patch that exists in the Catskills. Blueberries were deliberately encouraged here, and both intentional and rare natural fires have kept the summit open, the soils thin, and the berries prolific. It will prove very worthwhile to visit during berry season, which is roughly two weeks behind the normal season at sea level (toward late July is the typical harvesttime).

Consuming vistas will tempt hikers off the trail and onto the rus-set, open balds, especially during berry season. Off the berry patches in the scrubby hardwood margins it is possible to camp legally. Views of the Ashokan Reservoir can be had by foraging east through the woods. The low knob to the east is Little High Point (2800 ft.). Half of the knob is privately owned. At this time the state is interested in acquiring that parcel for the ultimate construction of a larger loop that would descend to the north, cut west across South Hollow, and connect with the Kanape Trail.

Three small but conspicuous boulders sit in an area to the north of the trail where sandstone bedrock surfaces in small patches. From a position roughly in the center of these open fields are Slide Mountain (4190 ft.) at 330 degrees and Balsam Cap. Moving left from Slide is an unnamed peak (3446 ft.), then Rocky (3508 ft.), Lone (3721 ft.), Table (3847 ft.), and Peekamoose (3843 ft.) follow. To the right of Slide is Friday (3694 ft.), Cornell (3870 ft.), and Wittenberg (3780 ft.). The Burroughs Range is the birthplace of the Rondout Creek, which winds around to the west and east again, emptying into the Hudson in Kingston. The Devil's Path mountains (Indian Head Wilderness Area) stand to the northeast, and to the right of Wittenberg are the rural uplands of Lexington, Hunter, and the rugged West Kill Wilderness Area, including Hunter Mountain (4050 ft.).

Following the loop adds an hour to this hike. If the weather deteriorates or darkness approaches, it is advised that hikers return the way they came. The trail continues along the western slope of the mountain. Although it would seem that the trail might proceed to the north here (following herd paths across the balds), it in fact goes off to the left (west), so watch carefully. Because trees and rocks are scarce here, so are trail markers and paint blazes. Backtrack if necessary to regain the trail. The trail turns into the forest to the north-northwest, toward Slide Mountain, and drops downhill through a section that is not adequately marked.

Continuing on the loop, the trail continues up and down gently through a mixed hardwood forest. Views are limited. At 4.1 mi., the trail turns 90 degrees to the left (south) and is not adequately marked at this time. Without the aid of a GPS, it is possible to miss it entirely (coordinates N41.55.807/W074.17.985). Although the trail has been difficult to follow in places so far, it becomes (and remains) self-guiding after the turn. Where the terrain opens to northwesterly views, ignore an established path to the right as the main trail bears left. The route swings southwest and descends gradually, changing direction 180 degrees, from northwest to southeast, and back into the southwest again toward Mombaccus Mountain and the saddle (where the summit ascent began at the 2.5-mi. point). Parts of the descent are steep and rubble strewn. At 5.5 mi., the loop is completed, and the trail turns right (west), reaching the saddle in a few hundred feet. The trail turns right (northwest) and descends to the trailhead at 8.0 mi.

Vernooy Kill Falls–Bangle Hill Trail (Long Path)

   to Peekamoose Road: 9.7 mi., 4 hrs.

Vernooy Kill Falls has become a popular destination for hiking and ski touring, and the matrix of roads and snowmobile trails provides some of the most ridable mountain-biking terrain in the forest preserve. This section of the Long Path crosses Bangle Hill into Sundown, where it continues over Peekamoose Mountain. Marking in this section needs improvement, and relatively few recreational hikers—other than those using the Long Path—hike in the area north of Vernooy Kill Falls. (At some point in the future the Long Path will be rerouted through the Lundy Parcel at the north end of Lundy Road.) GPS coordinates are provided for aid in identifying the several key trail junctions in this section of the Sundown Wild Forest.

   The trailhead is located off Upper Cherrytown Road. From NY 209, 0.6 mi. north of the traffic light in Kerhonkson, take Samsonville Road (CR 3) left (northwest) about 3.5 mi. from NY 209, bearing left onto Upper Cherrytown Road where Ridgeview Road comes in from the north. Continue bearing left. At a three-way junction, bear right on Upper Cherrytown Road and continue 3.0 mi. to the DEC trailhead parking area on the right (east) side of the road. The trail leaves immediately across the road from the parking area, following a marked (multiuse) hiking and snowmobile trail into a white-pine-and-oak woods. Signs are posted on Upper Cherrytown Road at the trailhead.

At 0.25 mi., the trail crosses a footbridge over Mombaccus Creek, ascending steadily through a burned-over area to the left of the trail, which has substantially damaged the understory of maple saplings. This 850-acre fire was started by a careless hiker (May, 2001), according to forest rangers. The trail ascends, pulling away from the creek, passing a woods road that veers left. Continue straight, still climbing. The trail soon levels and descends gently, passing a designated campsite to the left before arriving at Vernooy Kill Falls at 1.8 mi. The falls are small, appearing mostly upstream of the bridge in several tiers. A narrow chute flows under the bridge, and the creek flows past the single intact wall of an early gristmill built in the 1700s by Cornelius Vernooy.

A few herd trails explore the general area, upstream and down. The trail continues to the right (northwest) of the bridge and uphill a very short distance (300 ft.), following the snowmobile trail's north loop. The south loop continues across the bridge and goes on to Greenville.

Long Path blazes are not evident through this section (or the remaining distance to Peekamoose Road), but blue state-trail disks appear consistently. From this point forward, there is no destination signage. The trail ascends slightly and levels, following a dirt road. Watch carefully, when at 2.65 mi., the trail turns left (GPS N41.53.027/W074.21.756) and ascends gently. (To the right 0.2 mi. is Vernooy Kill Road, a trailhead parking area, and two designated campsites on a creek.)

Climbing gently to the north-northeast, at 3.9 mi. the trail turns to the left (west) again, where it joins another, more established woods road (GPS N41.53.884/W074.22.049). Cross an auto bridge and continue as several side trails appear, crossing another, smaller, deteriorating (at this time) plank bridge at 4.60 mi. The forest is dense hemlock with mountain laurel beneath. Water is abundant and the sandy road is typically wet and potholed. Pass a rustic hunting camp to your right (north), and soon thereafter a dirt road leaves to the left at 5.35 mi. Continue straight, watching to the right for a pair of poorly built cairns that mark the trail at 5.6 mi. The trail (now a footpath) turns right here (GPS N41.53.713/W074.23.628) and climbs to another dirt road. Turn left (southwest) at 5.9 mi. (GPS N41.53.784/W074.23.907). NOTE: To the right this road curves uphill slightly and ends at the site of a small stone shack. Hikers who have reached this point have gone too far and must backtrack a few hundred feet, watching for the markers, which are placed above eye level and are easy to miss.

At 6.1 mi. the trail turns right (north) and goes uphill (GPS N41.53.682/W074.23.992). Ascend easily. Within a few hundred yards the trail turns sharply to the left (west-northwest) and climbs to a height of land before descending easily, passing through thin hemlock stands, crossing a rocky creek (dry in late summer), and another, smaller but usually flowing trickle. The trail ascends to Bangle Hill, arriving at 8.7 mi. (2350 ft.). It is heavily wooded—there is no view. Following a steep descent down the north side, the trail turns west, nearly leveling as it traverses a steep slope, and follows a seasonal streambed downhill to join a woods road in a homogeneous sugar-maple forest. Now the trail descends very steeply, passing two skid roads to the left (west) and a deep gully to the right, at 9.7 mi. arriving at Peekamoose Road.

A small trailhead parking area is located across the road. The extensive Sundown Primitive Campsite on the north side of Peekamoose Road offers dozens of good tent sites. From here, West Shokan is 11.0 mi. to the northeast along CR 42. The Long Path continues from the north side of Peekamoose Road (CR 42), 0.4 miles to the east.

Section 9

Slide Mountain Wilderness Area

The Slide Mountain Wilderness Area is the Catskills' largest, mos popular wilderness. At 47,500 acres, it contains the Catskills' highest summit (Slide Mountain, 4180 ft.) and an extensive trail area making trips of several days' duration possible. Located in the north-western corner of Ulster County, the tract forms the watersheds of the Esopus, Rondout, and Neversink Rivers. The terrain is rugged and scenic, encompassing a group of trailed and trailless peaks, boasting thirteen named mountains more than 3000 ft. in elevation.

Hikers visiting the Slide Mountain Wilderness Area will be presented with many options for challenging single-and-multiday outings. The most popular of these is the Burroughs Range Trail (the Wittenberg-Cornell-Slide Trail), a skyline trail named for the Catskills' naturalist and guardian, John Burroughs. The Burroughs Range Trail can be hiked in a single day by avid hikers in good condition (who have spotted a car on each end of the trail), but the preferred method for many is an approach of two separate day hikes, allowing time to be spent enjoying the views from Wittenberg and Slide (Cornell's view is limited).

In the north of this area is the tremendously popular Giant Ledge, an easy day outing with significant scenic attractions. Panther Mountain is less frequently hiked as a destination in itself, but it is used as a thru-trail for extended hikes from the south Slide Mountain is the area's most popular destination by merit of its height, but most hikers do not consider its views to be as good as Wittenberg's. Still, the allure of Slide is great. Slide's summit view includes nearly seventy named Catskill peaks as well as a wide view of the Hudson Valley, Ashokan Reservoir, Green Mountains, Berkshires, Taconics, Hudson Highlands, and Shawangunks. This is the same view that Commissioner Cox, climbing Slide in 1886, pronounced to be "every bit as fine as anything to be seen in the Adirondacks."

Recently, New York State geologist Ingvar Isachsen discovered that a meteorite impacted the area around what is today's Panther Mountain some 375 million years ago. His discovery was backed up by his recovery of spherules—tiny iron droplets of condensed gas that

y. Satellite images clearly show the circular crater,
circuitous route of the Esopus Creek, which hikers can
udying their map.

ntains in the Slide Mountain Wilderness Area are
pruce-fir rocky summits and mountain spruce-fir forest
(3000—~ / ft.), the latter of which is very rare in New York State. Northern hardwoods persist at lower elevations. Hikers will find many wildflowers and ferns common to the area and that this wilderness contains the largest continuous old-growth forests in the Catskills, with several virgin tracts. Wildlife abounds, and there are significant deer-wintering areas and important bear habitat. (Porcupines may visit hikers for lunch or try to investigate backpacks on summits.) A distinct species of thrush that depends on boreal forest (Bicknell's Thrush) was discovered by E. P. Bicknell in 1881 and is believed to inhabit several peaks in the wilderness area.

Public use has caused significant impact in this wilderness area. Trailhead registrations show Slide Mountain with the greatest number of visitors annually, with Giant Ledge attracting similar numbers. The fewest hikers come in from Fox Hollow in the north. Average yearly totals run upward of 20,000 visitors, most arriving between mid-May and mid-October. The area's capacity to withstand use has been challenged with the steadily rising number of visitors each year and the Department of Environmental Conservation (DEC) asks for strict compliance in order to avoid deterioration of the wilderness character of this area. Trail maintanence is ongoing by the DEC, the New York–New Jersey Trail Conference, the Adirondack Mountain Club, and other groups. Hikers can do their part by using backpacking stoves instead of building fires, by camping in designated areas only, by staying on marked trails, and employing the principles of Leave No Trace (see page xxvii).

Wittenberg-Cornell-Slide Trail (The Burroughs Range Trail, Long Path)

to Terrace Mountain Trail: 2.6 mi., 1 hr. 30 min.

to Wittenberg summit (ascent 2500 ft.): 3.9 mi., 2 hr. 30 min.

to Cornell summit (Cloud Cliff): 4.7 mi., 3 hr.

to Slide summit: 7.0 mi., 4 hr. 30 min.

to Slide Mountain Parking Area: 9.75 mi., 5 hr. 30 min.

This is the Catskills' most popular interior forest route, traversing the Slide Mountain Wilderness Area and providing hikers with a scenic and memorable wilderness experience. The area is fragile and sensitive to the many visitors it has endured over the years. It has been determined by the DEC that more than 35,000 people a year use this wilderness area, most of them finding their way to the summit of Slide Mountain.

The trail begins at the Woodland Valley trailhead parking area at the end of Woodland Valley Road, just east of the state campground's main gate (see Phoenicia–East Branch Trail for directions from Phoenicia). A day-use fee (3 dollars at this time) is collected for each parked car during the months of the campground's operation. Consult the map and information kiosk in the parking area. Cross the road, and go left (east), with the campsite on the right (south). Trail signs are posted on the right, in view of the parking area.

In addition to blue state-trail markers, the aqua blazes of the Long Path appear here. (These will be removed if the trail is rerouted over Cross Mountain.) The trail leaves from the campsite, bearing left between campsites 45 and 46, and heads toward the creek, turning left (downstream), and crossing a footbridge.

The trail heads left (east) after crossing the creek and ascends over a rocky, well-maintained treadway, passing the trail register. The scratches visible on the rocks are from crampons. Moss-covered ledges and talus slopes under a canopy of mature forest characterize the steep ascent to a rocky hemlock knoll (2000 ft.). The trail ascends the lower northwestern extremis of Wittenberg—today an unnamed hill, but known in the late 1800s as the Big Knoll, from which bits of Hemlock (3240 ft.), Spruce (3390 ft.), and Fir Mountains (3630 ft.) can be seen, especially in winter. The trail relaxes now. This area, including the high peaks, was a part of the Hardenburgh Patent that became the private property of Robert Livingston.

Passing many picturesque rock formations, at 0.5 mi. the trail levels through a hemlock grove with a large bedrock monolith in its center. To the left (east) as the trail flattens, a small rock outcropping offers limited views to the south and east. Wittenberg, to the hard right (south), is among these, easily identified by its boreal green summit. This area is legal for camping (beyond 150 feet of the trail), but it is fragile. Old fire rings were built over the mosses, which have never recovered. A shallow ravine follows on the left as the trail bears right (south).

Fern, violet, and trout lily are profuse on these hardwood subslopes. The trail ascends through a northern hardwood forest and crosses a small seasonal creek, soon switching back hard to the left (southeast) at a point where an early roadway continues southwest, eventually disappearing. (The existence of a herd path here suggests that many hikers have missed this turn and continued straight ahead.)

Penetrating a talus slope tangled with hemlock, the trail cuts up 90 degrees to the right (south), turns left (east), ascends, descends, and passes a number of hemlock stands before crossing a seasonal creek. The trail descends slightly after the kill, following along the edge of a slope and offering scant views to the north. Several nameless and seasonal brooks follow, before the trail turns right (southeast) and uphill at 2600 ft., topping out on a flat where the vegetation type changes to beech and scrubby maple, with little spruce trees beginning to appear. Views of Wittenberg up to the right (west) appear as the junction with the Terrace Mountain Trail is reached at 2.60 mi., where trail signs appear.

Turning right (west) the trail ascends moderately toward Wittenberg. Climbing around to the north of Wittenberg's steep eastern slopes, a long rock outcrop offers some good views—views that are to a large degree redundant to those from Wittenberg's summit. Included are Overlook Mountain (3150 ft.), Plattekill (3110 ft.), Indian Head (3573 ft.), Sugarloaf (3810 ft.), Plateau (3850 ft.), and Hunter (4050 ft.). Hunter's fire tower can be seen by looking very carefully with binoculars at 42 degrees. Stony Clove, Diamond Notch, and West Kill Mountain (3890 ft.) are also seen.

At 3000 ft., the forest type shifts dramatically to spruce-fir. The trail ascends steeply now, with one ledge requiring all fours, reaching 3500 ft. at the site of an ideal but illegal campsite. The forest turns to a nearly homogeneous spruce-fir type and continues climbing, switching back through ledges and flats until the summit is attained at 3.9 mi. (3790 ft.). This open, east-facing ledge has attracted thousands of hikers annually. Fortunately, the summit is exposed bedrock and has proved resistant to the scars of high impact. (Arguably, some of the exposed bedrock is the result of intensive use.) In the opinion of many seasoned Catskill hikers, this is the region's premier scenic hike. Samuels Point stands to the east. To the right of Samuels Point is Friday Mountain (3694 ft., trailless), showing the scar from a May 1968 landslide. Balsam Cap (3623 ft., trailless) follows, with Peekamoose (3843 ft.) and Table (3847 ft.) to the right. Back to the north, the Blackhead Range is seen. Mount Tremper (2740 ft.) and its fire tower and all of the Devil's Path peaks can be identified. Ashokan High Point in the south and Sky Top in the Shawangunks' Mohonk Preserve are visible. The Ashokan Reservoir (built 1907–1916) is the showpiece of this view. Its multi-arched bridge over the dividing weir and Brown Station, the location of the aerating plant (and the beginning of the Catskill Aqueduct to New York City), is seen. A bit more to the right is the West Dike, and then the main dam beyond Samsonville Cove. The straight railroad right-of-way running east and west along the north shore is the relocated path of the Ulster and Delaware Railroad, which ran from Kingston to Oneonta (surveyed 1865, the railroad carried 676,000 passengers by 1913 and ceased passenger operations in 1954).

The trail continues west over flat stone and mineral soil past shoulder-high stone corridors, walled in by evergreens, and descends on its way to Cornell Mountain (3870 ft.). The trail flattens and is several feet wide in the saddle between Wittenberg and Cornell at 4.25 mi. in a section known as Bruin's Causeway. A few steep pitches follow, one crevice requiring all fours, where backpackers typically remove their packs and hand them up. It is especially tricky and potentially hazardous when the crack is packed with ice. The trail rises onto Cornell's summit (the "Crown of Cornell") into its thick mantle of virgin red spruce that extends over much of the mountain's western slopes. At 4.7 mi., a short spur to the left of the main trail leads to Cloud Cliff (Cornell's summit). The views here are disappointing in comparison to Wittenberg's, but day hikers are advised that the next view, at 4.8 mi., is spectacular, providing westerly vistas that are unavailable from Wittenberg. Most prominent of the mountains here is Slide itself, looming monstrously ahead, its namesake landslide (1820) showing prominently on the north slope. Peekamoose and Table show up to the left, and to the right (north) are Giant Ledge and Panther. Van Wyck (3206 ft.) and Woodhull (3050 ft.) show to the southwest, and trailless Hemlock (3240 ft.), Spruce (3390 ft.), and Fir (3630 ft.) appear to the northwest, over the northern shoulder of Slide.

NOTE: Most day hikers coming from the Woodland Valley trailhead turn around at this point. Hikers intending to continue across Slide Mountain should make note of the time and be prepared—this is the "Point of No Return."

The descent of Cornell's western slope provides several outcroppings with sustained views. Around 3300 ft. the trail begins to flatten, and the first of several intermittent streams flows across the trail (varies seasonally) at 6.2 mi. Opportunities for camping in the saddle are excellent, with its six designated (legal) campsites. Water in the saddle becomes scarce by late summer, and hikers should be prepared to carry extra water.

The trail continues west, climbing Slide's eastern slopes and passing a spur to a spring at 6.8 mi. (3900 ft.). Views from this spur are spectacular. Looking back into the northeast as the sun is setting, it is possible to see the sun reflecting off the cab of Mount Tremper's fire tower. The trail soon climbs a series of long, wooden stairways and stone steps, swinging southwest before it arrives at the summit ledge where a bronze plaque commemorates the Catskills' beloved naturalist, John Burroughs. It has been determined by trail-register sign-ups that the actual visitors to Slide Mountain are estimated at more than 35,000 visitor-days. Slide Mountain and Giant Ledge share 50 percent of these visitors. It is not unlikely that on a weekend at the height of the season (August 15–October 15) hikers may encounter as many as a hundred people on Slide's summit. Many hikers come to Slide because it is a relatively short climb from the Slide Mountain trailhead and because it is the Catskills' highest peak—the views are not as good as Wittenberg's.

The entire Devil's Path is visible from Slide's open rock summit, as well as Kaaterskill High Peak, Black Dome, and Blackhead. Mounts Tremper and Plateau are in the northeast. Cornell and Wittenberg are directly in the east. Friday and Balsam Cap appear to the right, as well as Ashokan High Point (150 degrees). Around 1890, a tower on Slide enabled visitors to see more than seventy named peaks and mountain ranges as far away as Vermont, New Jersey, the Hudson Highlands, and the Berkshires (similar views are available from many Catskill peaks).

Crossing the actual summit, where a fire tower and lean-to once stood, the trail descends gently to the west. Within moments, another vantage point appears to the right (north), again with extensive views, that add to those from the summit to include Giant Ledge, Panther, Halcott, Sherrill, North Dome, West Kill, Windham High Peak, Hunter, and others too numerous and clustered to identify. This view is in many respects better than the summit's. Descending easily, the trail widens (it once served as the fire tower road) and is heavily traveled. At 7.7 mi., the Curtis-Ormsbee Trail comes in from the left (southwest) at 3900 ft.

The Wittenberg-Cornell-Slide Trail continues downhill and curves through an unusual section of crumbling white quartz pebbles that some early guidebook writers called the Garden Path. This trail soon turns to uneven stone and cobble and descends consistently until reaching the junction with the Phoenicia–East Branch Trail at 9.05 mi. Here at the junction with the Phoenicia–East Branch Trail, the Wittenberg-Cornell-Slide Trail turns right toward the trailhead parking area.

Terrace Mountain Trail

  to Terrace Lookout: 0.3 mi., 15 min.

  to Terrace Mountain lean-to: 0.9 mi., 35 min.

Terrace is not a mountain in its own right, but literally a terrace projecting from the northerly shoulder of Wittenberg. Its main attractions are the lean-to and its surrounding flat ground, which has been used traditionally by large groups. At one time the Wittenberg-Cornell-Slide Trail began near the base of Cross Mountain Hollow and started out across the old suspension footbridge that spanned the Esopus Creek east of Woodland Valley Campground. Now the trail begins in the saddle between Terrace and Wittenberg along the Wittenberg-Cornell-Slide Trail.

The Terrace Mountain Trail heads north from the saddle, passing through a short tunnel of hemlock trees. The trail drops out of the evergreens into a hardwood forest, descending to the southeast slightly before turning north again where the trail opens onto a large, tilted rock terrace and spruce meadow, with tufts of grass, spruce-fir trees, old fire rings, and open bedrock with a northeasterly aspect. From the high (southerly) end of the terrace, near two benchmarks spaced 15 feet apart, are phenomenal, close-up views of Panther Mountain (3730 ft.) and Giant Ledge (3200 ft.). In addition, West Kill, Diamond Notch, Southwest Hunter, Hunter (at 44 degrees), North Dome, Sherrill, Halcott (10 miles distant), Stony Clove Notch, and several mountains of the Devil's Path are visited. Samuels Point (2885 ft.) is at 150 degrees. The trail continues to the north, crossing small, open rock meadows (none as good as the first) through a hardwood forest over a gullied treadway that flattens as it turns east, where a few very large hemlock trees appear. On the expansive wooded terrace of Terrace

Mountain, the lean-to stands in an open, grassy hardwood grove. A bronze plaque imbedded in the logs commemorates Jack Gebel of the Adirondack Mountain Club's Long Island Chapter.

From the front of the lean-to to the left 150 ft., the old Wittenberg-Cornell-Slide Trail goes off to the east. It is obscure, unmarked, and often identified by a tiny rock cairn. Although the trail has no legal outlet without bushwhacking to state land and fording the Esopus, it can still be walked and is in excellent condition. Hikers staying over at the lean-to can explore this old trail, which drops downhill to the south, switches back at Fiddler's Elbow, and descends through a maturing sugar-maple forest, dropping 1.2 mi. to the Esopus Creek and the site of the old cable footbridge, which was removed by the DEC several years ago (the concrete anchors remain). This route is, however, the fastest egress to Woodland Valley in the event of an emergency and is all downhill to the creek (1200-ft. descent).

Phoenicia–East Branch Trail (Long Path)

to Giant Ledge–Panther–Fox Hollow Trail: 2.7 mi., 1 hr. 30 min.

to Slide Mountain parking area: 5.35 mi., 2 hr. 45 min.

to trailhead parking area on Denning Road: 9.8 mi., 4 hr. 30 min.

The Phoenicia–East Branch Trail (aka Woodland Valley Denning Trail) begins in the scenic forest recesses of Woodland Valley, long known for its tumbling creeks, good trout fishing, and rugged mountain scenery. The trail is used as an alternate access route to the Giant Ledge–Panther–Fox Hollow Trail, as well as Slide Mountain (via the Wittenberg-Slide or Burroughs Range Trail), and beyond the steep topography of Fork Ridge, it follows an old woods road to Denning. Following its junction with the Wittenberg-Slide trail, the Phoenicia–East Branch Trail is a popular cross-country ski trail among local enthusiasts.

From the west end of Phoenicia at the junction of Old NY 28 and NY 28, travel 0.6 mi. west on NY 28, turning left (south) onto Woodland Valley Road, cross the Esopus Creek at 0.8 mi., and continue right on Woodland Valley Road. At 5.8 mi., park at the Woodland Valley trailhead parking area at the west end of Woodland Valley Road, across from the state campground. (This is the same parking area used to gain entrance to the Wittenberg-Cornell-Slide Trail). A day-use fee ($3 at this time) is collected for each parked car during the months of the campground's operation.

From the north side of the parking lot the trail climbs two flights of stone-and-tie steps, ascends, and turns left (west) to traverse Fork Ridge, leveling at 1900 ft. At 0.5 mi. a steep descent through a boulder-strewn hardwood forest leads to an impressive flight of fifty stone steps, built by an AMC trail crew in 1993. At 1.0 mi., the trail crosses a tributary of Woodland Valley Creek, situated in a rocky ash grove, and ascends through an area of isolated hemlock. At 1.2 mi. the trail turns to the right (west) at the site of a former trail junction. The trail widens and improves as the grade increases over an early roadbed (the old Slide Mountain–Woodland Valley Road). Crossing another seasonal tributary of the creek, the trail swings south at 1.7 mi. At 2600 ft. the terrain flattens, as it passes a designated campsite on the left (south), within 5 minutes' walk arriving at the junction with the Giant Ledge–Panther–Fox Hollow Trail at 2.75 mi.

Continuing west, the trail soon passes an obvious but unmarked, unsigned path on the left (southwest) at 2700 ft. This old road is still identified on some maps as the Slide Mountain–Woodland Valley Road. It is legally walkable for hikers going over to Slide's trailhead from Giant Ledge or Fork Ridge, and this is the recommended route, rather than descending to the hairpin turn on the Phoenicia–East Branch Trail, losing nearly 600 feet in elevation in the process. Traditionally, it is most useful to those completing the (usually hiked clockwise) circuit of the Burroughs Range Trail, from Woodland Valley over Wittenberg, Cornell, and Slide (who are at this point sorely in need of a level shortcut). This section of the old road is unidentified from either direction, and no signed routes indicate its distance or elevation advantage. The only sign, at the east end of Winnisook Lake where the road enters the woods, states: "Public Easement Across Private Land."

The Phoenicia–East Branch Trail continues straight ahead (west) descending over a very rocky surface and passing through a varied forest of large-in-diameter but low white-birch trees and a little hemlock stand at 2400 ft. Passing a signboard and trail register, continue downhill a few hundred feet to Slide Mountain Road at the hairpin turn and the Giant Ledge trailhead parking area at 3.40 mi. The Phoenicia–East Branch Trail turns left (south-southwest) and follows Slide Mountain Road (CR 47), passing Winnisook Lake at 4.1 mi., to resume at the Slide Mountain trailhead parking area on the left (southeast) side of CR 47.

At 5.35 mi., the Phoenicia–East Branch Trail continues from the Slide Mountain trailhead. This trailhead is the traditional, easiest approach to Slide Mountain (4190 ft.) from the Wittenberg-Cornell-Slide Trail junction (the old truck trail). It is also the dullest approach, and most hikers with the time will ascend the scenic Curtis-Ormsbee Trail (ahead) and descend via the Wittenberg-Cornell-Slide Trail, making a loop back to the trailhead on the truck trail (or continuing to Woodland Valley).

The Phoenicia–East Branch Trail crosses the west branch of the Neversink River, continues through a flat sugar-maple forest over impacted mineral soil for a few hundred feet, and climbs moderately steeply over large rocks and roots to the old truck trail, bearing right (south) at 5.75 mi., and leveling out. A piped spring is seen on the left. At 6.10 mi., the trail arrives at a T junction where the Wittenberg-Cornell-Slide Trail leaves to the left (east).

The trail continues straight ahead (south) over flat terrain. The road shrinks to the width of a footpath for a short distance; old campsites appear in the woods. Crossing a tributary on a wooden bridge, the trail climbs to the south at an easy incline. Within 20 minutes of the bridge, at 6.9 mi., the trail reaches a T and the beginning of the Curtis-Ormsbee Trail on the left (east).

The Phoenicia–East Branch Trail descends, still assuming the width and character of an old road as it heads south, providing seasonal views of Slide Mountain to the east. (From this point to the

Peekamoose-Table Trail, the Phoenicia–East Branch Trail is also a section of the Long Path.) The trail crosses a number of seasonal tributaries of Deer Shanty Brook—one of them spanning a deep gully with the remains of an old timber bridge with stone abutments. At 8.65 mi. the trail passes the junction with the Peekamoose-Table Trail on the left (west).

This intersection (or the Curtis-Ormsbee Trail) may be the origin of a proposed trail that would connect the Slide Mountain Wilderness Area to the Biscuit Brook trailhead, crossing over Wildcat Mountain. This 4.0-mi. trail would provide the opportunity for extended backpacking trips, joining two wilderness areas, and providing a link for the Finger Lakes Trail.

The trail soon crosses a footbridge and descends gradually over a stable road-wide surface, roughly following the east branch of the Neversink River in a deep forest setting, and arrives at the Denning trailhead at the northeast end of Denning Road near the confluence of Tray Mill Brook and the East Branch of the Neversink River at 9.8 mi. (2100 ft.). This trailhead is situated in one of the prettiest valleys in the Catskills. Many hikers embark upon day hikes of Peekamoose and Table from here to gain the 1000-ft. elevation advantage over the route from Peekamoose Road (CR 47), and, less frequently, make round trips to Slide via this trailhead and the Curtis-Ormsbee Trail.

Giant Ledge–Panther–Fox Hollow Trail

> *to* Giant Ledge (from trailhead): 0.85 mi. 45 min.

> *to* Panther Mountain: 2.55 mi., 1 hr. 45 min.

> *to* Fox Hollow: 7.50 mi., 3 hr. 45 min.

Giant Ledge has long been one of hiking's favorite destinations, owing to its easy access, dramatic scenery, and legal ridgetop camping. Overnight camping continues to be a popular activity that imposes upon the pristine nature of the ridge. However, this high-use area is being closely monitored and well kept; at this time, impact has been regulated and appears to be stabilized.

Access the Phoenicia–East Branch Trail junction at the hairpin turn (Giant Ledge parking area), 7.2 miles south from NY 28 on CR 47, locally known as Big Indian Hollow Road, Slide Mountain Road, or West Branch Road. (From the hairpin turn, hikers must first travel east along the Phoenicia–East Branch Trail 0.85 mi. to its junction with the Giant Ledge–Panther–Fox Hollow Trail.)

The Phoenicia–East Branch Trail heads east into the forest, arriving in few hundred feet at the map kiosk and trail register. The Esopus Creek headwaters run audibly to the left (north) and downhill. The trail climbs, penetrating a northern hardwood forest with large, low-crowned yellow birches. A few natural stone steps have been enhanced with contrived steps as elevation is gained. This section of trail is rock strewn but short. At 2680 ft., the trail flattens into a saddle as a woods road departs to the right (west) toward Winnisook Lake. (This unmarked but legal road can be used as a shortcut to and from the Slide Mountain trailhead.) The trail junction appears at 0.85 mi. on the left (north) amid cherry trees and snarls of blackberry underbrush. It is well identified.

Turning left (north) off the Phoenicia–East Branch Trail, the Giant Ledge Trail passes over large, flat stones through muddy areas. This brief level stretch gives way to a flight of wide steps built with vertically placed bluestone. After a short ascent, at 0.6 mi. (1270 ft.) a marked spur leads left (west) to a spring. Climbing from this junction, the trail tops out at 0.8 mi. (3250 ft.), passing a herd trail to the left (west) of a pair of long, flat rocks, which leads to two illegal campsites. The trail continues over rock on a level ridge to another short, unmarked spur on the right (east), the first and perhaps most significant of Giant Ledge's lookouts. These vertical drops are hundreds of feet high and must be considered extremely dangerous. The views are significant. It was from this interior cirque that a late-retreating glacier (perhaps the Catskills' last) scoured the walls of the surrounding slopes into steep, half-bowl profiles. From areas along the cliff, hikers can peer down at trees that have been smashed under break-away talus and others killed by drought, their skeletonized trunks visible in the forest below.

From left to right the view takes in West Kill and Ox and Stony Cloves to Hunter. Plateau is the longest, flattest summit ridge, to the right of Hunter. Most of the Indian Head Wilderness Area's peaks can be seen from Plateau to Overlook. Wittenberg, Cornell, and Slide (between the latter is Friday, 3694 ft.) are visible. (Don't lean too far out on the ledge to see Slide.)

The trail continues level as it travels straight (north) along the ledge, where several open shelves of rock appear to the right (east), each with its distinct character and expansive views. Blueberries are profuse. Following the first few ledges, at 0.85 mi. a spur trail departs from the main trail to the left (west), leading past two heavily used campsites (legal) to Giant Ledge's only westerly views of the Big Indian–Beaverkill Range Wilderness Area. Across Big Indian Hollow is Fir (3630 ft.), with Spruce (3390 ft.) and Hemlock (3240 ft.) to the left (southeast). Beyond Hemlock is Van Wyck (3206 ft.). To the right (northwest) of Fir is Big Indian (3710 ft.), Eagle (3610 ft.), Haynes (3420 ft.), and Balsam (3610 ft.). These peaks are traversed by the Pine Hill–West Branch Trail. (The position of this ledge is N42.02.318—W074.23.761, at altitude 3209 ft.)

As the Giant Ledge–Panther–Fox Hollow Trail moves north along the ridge, points looking to the right (east) continue, the ledges too numerous to identify singly. At 1.0 mi., the trail descends, sharply at times, leveling in a densely foliated area of northern hardwood and ferns. This is the saddle between Giant Ledge and Panther, leading to the (720-ft. vertical rise) ascent of Panther. As the trail ascends, at 1.8 mi. a short, unmarked spur to the right (east) at 3400 ft. opens to views of Slide and Wittenberg. Fork Ridge juts southeast into the cirque, down in the southern foreground.

The trail crosses over to the western side of the ridge, climbing through ledgy terrain to the 3500-ft. mark. A large rock (false summit) offering only strained views is attained shortly thereafter, at 3560 ft. For hikers coming up from Fox Hollow, this view is not worth coming across the long flat summit to see (better views exist at the summit).

The trail climbs a bit more, easily, to attain the summit ridge, which is virtually blinded by balsam fir. Panther's true summit is reached at 2.55 mi. (3730 ft.), offering a view of vast proportions. This little outcropping in the fir faces northeast, and although similar in many respects to the view from Giant Ledge, it offers a look at more northerly territory. West Kill and Hunter remain in sight, but now North Dome (3610 ft.) and Sherrill (3550 ft.) appear. The vague bubble-peak sticking up between Plateau and Sugarloaf is Kaaterskill High Peak. The Blackheads appear, but only two of them—Black Dome and Thomas Cole. Up against the northeastern skyline you can see a chip of the escarpment as it drops toward Dutcher Notch. The Devil's Path mountains, as well as Overlook and Mount Tobias, are visible. Hunter's fire tower can be seen, as can Mount Tremper's (90 degrees). The Burroughs Range is no longer visible, but low in the valley you can see the piscatorial town of Phoenicia alongside the Esopus Creek.

The trail descends amid white stars of bunchberry and peppermint-faced oxalis blooms (common wood sorrel), always looking east, then leveling on a flat in boreal Catskill alpine terrain. Little views appear, suspended over Woodland Valley. The trail drops downhill shortly into hardwoods again, crossing over large stones, through ledges and fern glades, and at 3.8 mi. crosses a bald, where discreet upper-elevation camping is possible (there are several such places) without damage to vegetation.

At 4.35 mi. (3200 ft.) another false summit is reached, with limited views to all but the north. This is a large, open rocky bald, from which many large peaks can be seen to the east and west. Most striking is the profile of Panther itself, close at hand and nearly due south. The trail descends now, through open northern hardwood forest, winding in a wide arc from northwest to northeast. The terrain flattens only briefly as it runs cross-slope under a steep hillside covered in rock and yellow birch. Very tall ash and sugar maple are the homogeneous type. Understory sunlight is limited, and with the high canopy providing so much shade, the wet soil enables excruciating stinging nettles to grow in a solid, verdant carpet of ground, covering acres.

Thick forest continues as the trail follows a rocky old road, long since abandoned. The trail turns to the east. At 7.1 mi. (1700 ft.), a spur to the left (north) leads 200 ft. to an open grassy area with a spring and lean-to. The main trail descends through the shady woods of Fox Hollow with its stream and tall hardwoods following the old settlement road to pass the trail register, on the left at 7.3 mi. The trail is heavily eroded now as it crosses a wet spot on a double-stringer bridge, bearing right to the parking lot, where a privy and trail signs are located.

Curtis-Ormsbee Trail (Long Path)

to Slide Mountain summit: 2.3 mi., 1 hr. 30 min.

This trail begins off the Phoenicia–East Branch Trail, 1.5 mi. from the Slide Mountain trailhead on CR 47. It was pioneered in the late 1800s by two avid hikers—"Father Bill" Curtis, an officer of the Fresh Air Club, and his companion, Allen Ormsbee. Both of them died of exposure in a snowstorm on their way to a meeting of the Appalachian Mountain Club on Mount Washington, in August 1900. The small marble monument commemorating them has been shot at and otherwise defaced. This trail provides the most enjoyable, scenic, and popular approach to Slide Mountain.

The Curtis-Ormsbee Trail runs east from the Phoenicia–East Branch Trail, remaining flat momentarily until beginning a steady rise at 3100 ft. After a short steep section at 0.4 mi., the trail opens up on a rock outcropping with good views to the left (north) at 3400 ft. The vista includes Doubletop (3870 ft.), Graham (3868 ft.), Wildcat (3160 ft.), Big Indian (3710 ft.), Fir (3630 ft.), Spruce (3390 ft.), and Hemlock (3240 ft.). Balsam Lake Mountain (3730 ft.) is behind Graham. The trail continues to climb, passing the 3500-ft. mark, when at 0.6 mi. a short, marked spur leaves the main trail 200 ft. to the right (south), to an outstanding ledge at 3550 ft., and views of Table (3847 ft.), Lone (3721 ft.), Rocky (3508 ft.), and Balsam Cap (3623 ft.). High Point (1803 ft.) in the township of Sussex, New Jersey, is easily identified (with binoculars) by its monument, a war memorial to the state's soldiers.

The trail eases to a gentle grade as balsam fir begins to take hold, and soon flattens, becoming muddy in spots. Climbing again through a forest of pure fir, the path curves to the north and back into the east again before leveling above 3900 ft. and arriving at the junction with the Wittenberg-Slide Trail at 1.65 mi. At the junction, the ground is dusted with white quartz pebbles.

Peekamoose-Table Trail (Long Path)

to Peekamoose summit: 3.35 mi., 2 hr.

to Table summit: 4.30 mi., 2 hr. 30 min.

to Phoenicia–East Branch Trail: 7.2 mi., 3 hr. 45 min.

From a rugged environment of waterfalls, boulders, and ravines at the Rondout's headwaters, the Peekamoose-Table Trail rises more than 2600 ft. in 3.35 mi. Park at the Peekamoose (Peak-of-the-Moose) trailhead, 10 mi. west of West Shokan along CR 42. Watch carefully for the trail signs and parking area on the right. The trail rises immediately from the parking area on the north side of Peekamoose Road. Trail signs are posted here.

The trail ascends to join an old road at 0.75 mi., where the trail register is located in a flat, open area. Beech trees give way to sugar maple and birch as old stone walls appear and a red-pine plantation is seen to the east. Mike Kudish points out that these trees were planted by DEC Forester Ed West, in the 1920s. Skid roads cross the trail, which now climbs, relaxing somewhat through a flat, grassy maple woods, soon crossing an open, east-facing slope exposed to the wind, where hundreds of trees were blown down during Hurricane Floyd in 1999. The downed, large-diameter hardwoods (ash and cherry) will remain visible for years to come. The opened canopy has provided light for mountain ash and wildflowers—asters, nettles, touch-me-nots. Marking and maintenance are good, and tantalizing (but ultimately frustrating) views of Breath Hill

(2536 ft.) and the ridges of Sundown Wild Forest exist to the right (southeast).

The trail rises in pitches, over ledges and flats, ascending steadily to reach a large "balance rock" on a flat slab of fissured, pink sandstone at 1.9 mi. This is Reconnoiter Rock (2900 ft.), which is viewless during leaf-out season. The trail is mineral soil now, continuing through a lush first-growth forest over rooty, red silt. At 2.3 mi. (3500 ft.) a ledge is reached, where herd trails have preempted the superior views existing just a bit higher in elevation. Ignore these, instead continuing on the main trail to the lookout above the 3500-ft. sign, where at 2.4 mi. a large ledge appears to the right. The view is excellent, including Big Indian (3710 ft.), Doubletop (3870 ft.), and Balsam Lake Mountain (3730 ft.) and its fire tower (319 degrees). High Point in Sussex, New Jersey, can be seen at 212 degrees. Van Wyck, Wildcat, and Woodhull lie among the southwestern hills.

The following terrain has several ledges worthy of exploration and feels like a summit, but there's still a good distance remaining to the true summit of Peekamoose. The trail continues flat through white-birch and red-spruce thickets, with black cherry over ferns. Leaving the fern glades the trail rises over red silt again as a spring appears to the left of the trail—nearly in the trail—draining into a cloudy puddle. The trail climbs into balsam and passes briefly over duff, rising onto the boreal summit at 3.35 mi.

Encased in thick balsam-fir cripplebrush, Peekamoose summit (3843 ft.) is punctuated by a solitary conglomerate boulder in the corner of a small clearing. Even climbing the rock won't provide views over the canopy of low fir trees. The trail descends beyond the summit on a treadway of sandy glacial till and flattens in a brief saddle before rising gradually, then more steeply through a boreal corridor to the viewless summit of Table Mountain at 4.3 mi. (3847 ft.). While it is possible to discover views from Table, it is difficult to do so without damaging the sensitive upper-elevation vegetation through the encouragement of herd paths, of which there are several. As the trail descends the north side of Table, marginal summertime views of Slide

Mountain appear to the north. Just below the 3500-ft. mark at 4.5 mi., a spur to the left (southwest) leads to the Boughton Memorial lean-to, with some views of Van Wyck. A lower spur trail to the right at 3430 ft. leads 100 ft. to a piped spring. The trail descends into the west and travels easily across-slope, passing a lookout ledge to the left (southwest), with a dangerous drop overlooking Van Wyck Mountain (3206 ft.). Increasingly large cherry trees follow and the trail drops down to 2700 ft., passing another southwest-facing, treed-in spur trail to the left with no summer views. Ascending to a knoll, the trail drops steadily thereafter through a ledgy hemlock woods, where designated campsite disks identify a spur trail on the right (north). The spur trail follows the spine of a hemlock bluff above the Neversink River for 100 yd. to a large and attractive campsite with room for a dozen tents. The main trail continues, descending slightly to pass another designated site on the left.

Keep a close watch on the trail markers as you come west through the various stream channels at the confluence of Deer Shanty Brook and the Neversink's east branch. This is beautiful country, and forest management has taken several steps to ensure that it remains pristine. One step was the removal of the lean-to so that the site complies with the 150-ft. rule (and because the proximity of the river discourages the building of a privy) and minimizes user impact in an area so close to a trailhead. (Several designated sites remain in the area.) The trail continues across the confluence of creeks here, where log bridges have been placed. The spring runoff is so boisterous it has defied efforts to place permanent footbridges. Be careful crossing these stringer bridges, which are slippery when wet and high enough to result in injury in the event of a fall. From the west side of Deer Shanty Brook, the trail climbs gently to meet the Phoenicia–East Branch Trail at 7.2 mi.

Section 10

Willowemoc Wild Forest

Hikers with young families and those desiring relatively easy backpacking shake-down trips will find this region of gentle hills and waterways ideal for their purposes. Several of the trails can be entered directly from the Mongaup Pond Public Campground. Within the Willowemoc Wild Forest is the Mongaup Pond Public Campsite, an ideal place to stay while using this forest. While there are no named summits in this area—the maximum elevation is 3100 ft. (streams and ponds are numerous) and the topography is not as mountainous as parcels to the east and north—the area offers unusually good opportunities for mountain biking and backcountry skiing and has the largest snowmobile trail system in the Catskills. Horseback riding is permitted here, except on marked foot trails or on ski and snowmobile trails that are covered with snow or ice. There are fifteen miles of single-use, "hiking only" trails, twenty-nine miles of marked snowmobile trails, as well as a great number of primitive camping areas in designated sites adjacent to excellent fishing streams (some of the best of these sites are located at the north end of Flugertown Road in the southeast of the area, along the Willowemoc Creek's headwaters). Other designated camping areas, free and open to the public, are at nearby Waneta Lake on CR 151, and along the northern perimeter of the forest, off Shin Creek Road. (There is one designated site on Beaver Kill Road east of Turnwood as well.) Fir Brook, along Pole Road, also offers good trout fishing and excellent public access.

This area is known for its trout fishing. The state fish hatchery at DeBruce, just outside the Mongaup Pond Public Campground, is a good place to see the spawning stock and to learn about the Catskills' trout populations. The Department of Environmental Conservation (DEC) releases more than a half million fish into Catskill public waterways each year.

This area is habitat to deer and bear, and many early accounts document the capture and killing of large panthers in the area around Willowemoc. The Willowemoc band of the Lenne Lenape Indians established a popular trade and travel route known as the Sun Trail here. The Indians sold this land to Johannes Hardenburgh in 1706, a transaction that ultimately protected the area and resulted in its protection and later its annexation as state forest preserve.

Big Rock Trail

   to Frick Pond (Quick Lake Trail): 1.7 mi., 50 min.

From the Flynn Trail Junction east of Hodge Pond, the yellow-marked Big Rock Trail drops sharply downhill, losing 600 ft. in elevation in the process. This 1.1-mi. section north of Times Square Junction claims the steepest vertical rise over any equivalent distance in the Frick Pond–Quick Lake trail system. As a rejoinder to the Flynn trailhead in a loop hike, it is preferable to travel south (downhill) on this trail as conditions allow, whether on horseback, skis, snowshoes, or foot, rather than ascending it to return on the Flynn Trail. The section west of Frick Pond (flat) is among the most attractive trails in the area and can be fashioned into a loop using the Logger's Loop Trail, avoiding Big Rock's steep section completely. From the Flynn Trail Junction, follow trail markers south.

   The trail drops downhill from the Flynn Trail, arriving in 1.1 mi. at Times Square, a four-way trail intersection. The Big Rock Trail continues straight across the junction (southwest), following along the west shore of Frick Pond. The Logger's Loop Trail, also yellow, goes left and right. At first the hardwood surroundings and sometimes muddy trail will seem dull, but soon hemlock takes over, emanating from a lush inlet marsh to the right (west), and two short bridges are crossed in idyllic surroundings. An enchanting 275-foot-long boardwalk—unusual for the Catskills—is then crossed, offering forest and lake views. The trail ends at its conjunction with the Quick Lake Trail, in view of Frick Pond to the left (northeast).

Flynn Trail

to Hodge Pond: 2.15 mi., 1 hr.

to Junkyard Junction: 3.2 mi., 1 hr. 30 min.

Beginning at the north end of Beech Mountain Road, across the road from the Frick Pond trailhead parking area, this foot trail provides the shortest access to the Beech Mountain Nature Preserve. As you face the signboard and map kiosk, the trailhead and signage is at your back (east).

The trail descends slightly into the woods, heading northeast at 2100-ft. elevation, passing the trail register within 50 ft. After skirting a private inholding (this is the Beech Mountain preserve's gatehouse parcel), the trail regains Beech Mountain Road (dirt) and turns right (north), ascending steadily. Sparse views appear to the left (west). At 2700 ft., arrive at the junction with the Big Rock Trail, a four-way intersection. The Mongaup Pond snowmobile trail comes in from the right (northeast), and continues across the junction onto the Big Rock Trail, on the left (southwest).

The trail goes straight (north) crossing the state-land boundary and entering the public easement into Beech Mountain Nature Preserve at a barrier gate at 1.8 mi. At 1.95 mi., at a wide, grassy T, the trail goes left (west). Marking is obscured by trees on the right (north) side of the trail as it turns west. No destination signage is present and marking is obscure or absent. The trail is up to 80 ft. wide here and in the rest of the preserve. The trail descends and arrives at a junction near the south shore of Hodge Pond. This very appealing mountain pond contains brook trout and can be legally fished with artificial flies only. No bait of any kind—alive or dead—is permitted. Permission to camp is available by permit only. No boats, rafts, or canoes are allowed.

At 2.15 mi., the trail crosses the outlet, leaves the pond, and ascends gently through the preserve lands. Preserve rules require that hikers stay on the state-marked trail unless fishing in Hodge Pond. At an unsigned Y, the trail bears left and climbs to a barrier gate, returning to state lands in the Willowemoc Wild Forest, and is

still an established woods road. The grass-covered trail flattens over
scarce patches of flat rock in a dense hardwood forest, until reaching
Junkyard Junction and the Quick Lake Trail at 3.2 mi. This is the end
of the Flynn Trail. From this point the Quick Lake departs both to the
right (west, for Quick Lake) and to the left (south, to Frick Pond and
the trailhead parking area on Beech Mountain Road).

Quick Lake Trail

to Quick Lake: 7.2 mi., 3 hrs. 40 min.

This long trail is popular among mountain bikers and cross-country
skiers. Trails in the area are generally wide and grassy, but provide little in the way of scenery. Perhaps the biggest attraction the Quick
Lake Trail has to offer is its isolation. Few if any other hikers will be
encountered west of the Logger's Loop Trail and Frick Pond.

Enter this trail from the north end of Beech Mountain Road, 1.0 mi.
outside (southwest) of the main entrance to the Mongaup Pond State
Campground (see Mongaup-Hardenburgh Trail for directions). The trail
leaves from the northwest corner of the Frick Pond trailhead parking lot.
A signboard with maps and information concerning the adjoining parcel
of the Beech Mountain Nature Preserve (accessible with restrictions) is
posted here.

The trail follows the established, rocky treadway slightly downhill and north, shortly reaching the footprint of an old road, now a
worn path invaded by vegetation. The trail turns left (west) here, passing the trail register and continuing west until reaching a junction in
an open field just east of Frick Pond (not yet visible), at Graveyard
Junction. A headstone commemorating Marjorie and Lyle Lobdell,
residents of an early farm that stood here, rests to the southeast.

To the right is the yellow-marked Logger's Loop Trail. Continue
left (west), to arrive at Frick Pond, where there are limited views
north to Mongaup Ridge. This 6-acre, seasonally low, beaver-
impounded pond is contained by receding, grassy banks and has no
recorded fish-collection inventory. It is believed to contain bullheads,

shiners, and pickerel. After crossing the outlet on a wooden foot-bridge, the trail crosses two small plank bridges as it approaches a junction, still in view of the pond. At 0.65 mi., the Big Rock Trail leaves to the (right) north.

The Quick Lake Trail continues straight following red markers. A nearly pure understory of fern growth characterizes this section of trail, which is seldom used as of this writing. Ascending easily through an open forest of black cherry, the trail heads gradually north, crossing a washout. A hardwood stand takes over as Iron Wheel Junction (2350 ft.) is approached. At this T at 1.5 mi., lies a small but heavy set of iron wheels, possibly those of a horse-drawn log transport. The Logger's Loop Trail goes to the right here. The Quick Lake Trail turns left (south).

Shared briefly by the snowmobile trail, the trail goes left, uphill, over a grassy treadway, and arrives at a Y at 1.7 mi. (The snowmobile trail leaves to the left and rises steeply to meet the red foot trail at Coyote Junction.) The trail bears right here, following the red trail toward Junkyard Junction. There is no destination or distance signage. As the trail climbs, red markers are sparse. The trail is road-width and self-guiding, washed out in places and grassy in others, the eroded, thin soils leaving a sandy surface. The trail ascends gradually through a quiet, densely forested woodland to reach Junkyard Junction at 3.1 mi. (2785 ft.), where the Flynn Trail (blue markers) turns right (east) toward Hodge Pond. The Quick Lake Trail turns left (west).

Immediately to the left is an open, flat, rock clearing, the site of the former Beech Mountain Boy Scout camp's junkyard—the junction's namesake. It has been recovered to its natural state, and only small bits of trash can be identified. The trail traverses a thickly wooded ridge. Following the north slope of a nameless ridge averaging 2700 ft., the trail soon turns into the south, providing thin, seasonal views to the west at 4.1 mi. This is the Westerly Vista—the foot trail provides no other views. The trail descends to Coyote Junction at 4.25 mi. (To the left, the snowmobile trail descends to the Quick Lake Trail and Iron Wheel Junction.)

The Quick Lake Trail turns right (west) at this grassy junction onto a flat section of trail shared by the snowmobile trail, and at 4.9 mi. it arrives at Bobcat Junction. Signage is poor and deteriorating. This section of the foot trail begins level and quickly loses elevation. (The snowmobile trail goes right, descends steeply, and offers open but narrow views of the northern lowlands.) The wide, grassy thoroughfare has no distinct treadway. There are vague summertime views westward, with little definition. Patches of exposed flat rock appear as the trail levels and again descends to Flatrock Junction at 5.85 mi., a four-way intersection of exposed, broken rock. Although from this vantage the foot trail looks less inviting than the snowmobile trail, it is the more interesting choice. The snowmobile trail leaves to the left. The Quick Lake Trail goes right (west), and descends, passing a low, crumbling ledge to the right. Marking is poor or absent. At an unnamed junction at 6.8 mi. (2200 ft.), the snowmobile trail joins the foot trail from the left (east) and descends to end at Quick Lake at 7.2 mi., arriving on the north shore near a crude campsite. The foot trail is the extension of an old estate road that descends a few hundred feet to the west, following Gee Brook into the Beaver Kill Valley, crossing private lands. This is the fastest egress from this isolated outpost in the western Willowemoc Wild Forest in the event of an emergency. The adjacent private parcels are heavily hunted and several clubs post lands here. Quick Lake is a low, sluggish pond, 6 acres in area and impounded by beavers. There are no plans to repair the ruined, human-made dam. The only break in the homogeneous hardwood forest is the few hemlock trees at the campsite (2000 ft.).

Logger's Loop Trail

to Quick Lake Trail: 1.75 mi., 1 hr.

to complete loop adding Quick Lake Trail: 2.75 mi., 1 hr., 45 min.

The trail begins at Graveyard Junction (junction with the Quick Lake Trail), 0.4 mi. west of the Frick Pond trailhead parking lot. At this open, grassy trail junction, the Logger's Loop Trail heads north, following cross-country ski-trail disks (yellow) and yellow foot-trail markers.

Following the easterly margin of an open field, the path enters the woods where a privy stands to the left. There is a designated campsite area here, although it appears overgrown and little used. Frick Pond can be seen through the trees to the left (west). The trail ascends very slightly, levels, and descends gently again to Times Square at 0.6 mi., a four-way intersection with the Big Rock Trail. Identify the Logger's Loop Trail across this intersection. This section of the trail, to Iron Wheel Junction, is open to snowmobiles. The trail continues through the intersection.

Following a brief rise, the trail levels through a sugar-maple forest, crossing the Hodge Pond outlet (0.5 mi. south of Hodge Pond) and several seasonal runoff gullies, each tending to washout and erode the trail in spots. The trail makes a sweeping turn into the south, providing skiers with more outstanding diagonal striding terrain. A pair of black plastic culverts, often plundered and unearthed by a boisterous inlet tributary of Frick Pond, is crossed shortly before Iron Wheel Junction and the end of the trail is reached at 1.75 mi. To complete the loop, turn left (southeast). The Quick Lake Trail arrives at the Logger's Loop Trail at 2.75 mi. Straight ahead at 3.25 mi. the Quick Lake Trail ends at the Frick Pond trailhead parking area on Beech Mountain Road.

Campground Loop (Mongaup-Willowemoc Trail)

around loop: 2.4 mi., 1 hr. 45 min.

This fun family walk combines the Mongaup Pond Public Campground road with a section of the multiuse trail on the pond's eastern shore. The loop is popular with hikers and cyclists and appropriate for children. Bring bug dope and snacks. It is easily entered from anywhere in the campsite on foot. (Consult the Mongaup-Hardenburgh Trail for directions to the campground.)

Find the trailhead between campsites #144 and 147 in Loop G. Trailhead parking is available just beyond site #151 on the right (north) side of the road. Follow blue foot-trail markers (this is the beginning of the Mongaup-Hardenburgh Trail) and red snowmobile markers through the campsite area. The lake appears on your right. Blueberries grow along the shore. The trail is flat and at 0.3 miles, arrives at a trail junction where the Campground Loop Trail turns right (southeast). There is no destination or distance signage. The trail crosses a long footbridge over the pond's northernmost inlet. At 0.4 mi., cross another bridge, as the trail follows the lake and climbs easily, then another bridge in a maple woods, and still another, until at 0.8 mi. a trail junction with signage is reached. Continue straight ahead (south). The lake is no longer visible to the north (right). The trail flattens and soon descends to another junction in a hemlock woods.

A sign here indicates Mongaup Pond Campground, straight ahead. No distance is given. Continue straight ahead, crossing a slightly muddy outlet marsh near the headwaters of Mongaup Creek. Soon the trail exits the woods at campsite #38. To complete the loop, turn left. The campsite road does not circle the lake. Passing the bathhouses and beach area through the campground's most scenic area, the road heads north and back to the point of departure at the trailhead.

Mongaup Pond Snowmobile Trail

to Flynn Trail: 1.5 mi., 1 hr.

This short section of multiuse trail represents the northwesternmost section of the Mongaup-Willowemoc Trail. Its intended purpose—to provide an alternative route to the Flynn Trail Junction from the interior campsite area of the Mongaup Pond Public Campground—is seldom taken advantage of. The trail is seldom used by hikers and shows very slight impact from mountain bikes. Access the trail just beyond campsite #158 in Loop G, where small signs are posted. Trailhead parking can be found adjacent to campsite #151, ahead on the campground road (for directions to the Mongaup Pond Public Campground see Mongaup-Hardenburgh Trail).

The trail follows the snowmobile-trail disks north, immediately crossing a small stone bridge over Sucker Brook. The trail is level for a short distance as it travels to the left (west) of a small wetland, until rising steeply over a good surface. As elevation is gained, short sections of the trail are washed out and rocky. Above 2700 ft., the trail levels and undulates. In a northern hardwood forest the snowmobile trail descends over a wide, grassy surface until reaching the Flynn Trail junction.

Wild Azalea Trail

Distance from Butternut Junction

to Hunter Road: 3 mi., 1 hr. 30 min.

to Karst Trail: 3.75 mi., 2 hr.

to Mongaup Pond via Karst Trail: 5.7 mi., 3 hr.

From Butternut Junction, east of Mongaup Pond Public Campground off the Mongaup-Willowemoc multiuse trail, the Wild Azalea Trail heads south-southwest. It can be used to provide a link in a very large loop around the campground and is ideal for all-terrain cyclists and skiers as well as for hikers. There are no views. At Butternut Junction, the trail leaves the yellow-marked Mongaup-Willowemoc Trail and follows snowmobile markers.

The trail ascends easily through thick, second-growth hardwood. Leaf litter covers the trail and a few blowdowns may be encountered. Crossing a wooden bridge over a tributary of Butternut Brook and leveling out on a knoll at 2540 ft., the trail passes through a stand of thin beech trees. At 1.0 mi., the trail turns northwest briefly, moving through a maturing hardwood forest, ascending slightly and leveling, passing through a lush clearing, thick with fern, blueberry, strawberry, and scattered cherry trees. Entering the woods again, the trail crosses a bridge at 2280 ft., ascends into open forest, crosses another open, grassy clearing, and arrives at the junction with Hunter Road at 3.0 mi. It then turns right (northwest), toward Mongaup Pond. This established gravel road borders private property to the south. Descending, the trail passes a power-line right-of-way and then a tiny tributary of Mongaup

Creek at the site of an early settlement. A few stone ruins remain in the dense underbrush. Domestic ornamentals appear—barberry, apple, Norway and blue spruce, day lily, and lupine. A short distance uphill and beyond the brook, the trail levels at an intersection, bending right. To the left, the trail follows what remains of Hunter Road as it heads toward Mongaup Pond Road, terminating just south of its intersection with Beech Mountain Road. To the right at 3.75 mi. are direction signs for the Karst Trail.

Karst Trail

to Mongaup Pond from Hunter Road: 2.0 mi., 1 hr.

The Karst Trail begins at the intersection with Hunter Road, south of Mongaup Pond Public Campground. Bearing right at the Hunter Road and Karst Trail junction (see Wild Azalea Trail), the trail leads to an an open field. Marking is poor, leaving no indication as to the correct direction of travel. Straight across the field on a vague treadway in the grass and a short distance into the woods is a fire ring and undesignated (legal) campsite. Instead, walk diagonally to the left (northwest) a short distance (where little or no evidence of a path is visible) and find the trail again at the edge of the woods, well-marked and moving northwest between a Scots-pine plantation on the left and a stand of large red oak to the right.

The trail soon ascends slightly into deep forest, then levels, following to the right (east) of a wetland. Ascending again easily the trail pulls away from the wetland and back again as it descends into hardwoods, the treadway hemmed in stinging nettles. The type shifts to hemlock, many ghostly skeletons of which may still be seen in the marsh to the left (west). At 2230 ft., arrive at the cutoff to Mongaup Pond State Campground.

To reach the campsite, follow left to cross a muddy clearing, leaving the woods at campsite 38.

Mongaup-Willowemoc Trail

Flugertown Road to Mongaup Pond Public Campground: 2.85
    mi., 2 hrs. 30 min.

Enter the trail from a point 0.5 mi. west of Flugertown Road at its
junction with the Long Pond–Beaver Kill Ridge Trail. Heading southwest, the trail is somewhat rocky, but flat, and soon crosses Sand Lake
Road, a well-used dirt right-of-way leading to private lands in both
directions. Cross the road, and very soon a small brook. Through
shady hardwood stands the trail is grassy and only lightly impacted,
the rocks showing scratches from snowmobile use. The trail follows
an embankment above lively Butternut Brook in a picturesque setting
and draws closer to the creek as it moves northwest, soon crossing
the brook on a wooden bridge. The trail ascends slightly, passing an
abandoned trail on the left, shortly thereafter arriving at Butternut
Junction at 1.0 mi. Each direction is identified with red foot-trail and
snowmobile markers.

The trail becomes grassier, crossing the gravelly washout of a
small creek, then a small footbridge. Heading west and soon ascending, eroding, and finally topping out beneath a tall hardwood canopy,
the route descends until reaching a T intersection with the Mongaup
Pond campsite loop at 2.85 mi. Turn left to enter the campsite at site
#38, from there bearing left again on the campground road to reach the
main entrance. Hikers completing the loop hike using the Mongaup-
Hardenburgh Trail and Long Pond–Beaver Kill Ridge Trail should turn
right (north) to return to their point of departure in Loop G.

Central Catskills

For the purposes of this guide, the Central Catskills include the Big Indian Wilderness Area, the Dry Brook Ridge Wild Forest, and the Balsam Lake Mountain Wild Forest Area. Sections of north lying detached parcels of the Shandaken Wild Forest (trailless), Halcott Mountain Wild Forest (trailless), and the trailless, western section of the West Kill Wilderness Area lie within the region. The Belleayre Mountain Ski Area management unit is attached to the Big Indian–Beaver Kill Wilderness Area in the north.

The Central Catskills include several long ridge trails—the Dry Brook Ridge Trail, the Mill Brook Ridge Trail, and the Pine Hill–West Branch Trail. Opportunities for hikes of several day's duration are possible in each forest area. This is the lonely, reclusive heart of the Catskills, with forests that attract few visitors in comparison to the neighboring hills to the east. Steep slopes and rolling ridgetops provide for rugged and often challenging hiking. Several long ridges and eight mountains more than 3200 ft. characterize the setting—primarily forested by northern hardwood groups (some in virgin tracts), along with isolated conifer stands and plantations.

Much of the Catskills were preserved for one major reason—the Hardenburgh Patent. Beginning as a petition to Queen Anne for a small tract of vacant land, Major Johannes Hardenburgh and company managed through a combination of exploitation (of the Indians), political power, and Hardenbergh's personal influence (he fought at Blenheim and was knighted by the Queen), to procure two million acres of Catskill lands. The reasons for this land grant are many and complex, but the result was the preservation of the Catskills for a long period of time, long enough to protect it from resale, subdivision, and diffuse ownership. The patent was divided up into Great Lots, and shared among its "investors," which included the Livingstons. (The deeds purchased from Nisinos, a sachem of the Lenne Lenape, cost less than 100 pounds sterling). The patent was a determining factor in the sparse settlement in the Catskills, which resulted in a great deal of taxable, open space, much of which was eventually purchased or appropriated by the state and annexed to the forest preserve.

Roads opened the way for settlers, many of whom left their names on mountains and hollows in the region—Haynes, Rider, Seager, McKenley. The region developed an active tourist following. Many small hotels and boarding houses appeared, among them Jim Dutcher's Panther Mountain House, the Slide Mountain House, and the Grand Hotel along the Ulster and Delaware railroad line. During this time, large tracts of land were purchased by the wealthy, among them Jay Gould, who purchased land in the Dry Brook Valley. Gould was the robber-baron who in 1869 fought with the Vanderbuilts for control of the Erie Railroad. Most of the lands in this area were purchased by tax sale from the county prior to 1930.

Section 11

Big Indian Wilderness Area

A ruggedly mountainous and remote hiking area, the Big Indian Wilderness Area includes more than 33,500 acres of steep valleys and hollows, long ridges, and the high peaks of Big Indian, Balsam, Eagle, and Haynes, as well as the trailless summits of Spruce, Fir, Hemlock, and Doubletop. There are roughly thirty-five miles of trail area (views are limited). The wilderness is nearly completely forested by dense northern hardwoods (beech, birch, maple, and often cherry), except for the higher summits, which are typically clad in fir.

The headwaters of the Esopus Creek, Beaver Kill, Willowemoc Creek, and the west branch of the Neversink River add considerably to the wilderness appeal of this area. Each are important and scenic trout streams with public-access areas convenient to most of the local trailheads and state campsites. The Esopus is noted for its spring runs of rainbow trout, and there is perhaps no other trout stream in the east as renowned or productive as the Beaver Kill.

The Beaver Kill–Big Indian Range forms the watershed divide between the Hudson River to the east and the Delaware River to the west. A number of the hikes in the area are characterized by long, relaxed approaches to the high ridge, where the hiker will pass through early settlement areas, old orchards, and stone ruins, followed by steep and direct ascents to the summit ridgeline. This wilderness area is not heavily used by hikers, possibly because it does not offer scenic vistas of the kind found in the neighboring wilderness areas. Instead, those in search of solitude and privacy will seek out this region. Many designated campsites exist along the trails, in addition to seven lean-tos, some of which are located near streams and wetlands.

The single most popular trail is the Pine Hill–West Branch Trail, which runs north-south from Pine Hill to the west branch of the Neversink River. This 14.9 mi. trail is most often walked from south to north, a strategy that employs only a slight elevation advantage, but which culminates in the ascent of Belleayre Mountain and provides access to the scenic rewards that are available from the Belleayre Ridge Trail at the northern extreme of the area (technically, both the Belleayre Ridge and the Pine Hill–West Branch Trail end in the adjoining

Belleayre Mountain Ski Center Intensive Use Area). Other trails in this
wilderness area are treated as access to the singular peaks in the range.

Pine Hill–West Branch Trail

to Biscuit Brook lean-to: 1.9 mi., 1 hr.

to Big Indian Mountain: 4.5 mi., 2 hr. 30 min.

to Seager–Big Indian Trail: 5.85 mi., 3 hr.

to Eagle Mountain: 6.95 mi., 3 hr. 30 min.

to Haynes Mountain: 8. 35 mi., 4 hr.

to Oliverea-Mapledale Trail: 9.1 mi., 4 hr. 30 min.

to Balsam Mountain: 9.85 mi., 5 hr.

to Belleayre summit: 12.3 mi., 6 hr.

to Pine Hill village: 14.9 mi., 7 hr. 30 min.

Seasoned hikers seeking the remote surroundings and isolated feel of
a large wilderness area will find this trail a welcome respite from the
much-busier trails of the eastern Catskills, while newcomers may be
discouraged by the relatively scant views. In any case, this is a remote
area, where few people will be encountered. At 15 miles, the trail is
also longer than many. (Additional proposed mileage would connect
this trail to the neighboring Slide Mountain Wilderness Area.) Logis-
tics can be simplified by spotting cars at each end of the trail or by
hiking the individual peaks via the side trails from either Big Indian
Hollow (Oliverea-Mapledale Trail, extending to Rider Hollow and the
Lost Clove Trail) or from the Dry Brook Valley (Seager–Big Indian
Trail, Mine Hollow Trail). The northern trailheads can be reached conveniently by bus from Pine Hill, but those traveling independently may
prefer to begin from the more traditional starting point on West
Branch Road (CR 47), which allows for an (trailhead) elevation
advantage of 600 ft.

From Big Indian, travel 12.5 miles south from NY 28 on CR 47, or Slide Mountain Road, and park at the Biscuit Brook trailhead parking area. (At this point CR 47 is called West Branch Road.) The trail begins 200 ft. to the right (east) of the parking area on the north side of the road.

The trail heads north and turns rooty in a shady hardwood forest, immediately passing the trail register to the right. Blue markers are frequent and the trail is self-guiding as it begins to turn left (northwest), crossing a small seasonal brook at 2185 ft. and beginning to ascend moderately steeply to the northwest. Large trees keep the area heavily shaded even on very bright days. The terrain levels as the path rises into the north-northeast at 2400 ft., passing a vague old woods road, which descends to the southwest, toward Frost Valley. Remaining level for a stretch, then descending amid witchhobble, fern, and wood sorrel on a mile-long, westerly slope of Spruce Mountain (3390 ft.), the trail passes a nameless tributary at 2350 ft. Crossing several seasonal runnels off the same slope, the route passes a small wet area to the left. At 2360 ft. the trail splits, with the main branch continuing right (north). Off a short spur to the left (west) at 1.9 mi. is the Biscuit Brook lean-to, situated above the brook itself, facing west among a few large hemlock trees. The spur continues to a flat, impacted tent space. This lean-to is an older structure with a hand-hewn floor, oakum chinking, and an uncharacteristic 4 x 4 timber roof.

The main trail continues north, following next to a small tributary of Biscuit Brook (lively in July), until crossing it on stepping-stones above a large pool at 2370 ft., a few hundred feet after leaving the lean-to. The trail ascends slightly and the main branch is crossed as the stream widens into a flood channel. Walking next to the brook now, ascending, alert hikers will observe a few maple trees with extremely large dbh (diameter breast height)—nearly five feet. At 3150 ft. the trail rises above and away from the creek although it remains in audible distance. Ravens croak in this otherwise near-silent, peaceful woods, where the trail turns west to begin its ascent of Big Indian Mountain with a series of switchbacks and levels at 3400 ft. in a subalpine community of oxalis, red cherry, beech, and small balsam fir. The walking is easy on the feet now, along this viewless but effortless flat, which reaches 3470 ft. and the site of an old junction where an unmarked, disused trail goes off to the left (northwest) and drops away toward Seager. Yellow-paint blazes denote the boundary of state and private lands here, a large parcel of the latter containing both Doubletop (3870 ft.) and Graham Mountain (3868 ft.) to the west. These mountains are seasonally visible to the west as the trail moves north along the western ridge of Big Indian Mountain (3710 ft.). Pass the 3500-ft. mark at 4.5 mi. where a well-established, cairned herd trail leads to the right for Big Indian's summit and a canister maintained by the Catskill 3500 Club. Climbing to 3600 ft., the terrain remains flat until at 4.9 mi. the trail descends north off the shoulder of Big Indian Mountain. None but winter views to the west greet hikers as the trail drops steadily and easily downhill. Hemlock reappears as an ascent leads to the junction with the Seager–Big Indian Trail at 5.85 mi. (3100 ft.).

The trail continues straight ahead (north) and turning northwest climbs through deciduous woods to a shallow ledge on the approach to Eagle Mountain (3610 ft.), reaching the 3500-ft. mark at 6.85 mi. A few scattered balsam appear as the trail rises to a point east of the true summit of Eagle Mountain at 6.95 mi., where an unmarked trail leads west over flat terrain 0.1 mi. (approximately) to the viewless summit (the Catskill 3500 Club does not maintain a canister on this summit). Balsam fir grows profusely beneath a hardwood canopy through the remaining upper elevations of the mountain, where limited seasonal views are possible but never expansive. Dropping into the saddle at 3300 ft., the trail is easy and relatively flat as it follows along the Delaware-Hudson watershed until the ascent to Haynes Mountain begins. The elevation change is barely noticeable—less than 150 ft. from the ridge's average elevation. Crossing a small, flat rock distinguished by a shallow crack, the trail rises gently over a grass surface. This lush but viewless expanse at 8.35 mi. is Haynes's summit (3420 ft.). The trail remains level only momentarily until beginning the northerly descent. Balsam Mountain appears to the northeast, looming large and appearing to be farther off than it is, only 1.5 mi. distant. The trail drops steeply to the junction with the Oliverea-Mapledale Trail at 9.1 mi. (3000 ft.).

To the southeast, the Oliverea-Mapledale Trail drops very steeply into McKinley Hollow. To the northwest, a more relaxed descent penetrates Rider Hollow. Continuing northeast on the Pine Hill–West Branch Trail, hikers will see red-berried elder—a favored bird food appearing in rich woods—and flowering, tall meadow rue, which appears alongside partridgeberry and Canada mayflower, the latter going to seed by late July. Climbing uphill consistently now, this section of the trail to Balsam Mountain is the steepest ascent along the Pine Hill–West Branch Trail since the southerly slopes of Big Indian. At the 3500-ft. mark, ascend through rocky balsam-covered ledges into a forest of cherry, over glades of thick fern, where the trail turns lazy curves through lush woods. At 9.85 mi., Balsam's summit (3610 ft.) is a primordial-looking wreckage of blowdowns, stumps, rotting snags, and rock piles—the most ravaged peak, appearance-wise, in the range. Again, there are no views. Vague herd paths, created by zealous hikers, head to the right (east), revealing little or nothing. Private postings have frustrated attempts to identify vistas elsewhere.

Balsam Mountain is not entirely without its rewards, however. The trail continues north to the site of a small, flat boulder on the right at 10.1 mi. (3550 ft.), where a cut vista provides a limited but unexpected view east of West Kill, Hunter (its fire tower can be seen), Blackhead, Black Dome, Thomas Cole, Windham High Peak, Rusk, Evergreen, Sugarloaf, Twin, and a piece of Indian Head. Overlook and its fire tower (107 degrees) are visible. The upper Esopus Valley and McKinley Hollow lie below, with the long, north-projecting ridge of Panther Mountain above.

The trail proceeds north-northwest, soon reaching another viewpoint around 3100-ft. elevation, where the terrain is steepest and the treadway is most heavily eroded. A short, unmarked spur leads right (east), to a flat, mossy rock above a ledge, looking north. This natural vista looks to the right of Belleayre Mountain, which occupies the northwest skyline, at Halcott Mountain, Vly, and Bearpen. The trail descends and flattens at 2800 ft. beneath a few very large specimens of beech and maple. At 11.1 mi. (2890 ft.), the trail arrives at the junction with the Mine Hollow Trail, which drops moderately steeply but also very quickly to the Rider Hollow trailhead, offering the shortest, easiest route onto and off the Big Indian Range. The main trail continues straight ahead, turning slightly to the north.

The Pine Hill–West Branch Trail rises following a short, flat section after the junction, ascending to 3000 ft., through a forest of large, cankered black cherry. Turning northeast, winter views of Panther Mountain are seen to the right. The trail climbs very steeply through ledges at it turns north again toward Belleayre's final approach. A relaxing grade yields to the open summit (viewless) at 12.3 mi. (3430 ft.). Two benchmarks (1942) are seen in the stone here, where a fire tower and lean-to once stood. A decrepit picnic table on the stone summit and a fire ring off a short spur to the north, are all that remains of a once popular campsite. To the left (northwest), the Belleayre Ridge Trail goes to the Hirschland lean-to and Belleayre Ski Center's Sunset Lodge (3325 ft.), which is open during the summer months (fast food, phone). The Hirschland lean-to is newer and in a more scenic location (at the top of the Roaring Brook ski trail) than the Belleayre Mountain lean-to, ahead and downhill on the Pine Hill–West Branch Trail. The trail turns right (east), following the road-width, graded trail (once a fire road and still negotiable via ATV) that soon descends, providing winter views of open country and ridges to the north (Halcott Mountain Wild Forest, Shandaken Wild Forest), passing the lean-to (in poor condition at this time) on the left at 12.75 mi. The Pine Hill–West Branch Trail continues to descend, flattening at the junction with the Lost Clove Trail at 12.95 mi. and turning to the north.

Carolinian hardwood forest follows, featuring large red oak. The trail continues straight ahead on blue markers (there is no destination signage) as an old woods road. Handmade trail signs Giggle Hollow Trail (originally Guigou), still unofficial at this writing, depart to the right (east) for Belleayre Beach and the Pine Hill public recreation area. The Pine Hill–West Branch Trail curves gently around to the left (west), descending easily. The trail moves across slope toward

Woodchuck Hollow and joins a private road at 1
ment), turning left (west) at the appearance of a
Descending, the trail goes around a locked gate a
Woodchuck Hollow Road. Still descending, arrive
Depot Road and the trailhead at 14.9 mi. (to the west
following the railbed to the Cathedral Glen Trail). It
legal—to park at the top of Woodchuck Hollow Road (pullover parking), but this area is not as secure or convenient as the Depot Road access. There is no trailhead signage for either the Cathedral Glen Trail or the Pine Hill–West Branch Trail; however, marking is adequate.

Mine Hollow Trail

to Pine Hill–West Branch Trail, 1.0 mi., 25 min.

This trail provides the shortest access to Balsam Mountain (3610 ft.). It begins off the junction with the Oliverea-Mapledale Trail in Rider Hollow. There are several designated campsites in the hollow and a good lean-to on the Oliverea-Mapledale Trail. The Mine Hollow Trail bears left (northeast) at the trail junction, where a small angle-iron suspension bridge spans the brook to the right (south) on the Oliverea-Mapledale Trail. Follow next to a creek on the level for a short distance, beneath a few very large hemlocks. The trail climbs away from the creek and into hardwoods (beech) at 2500 ft., swinging north at 0.4 mi. through a large hemlock stand. Continue uphill to the junction with the Pine Hill–West Branch Trail at 1.0 mi.

Seager–Big Indian Trail

to Shandaken Creek lean-to: 2.1 mi., 50 min.

to Pine Hill–West Branch Trail: 3.1 mi., 1 hr. 40 min.

Seager, situated at the head of the Dry Brook Valley below Drury Hollow, is in one of the Catskills' wildest, most scenic valleys and provides the most expeditious approach to both Eagle (3600 ft.) and Big Indian Mountains (3700 ft.) for both short day hikes and extended backpacking g the Pine Hill–West Branch Trail. The Seager–Big Indian Trail joins the Pine Hill–West Branch Trail equidistant between the two peaks at 3150 ft. The walk to the lean-to is easy—thereafter the trail climbs radically. Find the trailhead 9.7 miles north of Arkville at the end of Dry Brook Valley Road (CR 49). Bear right at the covered bridge just before reaching the trailhead parking area.

The trail heads southeast, following Dry Brook through a hemlock forest. The brook and off-trail area are contained within a private easement. The trail rises above the creek slightly, crossing Flatiron Brook adjacent to a small waterfall and natural rock pool (private). At the intersection of a dirt road at 0.9 mi., Camp Flatiron (private) is posted to the southwest. On the left (northeast), a small bridge crosses Dry Brook (private). Trail signs are posted here. The trail, following a dirt road, goes straight ahead as the road becomes wide and rocky while following the edge of the creek. The road soon crosses the creek, while the trail fords just upstream at 1.2 mi. This ford is difficult in moderately high water. Watch the markers carefully after fording. The trail turns right (southeast) on the same road that crossed Dry Brook a moment ago, goes 100 ft., and turns left (east, uphill), following markers to a grassy roadway, which the trail follows to the right (southeast), rising above the creek. The trail climbs easily into the east, now following Shandaken Brook, soon crossing it at 2400 ft. and ascending into the Big Indian–Beaver Kill Wilderness Area.

Even in dry months, a spring runs across the trail from the hill opposite the lean-to. At 2.1 mi., the trail crosses Shandaken Brook (dry in late summer) to the lean-to. This older structure is enclosed by a half wall in front. There is a privy to the north as well as a very small designated campsite suitable for a single tent, in a pinch. The trail continues along the north side of the creek, heading east. It rises moderately, relaxes, descends, and then climbs relentlessly until nearing the ridge. It rises again minimally as the junction is reached at 3.1 mi. Remarkably, reinforcing stones appear on the downhill side of the trail at this elevation (3150 ft.), indicating that this steep trail was once a road used to drive cattle to Oliverea.

Lost Clove Trail

to Pine Hill–West Branch Trail: 1.3 mi., 1 hr.

This trail rises steeply from scenic Big Indian Valley into the Shandaken Wild Forest, which lies at the northern extreme of the Big Indian Wilderness Area.

At the corner of CR 47 (Big Indian Hollow Road) and Lost Clove Road, 0.5 mi. south from NY 28, the trail is identified with signage. Turn right (northwest) to cross the Esopus Creek and at 1.0 mi. find the designated parking area on the right (north) side of Lost Clove Road. Initially the trail ascends gradually on a dirt skid road from the site of a log decking area at 1600 ft. (public easement). The ascent steepens, sidehilling its way up a southeasterly slope of Belleayre Mountain. The trail is road width and in good condition, although recent, extensive logging operations on private property have made some impact both on the road itself and in surrounding woods. Watch markers carefully as the trail passes straight through a diagonal intersection at 2200 ft. and climbs more gradually as it approaches the junction with the Pine Hill–West Branch Trail in a red-oak woods at 1.3 mi. (2850 ft.). Belleayre Mountain's summit is 0.65 mi. to the left (west).

Oliverea-Mapledale Trail

to Pine Hill–West Branch Trail: 1.8 mi., 1 hr.

to McKenley Hollow Road: 3.6 mi., 2 hr.

From the east end of Rider Hollow Road (2.5 mi. off CR 49A), at the trailhead parking area, the trail leaves to the east adjacent to Rider Hollow Brook. A signboard is located here.

The trail passes a designated campsite on the right and turns left to cross the brook, soon entering a small clearing of burdock, bee balm, milkweed, and berry bushes. Reentering the woods, within 100 ft. the trail reaches the Mine Hollow trail junction at 0.4 mi.

Bearing right over a small, angle-iron suspension bridge and left across a stringer bridge, proceed alongside the creek in a mixed red-pine, hemlock, and hardwood forest. Designated campsites to the right (southwest) offer camping on flat ground. At 0.5 mi. the Rider Hollow lean-to appears on the left (northeast) in an attractive streamside setting. (The area is busy on most weekends during good weather.) The trail crosses the creek at 2150 ft. and makes a long, low-angle climb on a dirt roadbed to the south among red pine and maple, amid stone walls and rock piles—evidence of early settlement and cultivation. Drawing closer to the creek again and descending to cross it at 1.1 mi. (2350 ft.), the trail turns south near a stand of tall tamaracks. Again crossing a streambed, the trail begins to climb, becoming steeper to the southeast as it leaves a sparse stand of large hemlock, at 1.9 mi. arriving at the four-way intersection with the Pine Hill–West Branch Trail at 3100 ft.

Continuing through the junction, the trail passes a designated campsite to the left (north) and descends, immediately steepening. The terrain is at its steepest where a seasonal creek crosses the trail from the south side, and a landslide scrape is seen directly left (northeast) of the trail. Mineral soil and loose rock makes this section (2500 ft.) potentially hazardous, particularly for those hiking in wet or icy periods, when this trail should be approached with calculated caution and preparation or else avoided.

Relenting to an easy grade at 2200 ft., the trail eases but still drops through open hardwood forest, making a long sweeping turn through the hollow at 1900 ft. and crossing the brook on two short sets of stone steps. This area is very attractive if not serene—a good staging location for hikers planning an ascent from the east side of the ridge. At 3.0 mi., the lean-to is set in an open hardwood forest of large sugar maple, near the brook, past which along the trail is a fine Norway-spruce stand on flat ground, deep enough to provide legal camping between the trail and the creek. Now following the footprint of a dirt road, the walking is easy and nearly flat. The trail crosses a washout and then the creek at 1800 ft., where cottages appear to the left (northeast) as the trailhead is approached. From a large washout that was once the original roadway into the hollow, the trail turns north, crossing a footbridge, and joins McKinley Hollow Road at 3.5 mi. A yellow trail arrow identifies the trail (it is not obvious to those coming up into the hollow—watch carefully). The McKinley Hollow trailhead parking area is 500 ft. to the right, across from the Mountain Gate Indian restaurant at 3.6 mi. Big Indian Hollow Road is 0.5 mi. to the east.

Belleayre Ridge Trail

> *to* summit of Belleayre Mountain from Sunset Lodge
> (elev 3325 ft.): 1.0 mi., 30 min.

Running from the summit lodge and ski lifts of the Belleayre Mountain ski area, east to the summit of Belleayre Mountain (3375 ft.), this pleasant dirt-road ridge trail provides access to the Big Indian Wilderness Area via the Pine Hill–West Branch Trail and provides access to the Cathedral Glen and Lost Clove Trails. It is often used by hikers who climb the service road from the ski center to its summit lodge, and more recently by backcountry skiers and mountain bikers creating loops back to Belleayre's base lodge. Views from the open slopes and from the deck of the summit lodge are extensive. From the lodge's deck to the south is Balsam Lake Mountain (fire tower), Millbrook Ridge, and Dry Brook Ridge across Chimney Hollow. Graham, Doubletop, and Eagle Mountains are visible, as well as Hiram's Knob in the low foreground. To the north from the ski slopes themselves are Vly and Bearpen, Monka Hill, Halcott, North Dome, Sherrill, West Kill, and Hunter. These are the only scenic vistas available from the matrix of Belleayre's summit trails, besides views from the ski trails themselves.

The Belleayre Mountain ski area is located off NY 28 in Highmount, New York. From the summit's Sunset Lodge (3325 ft.), which can be reached during winter and summer months from the ski lift or on foot, red state-trail markers appear on the south margins of a clearing. Unofficial, square orange markers also appear. The trail heads east over deep red silty soil on a service road and climbs gently into increasingly remote woods. At the top of a ski trail on the north side of the trail, ski area signs point the way to Highmount Rail Station and Belleayre Beach. At 0.5 mi., pass the Hirschland lean-to on the left (north), which is easy to miss for hikers coming west, perched above the Roaring Brook ski trail and facing north (it is a far better location and in better shape than the nearby Belleayre Mountain lean-to on the Pine Hill–West Branch trail). The trail continues straight ahead (east) passing the Cathedral Glen Trail to Pine Hill at 0.7 mi., and at 1.0 mi. arrives at the (viewless) summit of Belleayre Mountain (3430 ft.) in an open, grass-and-bedrock clearing. This was once the location of a fire tower and lean-to. The Pine Hill–West Branch Trail departs to the south. Ahead, downhill, is the Belleayre Mountain lean-to and the Lost Clove Trail into Big Indian Hollow.

Cathedral Glen Trail

to Belleayre Ridge Trail: 1.7 mi., 1 hr. 30 min.

From the village of Pine Hill, take Bonnie View Avenue to Mill Street, turning south to cross the historic stone arch bridge. Continue, passing under the railroad bridge of the old Rondout and Oswego line. (The railroad changed hands to become the Ulster and Delaware line in 1875.) Turn right immediately after the bridge (trail arrows are posted on a tree at the southwest street corner) and park on the left-hand side of the road (Depot Road, pullover parking). The trail follows the railbed northwest. Blue markers appear without destination signage.

Follow the right-of-way west for 0.5 mi., over intact ties and rails that soon become tunneled over in saplings. The Cathedral Glen Trail begins on the left (south) just before the small snowmaking reservoir (for Belleayre Mountain ski area) is reached. Locate the markers and "No Motorized Vehicles" signs. There is still no destination signage. The trail rises through an extensive and beautiful hemlock stand with the deep Cathedral Glen on the right. As hardwoods begin to take over, the trail enters the north side of an open clearing at 1.1 mi. The trail follows left (east) along the treeline, continuing straight uphill.

Ski area signs to the right identify the Roaring Brook and Discovery Lodge Trails. Marking is sparse.

The trail (now a grassy ski trail) becomes extremely steep for the next 0.5 mi. until reaching a second large clearing at 1.6 mi., where the Super Chief and Cathedral Brook ski trails converge. Watch carefully for blue markers as the trail turns left (east) into the woods, away from the ski area's trail system. Climbing, the trail is sometimes indistinct and is too seldom used to be fully self-guiding. Marking is sufficient. Continuing uphill the trail curves back into the south and joins the Belleayre Ridge Trail (a dirt road) at 1.7 mi., just east of the Hirschland lean-to (the Belleayre Mountain lean-to is below the summit at 3000 ft. along the Pine Hill–West Branch Trail). To reach the Hirschland lean-to turn right (west). Services are available at the ski area's summit lodge, 1.0 mi. to the right (west) at the end of the ridge trail. The summit of Belleayre Mountain itself (viewless) is to the left (east) 0.2 mi. on the Belleayre Ridge Trail.

Mongaup-Hardenburgh Trail

Distance from Mongaup Public Campground and Day Use Area
  to Mongaup Mountain: 1.6 mi., 50 min.

  to Beaverkill Road: 6.40 mi., 3 hr. 30 min.

Access to this trail is from the Mongaup Pond Public Campground in DeBruce. To find the campground, take Exit 96 off NY 17 at Livingston Manor, turn left, following CR 81 and CR 82, 6 mi. to DeBruce, turn left (north) on Mongaup Road, and go 3 mi. to the campsite.

Many hikers begin here to hike the Mongaup-Hardenburgh Trail to Beaver Kill Road and the Dry Brook Ridge Trail to Balsam Lake Mountain, but more people use this trailhead to hike the Mongaup Pond Loop, an 8.8-mi. outing from the Mongaup Pond Public Campground that uses the Long Pond–Beaverkill Ridge Trail and the Mongaup-West Branch Trail to bring them back to the campground. The Mongaup-Hardenburgh Trail begins between campsites #144 and #147 in Loop G. Trailhead parking is located just beyond site #151.

Follow blue foot-trail markers and snowmobile-trail disks along the edge of the lake. At 0.3 mi., a junction is reached, with signs to the left.

The foot trail goes left (north), beginning level and rocky but soon climbing, leveling at 2170 ft. A stand of hemlock trees is encountered at 2235 ft., as the trail ascends steadily but easily and remains self-guiding and well marked until a blowdown area is reached around 0.8 mi. (2300 ft.). Open sunlight and the resulting aftergrowth of vegetation has obscured the trail slightly for a short distance. Blackberry and mountain ash crowd the way where the loss of standing trees has deterred marking somewhat. Red-paint blazes appear. Obscured views to the south reveal parts of Mongaup Pond.

Blowdowns disappear as the trail rises steeply, topping out at 1.6 mi. (2989 ft.) where, to the trail's left, the words "The Top" are crudely etched on a conspicuous rock. This is the summit of Mongaup Mountain's middle peak. There are no views. The trail turns east, downhill, over a sparsely used treadway, following a saddle at 2550 ft. before climbing out of it to reach the east summit of Mongaup Mountain at 2.7 mi. (2928 ft.). It then descends Mongaup Mountain onto the Beaver Kill Ridge in a forest of dense hardwoods, moss-topped boulders, wood sorrel, and ferns. At 3.2 mi. (3000 ft.), the trail reaches the junction with the Long Pond–Beaver Kill Ridge Trail. The Mongaup-Hardenburgh Trail bears left (northeast) here.

Ascending slightly to 3150 ft., the trail follows a flat ridgetop briefly, descending again through a beech-and-cherry woods. There's plenty of flat ground nearby for tenting. A short distance off the trail here it is possible to find views (even in summer) to the east of Table (3847 ft.) and Peekamoose Mountains (3843 ft.). Of all places in the forest preserve, this one—generally lacking any unimpeded views—would seem to merit a cut vista. The trail descends again to a small fern-clad clearing where a rock to the right provides the singular view of Denman Mountain (3053 ft.). Descending off this knoll to 2985 ft. the trail becomes level. At 2950 ft., the trail rises steeply, and after a short distance levels again, thereafter rising gently. The spine of the ridge is reached at 4.75 mi. (3228 ft.), where the terrain flattens, offering winter views to the left (west) of the low-lying Delaware Ridge. Descending to 3200 ft. the trail remains level until it drops down off the northerly slopes of the ridge, descending moderately and switching back until reaching the suspension bridge spanning the Beaver Kill. It then rises on a long flight of stone steps to the trailhead parking area at 6.4 mi. This prime trout water is heavily posted. In fact, the entire Beaver Kill is posted in this area all the way up to Vly Pond, and postings are taken very seriously. Hikers can fish in the upper headwaters early in the spring when the water is high, or from public-access areas farther downstream.

Thru-hikers (this trail is popular with backpackers) to Balsam Lake Mountain will turn east here, following yellow markers 1.8 mi. and rise 300 ft. in elevation to the Balsam Lake Mountain trailhead parking area (see Dry Brook Ridge Trail for connections to the Balsam Lake Mountain Trail). The Neversink-Hardenburgh Trail (aka the Claryville Trail) departs from the southeast corner of the Balsam Lake Mountain trailhead parking area, while the Dry Brook Ridge Trail departs from the northeast corner.

Neversink-Hardenburgh Trail (Claryville Trail)

  to Fall Brook lean-to: 4.2 mi., 2 hr.

  to Black Bear Road parking lot: 9.0 mi., 3 hr. 45 min.

From Livingston Manor, the northern trailhead is reached by traveling east on CR 151 (Johnston Hill Road), passing Waneta (Juanita) Lake and the Beaver Kill State Campground, onto CR 152 in Lew Beach, passing Barkaboom Road to Little Pond State Campground, and arriving at the dead end of Beaver Kill Road and the Balsam Lake Mountain trailhead parking lot. A total distance of about 22 miles—much of it follows next to the heavily posted world-famous Beaver Kill trout stream. (Hikers will have passed the Mongaup-Hardenburgh trailhead to Mongaup Pond, 1.8 mi. west of the Neversink-Hardenburgh trailhead.)

From the parking area, two trails depart in opposite directions. Neither is adequately identified. The Dry Brook Ridge Trail leaves from the northeast corner of the lot, offering the shortest route to Balsam Lake Mountain summit and fire tower. The Neversink-Hardenburgh Trail (aka Claryville Trail) leaves from the southwestern corner and is not identified as such. Only a Finger Lakes Trail disk exists at the trailhead at this time. A signboard located in the parking lot will aid in orientation. This is a remote trailhead and a rather long walk into an area nearly as remote, and although there are roads at the trail's end there are no villages or services—or even telephones—anywhere nearby. Be prepared for all conditions.

The Neversink-Hardenburgh Trail follows southeast along the western edge of a field, revealing two large peaks to the left—Doubletop (3870 ft.) and Graham (3868 ft.). The trail enters the woods near the trail register, descends and crosses several stone waterbars, at 0.5 mi. crossing Black Brook on a footbridge. The trail is narrow, rocky, and sometimes leaf-littered, the overstory changing type from hemlock and birch to dense sugar maple, cherry, and beech. At 1.3 mi. (2400 ft.), the trail crosses Gulf of Mexico Brook on a 40-ft. bridge, soon thereafter reaching a dirt road, and continuing slightly to the right across the road. The trail descends to cross Vly Pond outlet, a lively brook with no bridge, downstream of a beaver meadow, and then rises into a hemlock grove, its surface strewn with cones and needles. The trail crosses the outlet of Tunis Pond, named for one of the last Delaware Indians to live in the Catskills; he lived on this pond's shore.

At 2.8 mi., the trail reaches a dirt road and follows it to the left (southeast) along the Beaver Kill. Hikers traveling north must pay close attention to this turn, as it is marked with only a yellow trail arrow and disk. Careful investigation will turn up the trail signs. (GPS N42.01.170/W074.34.329.) The trail heads upstream (southeast) on the dirt road and soon crosses a small bridge where a feeder creek comes in from the left (northeast). The road is sandy, wide, and well trafficked by the owners of a private hunting camp on an inholding at 3000-ft. elevation. Pass a designated campsite on the left. This site is little used and is normally a patch of ferns. The trail continues straight ahead at a junction where a bridge supported by railroad rails turns right (southwest), following the Beaver Kill straight onto a footpath identified with two yellow trail markers. (More obvious signage is needed here.)

Passing adjacent to the creek for a short distance, small sections of trail have washed into the creek. Fording on stones, the trail leads to a more severely eroded section of the kill where hikers momentarily walk in the streambed itself. Just as the trail seems to vanish altogether it takes shape again, continuing as a small path above a union of two tributaries. At 3.1 mi., 200 ft. to the left (east) on a thin spur, situated high-and-dry in a hemlock stand above the confluence, is an ideal designated campsite. The trail continues over an improved surface now, leading to an active beaver pond on the trail's left at 3.5 mi. Doubletop is visible to the northeast.

This section of trail is muddy, but soon hardens into the vestiges of a nineteenth-century road, marked as a hiking trail since 1935. The trail passes through a wet area shortly before reaching the Fall Brook lean-to at 4.25 mi. Porcupines have chewed the floor, but the shelter is sound. A privy is nearby.

The trail becomes wide and rocky now, serving as a seasonal streambed before the runoff finds its way into Fall Brook, leaving a comfortable treadway of duffy soil. Trending south, the route crosses a ravine carved by a tributary of Fall Brook, originating on a steep southwest-facing slope of the Beaver Kill Range.

As it approaches the northern end of Black Bear Road, the trail passes directly in front of a seasonal residence, crossing the front lawn and continuing on the lot's south side over an established dirt road. Once out of the forest onto Black Bear Road at 6.0 mi., striking views of the southeastern mountains appear to the left. Peekamoose (3843 ft.) and Table (3847 ft.) are easily identified by Table's long, flat summit. Passing through a detached parcel of the Willowemoc Wild Forest and (legally) back through private lands, the trail walks past several hunting camps, descending. Red Hill (2990 ft.) and its fire tower can be identified easily (seeing the fire tower may require binoculars). Slightly southwest is Denman Mountain (3053 ft.). Wildcat Mountain (3100 ft.) stands in the middle ground, with Woodhull (3050 ft.) just beyond the Neversink's East Branch. Farther along the road, hikers will enjoy a complete view of Slide Mountain's (4190 ft.) ridgeline contour and summit.

The trail descends Black Bear Road to the trailhead parking lot. Those hiking the Neversink-Hardenburgh from the south will most likely be using this lot, as it is no longer practical to park pullover style up above, as it once was. As in the north, hikers will be discouraged not to discover any signage for the Neversink-Hardenburgh Trail. Rely on the map.

Long Pond–Beaver Kill Ridge Trail

to Flugertown Road: 3 mi., 1 hr. 30 min.

to Long Pond: 4.1 mi., 2 hr.

to Black Bear trailhead parking lot: 7.4 mi., 3 hr. 45 min.

As well as connecting the Big Indian Wilderness Area to the Willowemoc Wild Forest, this northerly section of the trail forms the second leg in the 8.8 mi. Mongaup Mountain–Mongaup Pond loop. From its junction with the Mongaup-Hardenburgh Trail at 3000 ft., the trail leaves to the south, heading in the direction of Flugertown Road, following red markers along a high, wooded narrow ridge. A black-cherry woods opens up slightly to reveal views of Graham Mountain (3868 ft.), Doubletop Mountain (3870 ft.), and the Beaver Kill Range. Oak appears as the route descends southward to an easterly shoulder at 2754 ft. The trail has recently been remarked but is little used. Obscure summer views exist to the right (south). Descending and turning gradually to the southwest, the trail enters the Willowemoc Wild Forest and flattens at 2.0 mi. (2200 ft.), meandering through a thick hardwood forest with stands of pure sugar maple where meadow rue and wild leek (ramps) are common. Many large cherry trees have blown across the trail in this area and have been cut away by trail-maintenance crews. Assuming the footprint of an old road now, the trail is nearly flat as it descends to the junction with the Mongaup-Willowemoc Trail at 2.6 mi. (2200 ft.).

The trail turns left (east) on a section of trail shared by both the Long Pond–Beaver Kill Ridge Trail and the Mongaup-Willowemoc Snowmobile Trail, at 3.0 mi. arriving at Flugertown Road. In this area are several primitive, designated campsites along the Willowemoc Creek, a popular trout stream during high spring water levels. There are trail signs on the southeast side of Flugertown Road across from this fairly obscure trailhead at 2000 ft.

The trail turns right (south) on Flugertown Road, and in a very short distance (250 ft.) the Long Pond–Beaver Kill Ridge Trail enters the woods on the (unsigned) red-marked multiuse trail, proceeding left (south). A trail sign appears within 100 ft. at a footbridge crossing the Willowemoc. The trail crosses another bridge and ascends steeply for a few hundred feet. The incline relaxes and flattens into the south. On the right (southwest) side of the trail an unmarked, discontinued snowmobile trail heads back to the Willowemoc Creek. Continue straight, southeast, over flat and sometimes muddy ground to a junction in a hemlock forest at 4.1 mi. The trail is identified with red foot-trail and snowmobile-trail markers in every direction. To the right (south) is the Long Pond lean-to at 0.1 mi.

The trail continues east toward Black Bear Road as the forest type changes from hemlock to hardwoods. Following is a flat and grassy section that passes an unmarked spur trail leading right (west) toward the east shore of Long Pond. The DEC plans to mark this trail in the near future, in order to provide additional access to the pond. The trail continues flat and often muddy to a junction.

To the right (south) is a (visible) barrier gate leading onto a private inholding. Go left (north), soon reaching an intersection with Basily Road at 5.1 mi. (2240 ft., dirt). Bearing right (east), Basily Road climbs, the treadway becoming rocky but passable by four-wheel-drive vehicles (this section is a town road). The trail passes a designated campsite to the right and climbs to 2300 ft. where the road crests in front of a hunting camp. A road (private) leads north at this point. The trail continues north on the maintained road now, descending to Black Bear Road trailhead parking area, where signs are posted at 7.4 mi.

Dry Brook Ridge
Wild Forest

West

The main topographical feature of interest to hikers in the Dry Brook Ridge Wild Forest is its central ridge (3460 ft.) and the scenic vistas scattered along its length. Many hikers enjoy the quiet and solitude of this area. Many use the ridge trail as a thru-hike from north to south that culminates in the ascent of Balsam Lake Mountain (3730 ft.) and usually arrange for a shuttle from Mill Brook Road or the logistically more involved Beaver Kill Road in Hardenburgh. It is simpler to backtrack north from Balsam Lake Mountain back out to Mill Brook Road. The forest's eastern access at German Hollow is also its steepest. The northerly ascent to Pakatakan Mountain (viewless) is the conventional trailhead for thru-hikes of the ridge, although more popular is the Huckleberry Loop Trail, which provides access to the views of Dry Brook Ridge while omitting the miles of approach from north and south. The northerly leg of the Huckleberry Loop Trail (that portion of the trail north of Huckleberry Brook Road) is the single most popular approach to the ridge and views from the Penguin Rocks. Opportunities for camping throughout the unit are unlimited. Northern hardwood forest occupies most of the area (beech, birch, maple), with ash, cherry, basswood, and oak. Hemlocks are present in small, isolated stands. Large plantations of Norway spruce and red pine exist. Deer are present in large numbers, but bear are not abundant. The *Breeding Bird Atlas* indicates forty-seven confirmed species of breeding birds in the area, among them the red-shouldered hawk, hairy woodpecker (blue list), Louisiana waterthrush, and eastern bluebird.

There are three lean-tos in the Dry Brook Ridge Wild Forest, one is in German Hollow and another is north of Mill Brook Road on the ridge trail itself. The third lean-to—and the best choice for latecomers or trailhead bivouacing—is the Mill Brook lean-to, located within walking distance west of the southerly Mill Brook Road trailhead.

Dry Brook Ridge Trail

to Dry Brook lean-to: 8.25 mi., 4 hr.

to Mill Brook Road: 9.1 mi., 4 hr. 30 min.

to Beaver Kill Road: 13.6 mi., 6 hr. 30 min.

This long ridge provides seclusion and privacy for hikers in search of scenic isolation. In general, the terrain is lower and easier than the mountain trails of the neighboring Southern Catskills. Recent trail additions (the Huckleberry Loop Trail) have made this trail more accessible to hikers seeking moderate day outings to the top of the Dry Brook Ridge.

Turn left (southeast) onto Fair Street, 0.4 mi. west of Margaretville off NY 28/30. Turn left again (north) at 0.6 mi. onto south Side Spur, and at 0.75 mi. locate the trailhead on the right (east) side of the road. Pullover parking is on the left (west).

The trail ascends, leading 200 ft. to an old road, bearing left (northeast) past a shallow rock overhang and ascending through hemlocks and mixed hardwood forest. As the terrain flattens out, wild-forest signage appears. Long switchbacks follow, the first turning through a westerly curve at the site of a small hut (private) to the right (southwest) of the trail (this turn, which shortcuts back onto the woods road is not as obvious to those coming from the south). Hardwoods dominate as the trail turns south-southwest and the road is covered in pieces of broken bluestone, fragments of a quarry (which can be seen to the right of the trail) that was apparently mined to reinforce the road farther downhill. A sugar-maple forest follows as the trail flattens at 1900 ft., turning grassy and rising moderately steeply as the forest type changes to oak, and heads east. The trail then levels as it crosses the ridge, moving around a rocky knoll on the right approaching 2400 ft., and climbs again, easily now. A few very large cherry trees appear as the trail climbs through a section of dense forest where it flattens briefly before two steeper pitches that relax on the treed-in summit elevation of Pakatakan Mountain, at 2700 ft., and the junction with the German Hollow Trail at 1.75 mi.

The trail continues straight (south) from the trail junction and ascends, leveling before rising again in brief pitches through ledgy terrain and open hardwood. The trail travels along an easterly slope, descending, and is both poorly routed and in marginal condition along this section, in need of minor improvement. At 2970 ft. the trail turns right and uphill to the south-southwest and crests a rise in the ridge, arriving at the junction with the Huckleberry Loop Trail at 3.25 mi. (3100 ft.).

There is no destination signage here for southerly points along the Dry Brook Ridge Trail. Continue south, through a fern glade. The trail is level initially but rises gently just beyond the junction, circling a dry bog (which is sometimes full of rainwater) populated with sedges at 3150 ft. The trail adheres to the ridgeline elevation now, and the atmosphere of the ridge becomes light and airy—a welcome change from the heavy, dark, lower-elevation woods—and is self-guiding, although in a few locations it is invaded by low vegetation. At 4.8 mi. (3200 ft.), following a brief ascent, limited views appear to the right (west) from an isolated rock. Better views lie ahead a very short distance, off a very short spur (easy to miss, and initially looking less spectacular than it actually is) to the right (west). These are the Penguin Rocks, representing the best year-round views from the ridge. What's unusual about this outcropping is the appearance here of the three-toothed cinquefoil, which Dr. Kudish notes is "a largely arctic tundra plant . . . it occurs in only eight other places in the Catskills; the presence of this plant on the exposed ledges suggests that forest never invaded this site since the ice age." The cinquefoil blooms in early to midsummer. The views westward from this rock ledge are good and include the easternmost arm of the Pepacton Reservoir (where the east branch of the Delaware enters it—in reality, the Pepacton's waters are the dammed waters of the Delaware), and hills from Pakatakan in the north through the west-lying Cross Mountain, Barkaboom Mountain, and Touch-me-not Mountain. Across Cold Spring Hollow and the Huckleberry Brook Valley is Mill Brook Ridge, running west to east. Open pasturelands dot the valley below, and to the northwest are subtle glimpses into the hills beyond Dunraven, in the town of Andes. South, above Clark Hollow, is Woodpecker Ridge.

A nonconforming campsite exists just east of this spur, illegal due to its proximity to the trail (within 150 ft.). There is flat ground available all over the ridge for tenting beyond this site, irresistible for its proximity to Penguin Rocks. The trail continues southeast along this westerly side of the ridge where another spur leads right (west) to a large boulder at the top of a precipitous drop above a talus slope. After hiking through a viewless section of woods, at 3420 ft. the trail tops out at the edge of another ledge, achieving its maximum elevation beneath the ridge's summit knoll at 5.0 mi. (3460 ft.). The trail continues through cherry-and-beech woods until reaching the southerly junction of the Huckleberry Ridge Trail at 5.5 mi., which descends westward to Ploutz Road.

Straight ahead (south) the Dry Brook Ridge Trail descends and ascends before leveling, remaining at ridgetop elevation until decisively (and sometimes steeply) descending at 7.2 mi. through broken, low ledges, crossing an old but distinct woods road at the edge of private lands just under 2900 ft. This extensive elevation drop (800 ft.) brings you off the upper ridge and down to the lean-to at 8.25 mi., which faces west into the hardwoods at 2700 ft. Just 150 ft. north of the lean-to is a tributary of Mill Brook that dries up in late summer.

Following the lean-to the trail continues southeast, gaining elevation to 3085 ft., and descending thereafter over a few stone water bars, where conifers appear. Winter views are limited to the south here, restricted by heavy hardwood growth. The trail again descends gently across-slope, passing a small Norway-spruce stand to the left of the trail. Switching back in front of a crumbling ledge, the terrain levels, turning easterly in a transitional zone between a Norway-spruce forest on the right and hardwoods (sugar maple) on the left. This is perhaps the trail's most attractive forest, with a nearly pure fern ground cover. The trail switches back again, heading south and down a few small stone steps where small ledges appear to the right and broken-off boulders lie scattered across the forest, heaped with detritus and moss. Millbrook Road is soon visible. Signing out at the trail register on the left, arrive at the Dry Brook Ridge parking area at 9.1 mi.

This trailhead is the most popular access to Balsam Lake Mountain summit. (The shortest approach, however, is from the south, coming north on the Dry Brook Ridge Trail and taking the red-marked Balsam Lake Mountain Trail, but the access from Beaver Kill Road is remote.)

The Dry Brook Trail continues on the south side of Mill Brook Road, following a dirt road to the west, on the left side of Mill Brook Road (within view of the trailhead parking area). This wide fire-tower access road goes uphill (south) easily but steadily, passing the trail register on the left (east). The trail switches back to the 3000-ft. point, soon passing a spring on the right (west) about 50 ft. off the trail down a set of stone steps. The grade eases as the trail follows the westerly shoulder of a high ridge, with seasonal views to the west. At 11.6 mi. (2700 ft.), an unmarked trail to the left (east) enters a private parcel (with no legal public easement) to ascend Graham Mountain (3868 ft.). At 11.75 mi. (3270 ft.), arrive at the northern junction of the Balsam Lake Mountain Trail.

The trail continues straight ahead (southwest) at this wide, flat junction into an area that receives little use (most hikers using the area ascend Balsam Lake Mountain by either the north or south Balsam Lake Mountain trailheads, avoiding this section entirely). This old road descends along the side of a slope, varying in surface quality from rocks to grass. Uphill to the right (west), a talus slope appears, covered in yellow birch. Views to the east (left) are limited to the Black Brook Valley and the ridge above Young's Hollow. Uphill the talus is decorated with mountain ash, their scarlet berries showing by late July. Descending easily to 2900 ft., the junction with the Balsam Lake Mountain Trail is reached at 12.7 mi. in a hardwood forest.

The trail descends easily through hardwoods, soon approaching its terminus beside a scenic, open fern-covered pasture, passing an old tree farm on the right where Scots pine and European larch are escaping cultivation. To the left (east) is a deep, alluring forest of tall maple. At 13.6 mi., the trail ends in the Balsam Lake Mountain parking area at the location of the Neversink-Hardenburgh trailhead (which begins from the southwest corner of the parking lot). A signboard is posted here. The Mongaup-Hardenburgh Trail begins from Beaver Kill Road, 1.8 miles to the right (southwest) of the Balsam Lake Mountain trailhead parking area. Alder Lake is 8.0 mi. southwest on Beaver Kill Road and 2.6 mi. north on Alder Lake Road.

German Hollow Trail

to Dry Brook Ridge Trail 1.5 mi., 50 min.

Alternate access to the Dry Brook Ridge Trail from the north is available from Arkville via this steep trail through an old settlement area. It is a more direct but considerably steeper trail to the ridge than the Dry Brook Ridge trailhead itself, beginning in Margaretville. Its advantage lies in the lean-to and water source above the trailhead at Chris Long Road, and in the convenient, walkable distance to and from Arkville.

On the west side of Arkville, follow Dry Brook Road south, 0.3 mi. to Chris Long Road (dead end). Go right and at 0.2 mi. park on the left side of the road's end by a low stone wall just before reaching a private garage. The trailhead is visible across the parking area (on the west side) of this private parcel. The landowners have generously allowed day parking on their property but prefer that overnight visitors use the adjacent road parking.

Follow markers 150 ft. to the trail register. The trail climbs over a rocky, washed-out road and into the reclaimed pastures (1680 ft.) of a farm dating from 1869 belonging to J. H. Dean (Mike Kudish points out the existence of Tartarian honeysuckle, lilac, European Saint-John's-wort, and big-tooth aspen here). The trail climbs through a logged-over private parcel into second-growth hardwoods. Rising steadily, the grade eases as the lean-to is reached. A piped spring is located 500 ft. to the south at the end of an unmarked path on the north slope of Reservoir Hollow. The trail swings hard right nearly 180 degrees around the front of the lean-to and switches back into German Hollow, climbing steeply. After a stiff climb through an oak woods, the trail eases at 2700 ft. This brief reprieve is followed by easier ascents and flats. The trail finally levels out in a maple stand., trending southwest to the junction with the Dry Brook Ridge Trail at 1250 ft. (elevation gain) above the trailhead.

Huckleberry Loop Trail

around loop: 10.6 mi., 5 hr.

to Penguin Rocks via northern (Hill Road) leg: 3.2 mi., 1 hr. 30 min.

Loop trails are uncommon in the Catskills, and the Huckleberry Loop Trail was created in light of this fact. The trail also represents the only westerly access to the Dry Brook Ridge, an otherwise long and logistically impractical day hike. Signage and destination identification may be confusing, inconsistent, or absent. The trail is noteworthy for its easy access to the Dry Brook Ridge summit views (Penguin Rocks) and its plantations of Norway spruce.

Find the trailhead west of Margaretville from South Side Road, which runs adjacent to (and south of) NY 28/30. Two miles west of the village, South Side Road leads to Huckleberry Brook Road, which leads to Hill Road. Bearing left on Hill Road, find the trailhead 1.3 mi. on the left (north), with trailhead parking directly across the road. For hikers intending to walk the entire loop—a long outing in itself—the Huckleberry Brook Road trailhead may optionally be used and has a larger parking area (it is 0.6 mi. southeast beyond the intersection of Huckleberry Brook Road and Hill Road, on Huckleberry Brook Road, and 0.3 mi. south on the Huckleberry Brook Trail from the Hill Road trailhead parking area). Day hikers planning on visiting only the Penguin Rocks along the Dry Brook Trail (rather than walking the entire loop), may prefer to start on the recommended shorter leg from the Hill Road trailhead in order to optimize time spent on the ledges. In comparison, the southern leg of the loop (the section crossing Ploutz

Road from the Huckleberry Brook Road trailhead) is longer and less appealing. Hiking the loop from the north will also save hikers 500 ft. in elevation.

The trail leaves from Hill Road at 1900 ft., at the sign kiosk and register, and heads uphill (north) into an extensive stand of Norway spruce. Red pine follows. This changes to hardwoods as the terrain flattens and the route trends east, switching back and following the edge of the red-pine plantation. Oak woods follow. The trail is wide and roadlike. A fine stand of spruce again appears, followed by more red pine with a striking understory belt of striped maple. Soon crossing an old disused woods road and continuing to the east the trail relaxes, still ascending at 2500 ft. and climbing more steeply as it moves along the southerly side of the ridge. It then flattens out to allow seasonal views to the south across Cold Spring Hollow. Stunted northern hardwoods characterize the upper ridge as the junction with the Dry Brook Ridge Trail is reached at 1.7 mi.

The trail turns right (southeast). At 3.2 mi., ledges begin to appear on the right and continue for the next 0.5 mi. (see Dry Brook Ridge Trail for details). At 3.9 mi., the Huckleberry Brook Trail junction (south leg) is reached at 3400 ft.

The trail turns right (south) and descends through fern glades and sugar maple. The trail shows little use but is well marked. The grade eases below 3000 ft. as an early, reclaimed (by vegetation) settlement is reached, where evergreens and stone walls provide a welcome respite from the deciduous forest. Passing through walls that once defined a pasture, the trail continues to descend easily through red pine and at 5.1 mi. arrives at (seasonally maintained) Ploutz Road where apple trees, stone foundations, a trail register, signboard, and trailhead parking area are located above a tributary of Mill Brook. Mill Brook Road is 1.5 mi. to the left (south), the nearest egress from this point.

From Ploutz Road the trail heads downhill into the southwest, turning right (west) within 100 ft. of the trailhead parking area. A stand of large European larch (a deciduous conifer) thrives here in the wet headwaters of Mill Brook. The trail follows next to a crumbling stone wall through a Norway spruce and pine plantation and rises up a long slope on an old road, turning right (northeast) next to a stone wall and steepening. Oak yields to maple as the trail enters a dense plantation of Norway spruce. Blue-paint blazes, remaining from the trail's construction in 1995, accompany red markers. Walk between two boulders into hardwoods, ascending to pass southwest of and below a wooded knoll at 2832 ft. The trail swings west at 5.6 mi., (2600 ft.) to cross over a knoll at 6.6 mi. (2800 ft.).

Continuing west, the trail descends easily into a saddle at 2400 ft., enters another Norway-spruce forest, turns to the right (north) following a tilted block of sedimentary sandstone, and travels along the easterly margins of a hemlock woods. At 8.0 mi., at the edge of a large, open field, the trail is no longer self-guiding, whereupon it follows sparse markers along the northeasterly (right) forest edge and crosses the field following cairns (piled rocks) that have been erected in the open field itself (nearly hidden by tall vegetation at the height of summer), taking a generally northerly course to the woods where red markers are posted.

From the field's northern edge the trail ascends into hardwoods, passing another isolated sedimentary boulder among scattered hemlocks, sidehilling as it begins to descend and switching back east-northeast, dropping more steeply. The trail crosses several seasonal creeks and levels somewhat, bearing right (east). Although this section of the trail is little used, it has been worn to mineral soil in places and is nearing its carrying capacity. Additional pressure will require improvement or re-routing, made difficult by the extreme slope. Turning left (north), the trail directly descends the slope, joins a woods road, and swings northwest. The surface widens and improves as a wet, minor confluence is crossed amid hemlock and mixed hardwood, and finally becomes washed out, nearly disappearing as the trail turns sharply to the right, heading north (this turn is not adequately marked and is barely self-evident). The trail descends steadily and gently into red pine, turning to hemlock as Huckleberry Brook Road appears to the north (left) and crosses the bridge spanning Huckleberry Brook at 9.6 mi.

The trail turns right (east), following Huckleberry Brook Road, soon passing the trailhead parking area on the left. The DEC's Huckleberry Brook storage area appears on the left (north) at 10.3 mi. The trail crosses a small bridge onto the storage-area lot. Trail signs appear on the side of the storage building itself.

The trail turns right (east) across the front lawn of the storage area and enters the woods at the east edge of the lot, thereafter turning left (north) and ascending through an evergreen forest, arriving at Hill Road at 10.6 mi. The parking area is 150 ft. to the left (west).

Balsam Lake Mountain Wild Forest

Positioned at the head of the scenic Beaver Kill Valley, most of this wild-forest area lies within the Ulster County town of Hardenburgh, bounded by Mill Brook Road in the north, across which lies the Dry Brook Ridge Wild Forest. High mountain ridges, deep hollows, steep-sided valleys, a lake, and a number of streams and beaver dams characterize this 14,000-acre area. The highest elevation is the summit of Balsam Lake Mountain (3730 ft.), while the lowest is at Kelly Hollow (1800 ft.), a designated cross-country ski trail system.

Hikers visiting the area will find primitive camping opportunities (and a lean-to) at Kelly Hollow along Mill Brook Road and at the Little Pond and Beaverkill Public Campgrounds to the west off Beaver Kill Road. Additional primitive camping is available at several scenic sites along the Alder Lake Loop Trail, and at a limited number of designated campsites along Beaver Kill Road east of Turnwood, and Shin Creek Road, south of Turnwood. There are five lean-tos within this area as well. The most attractive is the Beaver Meadow lean-to, located along the Mill Brook Ridge Trail, east of Alder Lake. Northern hardwood slope forest covers most of this area.

There are several important fisheries in the area, most notably the Beaver Kill itself, which has earned the area the reputation as being the "cradle of American fly fishing." This river is a part of the system of rivers lying within the most productive eastern trout waters, known by fly fishers as "The Charmed Circle." This stream is heavily posted where it abuts the forest preserve and elsewhere, although hikers can find public access along the Neversink-Hardenburgh Trail and in the villages east of Beaver Kill Road.

Scenic resources in this wild-forest area are significant and have a great deal to do with the placement of the first fire tower in the state on Balsam Lake Mountain's summit as early as 1887. Because it is a fairly isolated, high western summit, the mountain provides far-reaching views in every direction.

The Department of Environmental Conservation estimates that nearly 4000 recreationists use this forest area annually, which is far below the large quotas of the eastern wilderness areas. Approximately

1500 of these hikers are climbing the summit of Balsam Lake Mountain. The next largest user group are fishers, campers, and day hikers who use the Alder Lake area. Hikers will accordingly enjoy considerable privacy, access to shelters, good scenery—and excellent fishing—while visiting this wild forest.

Mill Brook Ridge Trail

  to Beaver Meadow lean-to: 1.5 mi., 1 hr.

  to Balsam Lake Mountain Trail: 5.85 mi., 3 hr.

From the trail junction at the eastern shore of Alder Lake, the Mill Brook Ridge Trail follows yellow markers east. The trail ascends, evening out through hardwoods over a good surface next to Alder Creek, penetrating a notch between Mill Brook and Cradle Rock Ridges. At 2300 ft. the trail begins to level, passing close along the northerly margin of a beaver meadow. Coneflowers crowd the heads of little feeder creeks where aster and meadow rue appear. There are a few huge specimens of beech and maple in the area. The trail ascends again, with the creek still to the right (south). At 1.4 mi. a short unmarked spur leads right to the edge of another beaver meadow that is presently drained. A small brook (the headwaters of Alder Creek) runs through the center. The trail skirts the north edge of the meadow, arriving at the junction of the spring and lean-to spur trails at 1.5 mi.

A slow-running piped spring is 100 yd. to the left (northwest) on a spur. To the right (southeast), toward the meadow and looking out across it, is an excellent lean-to, one of the most attractively situated shelters in the Catskills. The trail passes the lean-to's privy 100 ft. beyond the junction. Ascending, the trail passes another beaver meadow to the south. Rising and leveling moderately and in stages, the trail ascends as it heads southeast, passing a treed-in lookout to the northwest at 3400 ft. as it turns into hardwoods to reach the crest of a viewless knoll at 2.85 mi. (3480 ft.). The trail descends to the east, dropping several hundred feet into a saddle above Beecher Lake, which is sometimes visible through the forest to the south. The treadway becomes rocky and uneven, tunneled over by birch and cherry trees. Climbing out of the saddle to 3300 ft., and offering no summer views to the south, the trail rises to a peat-covered lookout punctuated by one large south-facing rock at 3.9 mi. Mongaup Mountain, the Beaver Kill Ridge, Woodpecker Ridge, and Cradle Rock Ridge are visible.

The trail continues flat until dropping off the easternmost section of Mill Brook Ridge at the location of a ledgy lookout point with obscured views of the Balsam Lake Mountain fire tower. A minimal descent settles onto level terrain as the route traverses hardwood forest around the top of a steep ravine above Balsam Lake, passing close to a number of steep and at least in one instance, vertical, ledges. Woodpecker Ridge comes into view to the right as the trail climbs into the northeast briefly and negotiates a flight of makeshift steps, switching back southeast on a longer ascent. At the 3500-ft. mark, balsam fir appears. Shortly beyond the 3500-ft. sign the trail switches north again, arriving at a bare ledge at 5.75 mi. with westerly views. Turn east at right angles to the lookout, entering an upper-elevation forest of mountain ash and balsam fir. The trail arrives at the junction with the Balsam Lake Mountain Trail at 5.85 mi. (3600 ft.). Balsam Lake Mountain (3730 ft.) and the fire tower are to the left (north) 0.1 mi., on the Balsam Lake Mountain Trail.

Alder Lake Loop Trail

around loop: 1.5 mi., 1 hr.

to Mill Brook Ridge trailhead: 0.75 mi., 20 min.

Alder Lake is an out-of-the-way trout pond and camping destination in the western Balsam Lake Mountain Wild Forest region. The trail is used by family campers, day hikers, and backpackers who wish to approach Balsam Lake Mountain "the long way"—from the west (see Mill Brook Ridge Trail). Alder Lake can be reached from the north by following Mill Brook Road 10.6 mi. west from Stewart's Turn in Seager (Dry Brook Road, CR 49) and coming south on (rough) Cross

Mountain Road 4.3 mi. to the Alder Lake trailhead parking area. It is easily accessible from the west, from Exit 96 off NY 17, by following CR 151 and CR 152 east (Johnson Hill Road) to Lew Beach and continuing east on CR 54 (Beaver Kill Road) to Turnwood (about 18 mi.). Alder Lake is just north of Turnwood off Alder Lake Road.

From the Alder Lake trailhead parking area and map kiosk, proceed past Coykendall Lodge, a now derelict mansion built by Samuel D. Coykendall, railroad and canal builder, in 1899. Several attempts to renovate the building have failed. This is the parcel formerly known as Alder Lake Scout Camp.

The lake and dam are visible from the lodge to the right (south). The trail bears right and crosses the dam. (Tent campers will wish to use the designated sites on the north shore.) The trail does not initially follow directly along the lakeshore, where a herd path leads to several highly impacted campsites, but heads to the right (west) where a solitary signpost indicates the trail's location. From the signpost the trail goes south and uphill gently, within a few hundred feet turning left (east), passing under power lines at a brushy intersection of goldenrod and bushy aster. Red trail markers are consistent, and the trail is in good shape, soon becoming a woods road and crossing a footbridge. The lake is to the left (north) after several hundred feet. Yellow birch is abundant as the trail crosses another footbridge. Herd trails, perhaps leading to primitive tent sites, are numerous. At 0.75 mi., the trail reaches the junction with the Mill Brook Ridge Trail on the right (east) and continues on the dirt-road treadway. A piped spring appears on the trail's left-hand side, in view of the junction. After crossing a pair of small wooden footbridges where hummingbirds sip at bee balm, the trail swings into the west, passing several designated campsites, most of them heavily used but well maintained and attractive. A few have stone chairs and tables, often with supplies of firewood left behind by other campers. The area becomes busy on most weekends, attracting perennial visitors who are avoiding the crowds at the nearby public campsites. Common to the area is the water-loving hawthorn (with a pear-shaped leaf and fruit that looks like a rose hip) and arrowhead alder in thickets, which are planted for wildlife cover and crowd the trail near the west end.

The trail continues west along the lake's north shore to the grassy lakefront of Coykendall Lodge at 1.5 mi.

Balsam Lake Mountain Trail

Distance from southerly junction with Dry Brook Ridge Trail

to Balsam Lake Mountain summit: 1.6 mi., 1 hr. 30 min.

The shortest route to the Balsam Lake Mountain Trail is from the Dry Brook Ridge Trail's southerly terminus (Balsam Lake Mountain trail-head parking area). This is the fastest (and steepest) way to the summit of this large westerly Catskill peak. By virtue of its fire tower, the views from Balsam Lake Mountain are extraordinary. The trails in this area are popular, but remote.

The trailhead parking area is at the eastern extreme of Beaver Kill Road, which can be reached most easily from Exit 94 off NY 17, by traveling east on CR 151 and CR 152 (Johnson Hill Road), to Lew Beach, and continuing on CR 54 (Beaver Kill Road) to its end (about 22 mi.). Beaver Kill Road can also be reached from the north by turning left (east) off Alder Lake Road onto Beaver Kill Road (see Alder Lake Loop Trail for details). The Balsam Lake Mountain Trail can also be accessed from the north off the Dry Brook Ridge Trail, using the Dry Brook Ridge trailhead on Mill Brook Road, 2.2 mi. west of Dry Brook Road (CR 49) at Stewart's Turn.

The Dry Brook Ridge Trail (blue markers) leaves from the north-east corner of the Balsam Lake Mountain trailhead parking area and leads 0.9 mi. to the Balsam Lake Mountain trailhead (red markers). Signage is poor at the Dry Brook Ridge trailhead. There is good signage at the junction.

At the junction of the Balsam Lake Mountain Trail and the Dry Brook Ridge Trail, the Balsam Lake Mountain Trail goes left (north) following red markers and climbs steeply to the lean-to spur at 0.5 mi. on the left (west) side of the trail. The spur is 0.2 mi. long, and leads through a patch of cow parsnips across a seasonal creek emanating from an uphill spring. To the west there are only obscure, seasonal views of Woodpecker Ridge. This is the Eleanor Leavitt Memorial lean-to (in excellent condition), built in recognition of Mrs. Leavitt's involvement in conservation issues.

The main trail continues and rises steeply, ascending a few stone steps past a spring. The trail flattens above this point, where an older campsite (illegal) appears on the right (east) near the 3500-ft. elevation mark. The trail eases now, in scrubby beech-and-cherry woods as summit elevation is approached and the junction with the Mill Brook Ridge Trail is reached at 0.75 mi.

Continuing straight ahead (north) and nearing the summit, the trail ascends slightly into a nearly pure fir forest. The tower stands in the corner of the small summit clearing at 0.85 mi., with an observer's cabin and privy nearby. Views from the tower are excellent. On weekends an observer may be present. To the east and slightly south are Peekamoose, Table, and Lone Mountains. In the foreground is Doubletop. Moving north, Slide dominates the far horizon. Graham, Giant Ledge and Panther, Indian Head, Twin, Sugarloaf, and Plateau can be seen. Hunter, West Kill, Blackhead, Black Dome, and Thomas Cole are visible to the northeast. In the foreground is Red Hill, its fire tower visible. On the right of Red Hill is Denman Mountain. The peaks of the Big Indian Range can be identified.

The trail continues northeast from the summit, descending through boreal forest on a steep truck trail. The descent continues easterly, dropping below the 3500-ft. level, and the trail ends at its junction with the Dry Brook Ridge Trail at 1.6 mi.

Kelly Hollow Trail

around loop: 3.8 mi., 1 hr. 30 min.

around short loop: 2.1 mi., 50 min.

to Beaver Pond and lean-to: 2.0 mi., 50 min.

Beautifully situated within a trio of nameless tributaries above Mill Brook, this designated cross-country ski trail makes a fine year-round day outing or overnight destination. It is convenient to both the Dry Brook Ridge and Alder Lake Loop trailheads. Car and tent camping in designated sites at the western trailhead, in addition to the (access by foot only) lean-to at Beaver Pond make this a popular destination for hikers and, especially in late summer, long-term campers. (A permit is required for stays longer than 3 days.) Unlimited opportunities for tent camping exist in the serene pine-and-Norway-spruce forests throughout the hollow. Larger parties should restrict themselves to the impacted, designated sites inside the west entrance.

The trail leaves from the eastern trailhead and designated parking area on Mill Brook Road, 6.6 mi. west of Dry Brook Road (CR 49). (The western trailhead and designated camping area is 0.3 mi. farther to the west.) A privy is situated near the parking area. Locate the yellow cross-country ski trail markers, which the trail follows south into a mature red-pine stand, turning left (east) over a creek to join an old road. The trail then turns right (south) and heads uphill through a barrier gate. A stone wall appears on the right (west) as the trail ascends next to a brook, where hemlock becomes dominant. At 0.5 mi., the trail continues straight ahead (south) at the Short Loop junction, where signs are posted. (The Short Loop departs downhill to the right, crossing a footbridge above a scenic glen, rises to Halfway Point, spans the brook's west branch, and joins the main trail again. The Short Loop receives little use and is often blocked with blowdowns. The west-branch plank bridge is in poor condition at this writing. Those wishing to shorten the hike can follow the short loop west to rejoin the long loop at the 2.6 mi. point, then turning right to the west-end trailhead.)

Avoid the Short Loop (a visit to the footbridge, visible from this junction, is worthwhile) and proceed straight ahead toward Beaver Pond. To the left (east) a large Norway-spruce plantation begins. The trail crosses the head of a sluggish creek in a strip of hardwoods before reentering the plantation, the latter so heavily shaded that there is little-to-no plant growth. At the top of the east branch, the trail turns west and north in a long, flat arc above the hollow. Hardwood yields to spotted spruce and hemlock, turning to nearly pure hemlock as the trail rises slightly to the well-situated lean-to at Beaver Pond, which sits in a north-facing depression of Mill Brook Ridge among tall spruce trees at 2.0 mi. The pond is frequently dry, depending upon beaver populations. The trail continues along the east edge of the pond, heading south. Marking is poor and the trail is crowded with brush and brambles, yielding large batches of black raspberries in late summer. Circling the lake to the northwest the trail improves as it joins an old dirt road through a farmed area of which only stone walls remain, turns right (north), and descends easily.

Descending more steeply now, at 2.6 mi. the trail passes the Short Loop on the right (east) and crosses a footbridge as it flattens out. Soon a graveyard appears to the left, and the trail joins the main camping-area road on the west end of the hollow. Go around the barrier gate, keeping the designated campsites to the right, at 3.5 mi. reaching Millbrook Road. At 150 ft. to the right (east) of the west entrance along Mill Brook Road the cross-country ski trail signs lead back into the woods, heading east. This connector trail will save hikers from walking the (short) road distance back to the east-branch parking area (the road is also pleasant, and never busy). The trail is not consistently self-guiding and marking on this section is poor. Keeping Mill Brook Road visible to the left (north) arrive at the parking area at 3.8 mi.

Mill Brook Lean-to Spur Trail

to Mill Brook lean-to, 0.2 mi., 10 min.

The Mill Brook lean-to is a convenient camping spot, located a very short distance off Mill Brook Road, less than a mile west of the Dry Brook Ridge trailhead parking area. Come west from Stewart's Turn at the corner of Mill Brook Road and Dry Brook Road (CR 49), passing the Dry Brook Ridge trailhead parking area at 2.2 mi. Continue another 0.9 mi., and park on the right side of the road by the lean-to spur.

The lean-to spur trail crosses a tributary of Mill Brook and climbs easily though a hemlock woods 0.2 mi. to the lean-to. The forest setting and proximity to water makes this a popular shelter, yet it remains clean and well maintained by the Adirondack Mountain Club.

Western Catskills

The Western Catskills include the Middle Mountain and Cherry Ridge Wild Forest, where the landscape is characterized by open fields, mature hardwood forests, and hills with steep slopes leading to long, flat ridges. The main trail in the area is a ridge and valley route joining several other trails, collectively known as the Delaware Ridge Trail, leading from Russel Brook Road in the west to Alder Lake for a distance of twenty-seven miles with seven road crossings. These trails are among the quietest and least used in the Catskills. Vistas, although present, are infrequent, but several natural lakes in the area are open to camping and fishing.

The Western Catskills shared many of the industries common to the rest of the range, with the addition of acid manufacturing, another extractive and ravaging forest-product industry. Because the acid-manufacturing process depends on hardwood, the post-tanning-period Catskills were well suited to the task. Early postcards of the Western Catskills, particularly around the villages of Roscoe and Rockland, show the clear-cut landscapes resulting from the acid-production industry in the late nineteenth century.

True to form in the succession of regional development, the railroads were followed by a brisk recreational and tourist industry, most of it focusing on hunting and fishing. It is a reputation the area maintains today. Perhaps no other spot in the east is as renowned for its trout fishing—in the 1980s, the Fly Fishing Federation of America labeled Roscoe "Trout Town, USA." Lying at the confluence (Junction Pool) of the Beaver Kill and Willowemoc—easily ranking among the country's most historic and legendary trout streams—the town sustains its status as an angler's mecca. Nearby Livingston Manor is host to the Catskill Fly Fishing Center and Museum. It was along the banks of the Beaver Kill that Theodore Gordon, the father of American fly fishing, developed his artificial dry-fly patterns (such as the Quill Gordon) that so effectively imitate the mayflies that trout feed on.

The Western Catskills are accessible from Mongaup Pond, Beaverkill, and Little Pond Public Campgrounds.

Section 14

Cherry Ridge
Wild Forest

West

Located in the town of Colchester in Delaware County, this 17,500-acre wild forest is mountainous, with trails ranging from moderate to steep. The forest is characterized by its several wetlands, more than 22 miles of snowmobile trails, 10 tributary stream systems, and 20 miles of foot trails. The dominant ridge trail is part of a continuous trail system spanning the Delaware Ridge. Elevations in this wild forest run from 2200 ft. to 2800 ft. and the area is almost entirely covered in forest of the Allegheny hardwood group, including cherry, red and sugar maple, American beech, yellow birch, and hemlock.

This wild forest contains three lean-tos and is ideal for day and overnight hikers seeking solitude and quiet in a little-used area. Several of the wild forest's most westerly trails are used by mountain bikers, in particular the Trout Pond–Mud Pond Loop. North of Trout Pond, however, the terrain is difficult and self-limiting to multiuse recreationists.

The Russel Brook trailhead is the one most commonly used by hikers, and the main attraction of the area around the trailhead is the falls and hemlock forests close to the road itself.

No threatened or endangered species exist in this area, although both the Cherry Ridge and Middle Mountain Wild Forest areas are believed to be host to the timber rattlesnake—a threatened species. Hikers should avoid exploring quarries or ruins during the warm, early months of spring when rattlers are active. Many of the area's fourteen wetlands (two of which are large enough to enjoy federal protection under the the Freshwater Wetlands Law) are host to beaver populations and help to create a greater diversity of wildlife. Trout Pond has been a popular fishing destination in the past and maintains a population of the Catskill strain of brook trout.

Trout Pond Trail

to Trout Pond lean-to: 1.4 mi., 30 min.

to Campbell Brook Road: 3.3 mi., 1 hr. 30 min.

to Campbell Mountain Trail: 5.4 mi., 2 hrs. 45 min.

From Exit 93 off NY 17 (Butternut Grove, Cooks Falls), the Trout Pond Trail begins 3.7 mi. east on Russell Brook Road. At 1.2 mi. from NY 17, Russell Brook Road is seasonally unmaintained. Both the Trout Pond and Mud Pond trail segments west of Trout Pond are used by mountain bikers and cross-country skiers.

Signs are posted next to the gated road adjacent to the trailhead parking area on the northwest side of Russell Brook Road. The trail follows this access road and descends a short distance to Russell Brook, crossing a pair of wooden bridges. The ruins of an early bluestone dam and bridge can be seen 200 ft. to the right (northeast, upstream). A heavily used, designated campsite is situated to the right (east) of the trail, within view of the trail register. Ahead 200 ft. is the Trout Pond Trail's junction with the Russell Brook Trail.

A stone foundation—the first of many to be seen in this early farming area—appears in the woods to the left. The trail bears right (north) toward Trout Pond over a wide, rocky road through hardwoods at 2045 ft., ascending easily and passing an unmarked spur to the left that leads 400 ft. to a designated campsite. Trout Pond comes into view at 1.0 mi., where an unmarked spur leads to a shingle beach on the south end of the pond. Beyond the concrete spillway, a rough (unmarked) path continues around the lake to the west. On the trail's right (east) amid tall hardwoods and a patch of striking, scarlet bee balm an arrow indicates the direction to the lean-to. A privy stands to the east of the trail here. The trail follows beside Trout Pond's northeastern shore, passes a legal, undesignated campsite on the right, after which a spring appears to the right of a footbridge where the DEC maintains a trout-spawning box. This piped spring provides a steady supply of cold water to a contrived spawning bed on the pond's east shore. Fishing in Trout Pond (brook trout) has proven productive in the past.

Ahead a very short distance is a trail junction, in view of the lean-to. To the left, the unsigned snowmobile trail leaves around the north end of Trout Pond, heading southwest to Mud Pond.

Rebuilt in the late summer of 2001, the Trout Pond lean-to is constructed of flat-sawn timbers, an unusual contrast to the old-style shelters made of peeled logs and hand-hewn planks. The Trout Pond Trail turns right (north) at the junction at 1.4 mi., climbing steadily into the northeast, at 2500 ft. arriving at a height-of-land where the Trout Pond trail continues left and a snowmobile trail leaves to the right (southeast) for Morton Hill Road.

Descending, the trail switches back before leveling into the east, thereafter descending steeply to a footbridge spanning the headwaters of Campbell Brook (dry in late summer) at 2100 ft. The trail flattens as hemlock appears in a pure stand before a second footbridge is crossed and the trail rises through hardwoods, deteriorating underfoot but remaining self-guiding and adequately marked. Stone walls denote the bounds of early settlements where late, second-growth hardwoods are taking hold. Passing around a barrier gate, the Trout Pond Trail crosses Campbell Brook Road at 3.30 mi.

Continue to the left (north) on Campbell Brook Road, within 400 ft. turning right (east), regaining the Trout Pond Trail. Climbing gently uphill into hardwoods, the quiet trail is fringed with blackberries and beech trees. At 3.7 mi. (2500 ft)., the trail levels through a flat summit knoll with no views. A downhill stretch to the southeast follows amid very tall hardwoods where a small quarry-talus heap, partly concealed by vegetation and detritus, appears to the right. The trail crosses a footbridge on the northerly headwater branch of Campbell Brook after which an interesting house or barn foundation is seen on the left as the trail enters a stand of maturing Norway-spruce trees. The trail (almost continuously an old dirt roadway) rises through this early farmstead area, where pioneer species (those taking hold after a fire or other disturbance) have taken hold in the open, grassy terrain and asters, Scots pine, apple, and escaped cultivated plants are growing. Ascending to 2175 ft., and passing around a barrier gate at 5.4 mi. where a signboard stands at the shoulder of Campbell Mountain Road, the Trout Pond trail ends. The Campbell Mountain Trail begins directly across the road. Finger Lakes Trail (FLT) disks may be posted here, where there is a small parking lot designated as a snowmobile-parking and off-loading area. This spot is isolated.

Mud Pond Trail

to Mud Pond: 1. 3 mi., 30 min.

to Trout Pond lean-to: 3.1 mi., 1 hr. 40 min.

This quiet trail leads to a mountain pond through deep woods and is the westernmost trailhead on state land in the Catskills. The forests in this area have reclaimed a number of old farms and orchards, of which hikers will see some remains.

From Exit 93 off NY 17 (Butternut Grove, Cooks Falls), the Mud Pond Trail begins 2.3 mi. east on Russell Brook Road (1.2 mi. from NY 17, Russell Brook Road is seasonally unmaintained). Both the Trout Pond and Mud Pond Trail segments west of Trout Pond are used by mountain bikers and cross-country skiers. The trail leaves to the north from the trailhead pullover parking area.

The trail enters the wood passes the trail register on the right and climbs, passing beneath a transmission line over the West Delaware Aqueduct right-of-way (1673 ft.). At 0.2 mi., a beaver pond appears to the west as the trail levels, draining through a small hemlock grove and into wet meadow to the east. The trail traverses one of the many old roads that penetrate the surrounding wild-forest area, passing through a shallow, picturesque hollow, carved by the outlet stream of Mud Pond. The trail ascends and levels, and at 1.0 mi., Mud Pond is visible to the right. Turning right (east) 90 degrees at a trail arrow where a snowmobile spur departs west to the head of Dry Brook Road (private), the Mud Pond Trail continues east, crosses Mud Pond's seasonal inlet creek, and passes several hand-laid bluestone foundations on the Mud Pond (right) side of the trail. At 1.3 mi., watch carefully for the easily missed, unmarked spur trail to the right, leading 400 ft.

to the pond. Just beyond the spur along the main trail, an undesignated campsite and fire ring exist to the right (south). At 1.5 mi., arrive at a junction where the Mud Pond Trail turns left (north), and the Russell Brook Trail (blue, snowmobile corridor 20A) continues straight ahead (southeast) to the Russell Brook Road parking area. Bear left.

Rising through sugar maple, the trail crosses the site of an early pasture, in the process of natural reclamation by a forest of vigorous maple saplings. Ascending with Russell Brook to the left (west), the trail rises to a point east off of Cherry Ridge at 2.5 mi. (2500 ft.). Now the trail descends to the east, crossing Trout Pond inlet and approaching the north shore of the pond, where a designated campsite lies just to the right (west). A new, well-built lean-to stands within sight of the Trout Pond Trail junction at 3.1 mi.

Russell Brook Trail

to Mud Pond Trail: 1.1 mi., 20 min.

This trail follows an early woods road to join the Mud Pond Trail and offers several attractive camping possibilities.

Beginning at the junction with the Trout Pond Trail a few hundred feet north of the Russell Brook Road parking area, this trail provides the shortest access route to Mud Pond and enables a loop connection for walks around both Trout and Mud Ponds (assuming that Russell Brook Road is used to complete the Mud Pond loop). Ascend over rolling terrain as Russell Brook appears to the left (south), becoming a deep, dry gully by late summer. Campsites are designated at both sides of a footbridge spanning the brook. The trail soon descends, arriving at the T junction with the Mud Pond Trail at 1.1 mi.

Campbell Mountain Trail

to Campbell Mountain lean-to: 1.1 mi., 35 min.

to NY 206: 2.4 mi., 1 hr. 40 min.

to Pelnor Hollow and Little Spring Brook Trails: 5.8 mi., 3 hrs.

This trail crosses isolated Campbell Mountain before descending to cross NY 206 and climbs across Brock Mountain before connecting to the Pelnor Hollow Trail and points east and south. It forms a major link in the Delaware Ridge Trail.

The trail begins on Campbell Mountain Road, a continuation of the Trout Pond Trail to the west. A parking area is located here, 0.8 mi. north of Jug Tavern Road on Campbell Mountain Road.

The trail begins past a barrier gate, and climbs gently through a mixed forest of white pine and hardwoods. Turning south and north again around a knoll (2461 ft.) the trail flattens momentarily as it heads southeast, with red oaks increasing. Passing a small but obvious footpath to the right (south) at 0.4 mi. (which heads off in the direction of Wedemeyer Road), hikers may hear highway noise filtering up through Cat Hollow from CR 7 (NY 206). The trail descends through an oak-and-maple wood, and passes an old, discontinued trail to the right across a seasonal rill, arriving at the lean-to spur at 1.1 mi. (2100 ft.). A sign indicates the shelter to the right, across the same (former) kill, which is dry in late summer. Continuing downhill, the trail switches back at a large quarry site to the left (north), where the hiker is guided by trail arrows. Through the 1800 ft.-elevation, a microburst has felled a substantial section of forest on the hollow's western slope. Continuing south the trail flattens, entering hemlock woods and crossing a tributary that flows 2.0 mi. north into the Pepacton Reservoir. A gratifying, dense Norway-spruce plantation follows—one of the few such stands encountered this far west in the Catskills—and thick yellow blooms of coneflower appear in this neighborhood of reclaimed farmlands. The trail curves left (north) and rises out of the woods along the side of a slope, reaching CR 7 (NY208) at 2.4 mi. This is a fairly busy highway. Signs and a register are present. Pullover parking is available.

Carefully cross the road and regain the trail on the east side, beginning the ascent of Brock Mountain (2512 ft.) as it climbs an embankment into the woods, heading northeast. Old stone walls stand to the right (south). Climbing through hardwoods followed by an extensive red-pine woods, the trail deteriorates into a rough path, at first ascending steeply, then relaxing in a mixed-hardwood area before climbing again, leveling off at roughly 2400 ft. Extensive tailing piles from a large quarry appear immediately to the trail's left (north), extending northeast. The talus field and strip mines are accessible from a small (vague) access path on the left (north) of the main trail. The quarry itself is overgrown and unspectacular—far inferior to those of the eastern Catskills—but it's worth a small detour a few hundred feet along this path to see the intriguing remains of an (early 1900s) dump truck—a solemn memoir of another era. Continuing east, the roadlike trail improves over the route of the original quarry road, which joined present-day CR 7. Ahead, be cautious to watch for the trail's 90-degree left-hand turn (north) as the quarry road continues straight ahead, passing through a now private inholding. Although the road is sometimes "blocked" with sticks to alert hikers, it's easy to continue on this more established, but incorrect route. Follow the trail to the southeast as it ascends, passing north of Brock's southeastern summit at 3.8 mi. (2760 ft.). The trail is level for a short distance, soon passing through a high (2700 ft.), grassy area punctuated by a small, flat clearing on exposed bedrock. The trail immediately descends through a forest of tall maple and scattered large, flat boulders, dropping nearly 500 ft. in elevation over the next 0.5 mi. At 4.6 mi., the trail reaches a woods road (dirt) that runs north-south. Signage is absent, marking is poor. A stone wall stands directly across the road. To the right (south) red snowmobile markers lead to School House Road (private). The Campbell Mountain Trail continues to the left (north), where snowmobile markers and (scant) blue markers head in the direction of Miller Hollow Road spur. Watch carefully as the Campbell Mountain Trail follows the snowmobile trail a distance of approximately 200 yd. before turning hard right (east) and sidehilling along a north-facing slope. As you travel east, within a few moments an unmarked woods road leaves to the right (south) onto private property toward School House Road. The main trail turns into the north, descending slightly, and turns southeast, leveling and again descending, passing through an extensive, well-made stone wall and into a maturing Norway-spruce forest.

At 5.6 mi., the trail arrives at a junction where a red-marked snowmobile trail leaves to the left (north) on a dirt road, ultimately joining (private) Berg Brook Road. The trail to the right, toward Little Spring Brook Road (still the Campbell Mountain Trail), leads to the Pelnor Hollow Trail. This intersection is marked only with blue and red markers, with a trail arrow pointing right (south). Avoid the red snowmobile trail to the left, and turn right (south) following the grassy trail, within minutes reaching a T junction, where as of this writing, signage appears on a post beneath an apple tree at 5.8 mi. This is the end of the Campbell Mountain Trail. The Little Spring Brook-Trail leaves to the south, and the Pelnor Hollow Trail goes left (east) to join the Mary Smith Trail.

Pelnor Hollow Trail

to Mary Smith Trail: 0.8 mi., 30 min.

to Pelnor Hollow lean-to: 3.1 mi., 1 hr. 30 min.

to Pelnor Hollow Road: 4.0 mi., 2 hr.

The Pelnor Hollow Trail begins at the intersection of the Campbell Mountain and Little Spring Brook Trails and rises to the east before turning south to meet the Mary Smith Trail. Heavily forested, the trail provides an egress/ingress route from the Delaware Ridge Trail to the south, via Berry Brook Road and Pelnor Hollow Road, just west of the Beaver Kill Public Campground. The area (especially the Pelnor Hollow lean-to) is popular with hunters.

The Pelnor Hollow Trail heads east following blue markers, crossing a seasonal creek into an extensive forest of red pine and Norway spruce, providing excellent camping potential for thru-hikers between here and the Pelnor Hollow lean-to. Climbing steeply and switching back through hardwoods, at 2500 ft., the trail turns south, flattening along a west-facing ridge with low ledges on the left. A break in the forest looking west is the location of Split Rock Lookout, a prominent vista. This area is also attractive for camping because the open ledge provides some visual relief as well as summer exposure to prevailing breezes. Approach cautiously, especially during snowcover or low light, watching for a shallow but potentially hazardous (20 ft.) crack where the ledge has fissured away from the ridge. To reach the ledge (not necessary in order to get the full view), go around to the left of a large boulder, avoiding the temptation to jump across the mossy crevice. Views to the west across the Little Spring Brook Valley provide a welcomed contrast to the enclosed woodlands of the Cherry Ridge Wild Forest area, exposing Brock Mountain (2512 ft.), Cherry Ridge (avg. 2600 ft.), and the hills of Hamden in the northwest. Climbing steeply but briefly, the trail arrives at the junction with the Mary Smith Trail at 0.8 mi.

Heading south, the trail becomes obscured by ground vegetation but soon provides an open and clear track, which is well marked and self-guiding. Descending slightly before climbing to the enclosed crest of a nameless ridge at 2672 ft., and turning briefly into the northwest and leveling, the trail soon descends south again as it approaches Pelnor Hollow. Amid the ash, red oak, and gray birch, hikers may see an occasional shagbark hickory tree and old snowmobile-trail markers. At 2.3 mi. the lean-to—well-situated in an open forest of tall maple— is reached, where a beaver pond is visible a short distance downhill to the southeast.

Continue south through a flat area of thin beech trees, turning through the west and descending to the (dirt) Pelnor Hollow Road at 4.0 mi. The lack of trailhead parking here is problematic for hikers heading north to the lean-to, and the road is both rough as well as heavily posted.

Little Spring Brook Trail

to Little Spring Brook Road: 0.6 mi., 20 min.

This short spur descends from its intersection with the Pelnor Hollow Trail and Campbell Mountain Trail, passing a small pond on the left (east), crossing its outlet (Little Spring Brook), and ending at the northern terminus of Little Spring Brook Road (off NY 206/CR 7, aka Cat Hollow Road). Trailhead parking on Little Spring Brook Road is limited to room for a car or two (pullover) near the driveway of a private residence, where a hand-painted sign identifies the parking pulloff. There is destination signage along the trail. Marking exists. This trail represents one of the few (legal) trails leaving/entering the Middle Mountain Wild Forest area and Delaware Ridge Trail from the south, between the much longer Pelnor Hollow Trail and the trailheads along the north-south-running area roads.

Section 15

Middle Mountain Wild Forest

West

The trails in the Middle Mountain Wild Forest are steep and more difficult than the hiker might expect from their westerly, marginal position in the range and their relatively lower elevations. The highest elevation in the 10,000-acre mountainous forest area is Middle Mountain itself (2975 ft.). Other named mountains in the unit include Cabot, Beech Hill, Touch-me-not, and Hunt Hill. Northern hardwoods are the predominant forest type, with isolated stands of plantation conifers and scattered stands of hemlock trees. Huggins Lake and Big Pond are two attractive ponded waters in the unit, and each contain trout. All of the low-gradient streams in the area flow to the Delaware River.

There are 12.8 mi. of trail in this wild forest, most of these miles comprising the summit or Delaware Ridge Trail system of individually named trails. Two sate campgrounds exist in the area and make ideal staging grounds for day hikes in the area (Little Pond and Beaver Kill Public Campgrounds). In an effort to connect the trail systems of the Western Catskills to those in the east, this wild-forest area was joined to the east-lying Balsam Lake Mountain Wild Forest by the construction of the Mill Brook Ridge Trail via Alder Lake.

On the trails, very steep initial ascents are followed by upper-elevation ridge forests, often with limited vistas. Huggins Lake is the only trail in the area that attracts multiple use in the form of an occasional mountain biker or cross-country skier, but it too has a steep trail. Many campers day hike the Campground Trail and Little Pond Trail, making an easy loop from Little Pond Public Campground. Primitive, designated campsites exist throughout the area, the most attractive of these are within a short walk of the trailhead parking area at Alder Lake. There are no lean-tos, but interior forest and ridgetop camping is ideal throughout the wild forest. This area is popular with deer hunters and has yielded more than five bucks per square mile. Bears are sometimes sighted in the area. Hikers using the forest during hunting season should exercise the proper precautions.

Mary Smith Trail

Distances from Pelnor Hollow Trail

> *to* Holliday and Berry Brook Road: 1.2 mi., 30 min.
>
> *to* Mary Smith Hill Road: 4.5 mi., 2 hr. 15 min.

At 2650-ft. elevation, 0.8 miles southeast from the beginning of the Pelnor Hollow Trail, the Mary Smith trail descends to the northeast. The trail quickly descends, becoming steeper before leveling in a mixed hardwood forest of basswood, birch, and large ash trees. Ferns and viburnum crowd the well-marked trail, which gets little use. Nearing Holliday and Berry Brook Road, the path first passes under power lines, beneath which is buried the East Delaware Aqueduct (not visible). This system carries water from the Cannonsville, Pepacton, Neversink, and Rondout Reservoirs east to the Croton watershed and its dozen reservoirs to supply New York City's drinking water.

Relocating the trail on the other side of the power-line right-of-way will demand a bit more attention from hikers coming west (because of the recessed treeline on the west side, there is nowhere to post a trail marker). The trail crosses the right-of-way diagonally, but is not self-guiding across the clearing. Watch carefully for markers. The trail picks up again slightly to the left, after passing under the power lines. Blackberries are abundant. The state has posted signs here prohibiting target practice (hunters prefer to site their rifles where they can place a target several hundred feet distant—the power line is an ideal place for this).

The following flat section of trail crosses a private easement. Hikers planning to camp near the trailhead should do so only after entering the wild-forest boundary. A grassy area leads to the road where signs are posted. There is a large parking area on the east side of Holliday and Berry Brook Road, where the Mary Smith Trail continues from the north end of the lot. Finger Lakes Trail signs and markers are posted here. Roughly 5.0 miles to the south on Berry Brook Road is the Beaver Kill Public Campground. The trail continues, following red markers as it leaves the parking lot, crosses a private easement, and quickly climbs into the northeast amid oak and maple trees, turning south and switching back at the site of a shallow overhanging rock. Here the path relaxes, penetrates a broken ledge, and begins to level at 2600 ft. on a westerly knoll approaching the summit of Mary Smith Hill (2767 ft.). Watch for a yellow arrow, where the route turns sharply to the right (southeast). The treadway is crowded with brush by late summer, but this vegetation—primarily viburnum and berry bushes—thins as the trail moves east. Marginal, seasonal views exist to the right (south). Following along the flat ridge for a mile beyond the summit, the trail arrives at a boulder and the site of a narrow (30 degrees) cut vista looking south across Huggins Hollow. The off-trail area is flat, legal, and suitable for tenting. The trail continues downhill into a maple forest, switching back steeply to the northeast, ending at Mary Smith Hill Road at 4.5 mi. (2300 ft.). Across the road on the left (north) is a designated campsite. Trailhead parking is a short distance south.

Middle Mountain Trail

Distance from Mary Smith Hill Road

> *to* Middle Mountain Vista: 1.1 mi., 30 min.

> *to* Beech Hill Road: 2.0 mi., 1 hr. 30 min.

On Mary Smith Hill Road, 3.1 mi. north of Lew Beach four corners on Beaver Kill Road, the Middle Mountain Trail heads east, forming another link in the Delaware Ridge Trail system. At the edge of the road's right (east) side, next to the trail register and a designated campsite, locate the trail signage.

Follow the established pathway east into the woods, which for a moment remains flat. Stone walls appear to the right as the track rises into hardwoods. Altitude is gained quickly and steeply. Views to the west of Mary Smith Hill are seasonal, improving as the trail relaxes and switches into the southeast, rising gently. Turning east, the bulk of the remaining ridgetop elevation is achieved at 2975 ft. on the summit of Middle Mountain (viewless) at 0.9 mi. The trail continues on the level to Middle Mountain Vista at 1.1 mi., a narrow but welcome cut view (30 degrees) looking south across Whitcomb Hollow and Lew Beach toward Mongaup Mountain. The trail descends hereafter, where Jack-in-the-pulpit gone to red berries (in season) appear. After descending, a shallow saddle is crossed at 2650 ft.; the corresponding ascent follows to Beech Hill at 1.5 mi. (2844 ft.), where the path is level amid ferns and cherry trees. (Be prepared to dodge copious bear scat while the red cherry is in fruit in July and August.) Seasonal views exist to the northeast toward Cabot Mountain (2970 ft.). The trail descends steadily off the northeast face of Beech Hill until reaching a dirt road. One hundred feet to the left (west) is private, posted property. Turn right (east), following the road (it is not well marked) to Beech Hill Road at 2.0 mi. A Finger Lakes Trail sign identifies the trailhead. To the right (southeast) 0.25 mi. is the trailhead parking area and the Touch-me-not Mountain trailhead.

Touch-me-not Trail

Distances from Beech Hill Road

  to Barkaboom Road and Big Pond: 3.9 mi., 2 hr. 30 min.

  to Alder Lake Road: 6.8 mi., 4 hr.

Named for the flower that is so prolific along its course, the quiet Touch-me-not Trail forms the easternmost link in the Delaware Ridge Trail. Find the trailhead 0.25 mi. south of the Middle Mountain trailhead on Beech Hill Road, and 3.0 mi. north of Beaver Kill Road, northeast of Lew Beach (this is near the corners of Delaware, Sullivan, and Ulster Counties). A large trail sign and Finger Lakes Trail signage appear at the parking area.

The trail heads northeast into the woods following the northern edge of a pine plantation in an open field of goldenrod, entering the woods to the east. Norway spruce appears on the south side as the trail descends slightly along a disused dirt road, soon ascending among a few rotting blowdowns colonized with brassy-orange golden trumpets. The climbing continues to the 2800-ft. level, where the trail turns southeast, becomes level, descends slightly, and again climbs easily to nearly summit elevation, where it turns northeast again. At the flat summit of Cabot Mountain at 1.4 mi. (2970 ft.), the anchor rod of a benchmark may be seen in a stone midtrail, but the benchmark itself is gone. At 1.5 mi., the trail arrives at a lookout point. This is a vertical ledge, where vegetation projects slightly over the edge of the rock itself. Use caution. Balsam Lake Mountain (3723 ft.) is seen to the left, but the fire tower is nearly impossible to spot without binoculars. South of Balsam Lake Mountain and farther back on the horizon is Doubletop (3860 ft.), with the Beaver Kill Range in the foreground. Little Pond (the location of the public campground) is visible directly below, with its sandy beach along the north shore.

The trail leaves across the top of the ledge heading north and descends steeply into the east, leveling at 2500 ft. in the saddle above Little Pond at 2.0 mi. The Little Pond Trail descends to the south at this point. No destination signage exists at this time, but directional marking is adequate. Pointing back into the west, a trail arrow here is hand-painted with the words "Beech Hill." From this point the trail continues east, following red markers. Watch carefully as the trail swings north, rising through a low ledge (a herd path continues a short distance to the right (southeast) before the ledge, indicating that this turn is frequently missed). Large oak and cherry trees characterize Touch-me-not Mountain at 2.8 mi. (2760 ft.), the treed-in summit approximated by the junction with the Campground Trail, which descends to the right (south) to Little Pond public campground. Signage here is good.

The trail descends to the east, easing as elevation is lost through the thick northern hardwood forest. Soon the trail joins an old woods road as it approaches Big Pond. This area has received high impact from indiscreet campers—there is broken glass and trash scattered along the trail here. Pass the trail register and drop down to Barkaboom Road at 3.9 mi. A Finger Lakes Trail signboard and red markers appear here at the trailhead. Destination signage is absent, but distances to points east can be found at the parking area to the right at 4.0 mi., a short way to the right (south) on the east side of Barkaboom Road.

There is also a small parking area here at the trailhead. A signboard at the open, grassy south end of the pond contains a map and information pertaining to both Big Pond as well as the wild-forest area. Big Pond has several designated campsites along its eastern shore, which can be reached by boat (no motors are permitted) or on foot via an unidentified trail that leaves from the trailhead parking area. This area is intensively used. The lake has a substantial population of large trout.

At the trailhead, signage indicates Alder Lake. Regain the Touch-me-not Trail from the south edge of the parking area where it goes east, passing a stand of conifers and the location of an early homestead on the left, of which only a foundation remains. Walking through an open field, the trail descends slightly into a maple woods. The trail soon ascends, switching back through open forest, climbing through Norway-spruce stands and thickets before relaxing through a hardwood forest, following the easterly edge of a ridge at 2500 ft. Now heading northeast, the trail enters an old farmstead area, where reclaimed pastures are now maturing forests of sugar maple, and passes stone walls and a pair of foundations on the right (east) and other evidence of settlement. There is no running or standing water until a seasonal creek, above a beaver meadow on a tributary of Alder Creek, is crossed at 2300 ft. Having crossed the rocky creek bed, turn left at an intersection where an old road goes off to the right. Climb easily, leveling on a rise where the trail turns right (east) and again ascends gently through an abandoned apple orchard and clearing. Large boulders appear to the left of the trail as it crosses several seasonal rills. The trail descends now, swinging left (north) to join the main confluence of Alder Creek, finally crossing it and rising to meet Alder Creek Road at 6.8 mi. Ahead (east) on the dirt road is Alder Lake at 0.3 mi. To the right 2.5 mi. is Beaver Kill Road (Turnwood).

Campground Trail–Little Pond Loop Trail

to Little Pond Campground and back: 3.6 mi., 2 hr.

In concert with the Little Pond Trail (and a section of the Touch-me-not Trail), the Campground Trail makes possible a fairly short and moderately strenuous loop of 3.1 mi., one that is popular with campers at the Little Pond Public Campground and Day Use Area (NYSDEC). The Little Pond Campground is located 14 mi. northwest of Livingston Manor on Barkaboom Road, off Beaver Kill Road (CR 54). Enter the campground, pay the day-use fee, and locate the trail directly behind the shower house in the campground's day-use-and-swimming-area parking lot.

The trail and trail register are found to the right of the trail signs. The Campground Trail enters the woods heading north and soon turns northwest and flattens out—for the time being. The trail rises steeply beyond 2300 ft., climbing north through clumps of large sedimentary rock covered in scales of lichen. This ascent continues until the Touch-me-not-Trail junction is reached, on the western summit area of Touch-me-not Mountain at 0.7 mi. (2750 ft.). The Campground Trail ends at this point. Arrive at the wooded junction with the Touch-me-not Trail and the Little Pond Trail at 1.5 mi.

There is presently no destination signage for the Campground Trail, but directional marking is good. To continue on the loop, hikers must turn left (north-northwest) on the Touch-me-not-Trail, which provides only broken winter views to the southwest (Middle Mountain area). Follow the trail, descending through an ash, oak, and cherry woods with some huge specimens of cherry (the small, purple berrylike drupes that appear along the trail in late summer are black cherries—a preferred food of the black bear). Dropping down through a narrow cleft in the bedrock, walk level along the ridge, arriving at the intersection with the Little Pond Trail at 1.5 mi. Marking is good; signage is poor. A trail arrow pointing west is hand painted with the words "Beech Hill" (not, as you might expect, Cabot Mountain), where red markers continue along the Touch-me-not Trail. To the left (south), yellow trail markers identify the Little Pond Trail, which is roadwidth and well-traveled. Go left (south). Within a few minutes' walk of the junction a large, open field (Beaver Kill Vista) is entered from the north. Along the northwest side is a dense stand of Norway spruce, and in a depression to the right of the trail is a shallow pond. Pastoral, lowland views open up to the east over Turnwood and into the rolling hills of the Mongaup–Beaver Kill Ridge—this is the western foothill region of the Big Indian–Beaver Kill Range Wilderness Area and the upper realms of the Beaver Kill Valley. Near the south edge of the clearing, a small stone foundation sits to the left of the trail. After reentering the woods the trail forks to the left at a trail arrow and descends into Norway-spruce forest, with red pine joining in on the right. This descent continues gradually into hardwoods. The wide, rocky trail passes a beaver meadow to the left, the seasonal outlet forming a deeply etched hollow in the soft soil, where hemlock grows. At 3.1 mi., in campsite #70, the Little Pond Trail meets Little Pond itself. Hikers coming around the pond loop from the west may walk past this junction without seeing the east-facing trail signs.

The Little Pond Trail continues to the right (west), circling the pond and arriving at the trailhead and remote campsite boat launch/parking area at the site of a solitary stone chimney. The home, which stood at this site, belonged to the Garrison family, who gave these lands to the state. Photos of the old estate can be seen at the campsite office.

Those seeking to complete the loop by returning to the Campground Trail should turn left (east) here, walking through the woods to the rear of the remote walk- or boat-in sites numbered 70–75. This will bring hikers in a full circle, back to the day-use and swimming area at 3.6 mi.

Huggins Lake Trail

to Huggins Lake: 1.9 mi., 45 min.

This trail has gained in popularity in recent years, going from relative obscurity to a destination with its own trailhead parking area. Mountain bikers, skiers, and hikers enjoy the trail, which has posed a management problem because of its use by all-terrain vehicles. The addition of an access barrier has reduced these activities, and hikers can anticipate quiet, peaceful surroundings.

From Holliday and Berry Brook Road, 2.5 mi. north of the Beaver Kill Public Campground, the trail departs from the trailhead parking area, passes around a barrier gate, and leads east and uphill into hardwoods. Signage is posted on the road, but marking along the trail, which is a wide and self-guiding dirt road, is poor or absent. The trail bears left at the first fork after only a few minutes of hiking. (This junction lacks a trail arrow.) Climbing to 2285 ft., the trail levels, passing to the north of a hill (2310 ft.) and descending southward.

The lake comes into view to the east and again as the final approach is made, as the trail switches back to the left (north). Huggins Lake lies cached in a shallow bowl that forms the head of Huggins Hollow. A dam at the lake's south end controls its flow of water into the Beaver Kill. Many wildflowers will be found blooming here throughout the summer—among them aster, sunflower, coneflower, and fleabane. Arrowwood grows next to the lake and produces blueberry–like drupe bunches by late summer (Native Americans used the shrub for arrow shafts). A campsite is designated to the north of the outlet, a hundred yards from the dam. The short (but hilly) round trip makes for an easy day hike.

Appendix A

Elevation of Major Peaks in Catskills

Name	Elevation
Slide	4190
Hunter	4050
Black Dome	3990
Blackhead	3950
Thomas Cole	3950
West Kill	3890
Graham	3868
Cornell	3870
Doubletop	3870
Plateau	3850
Table	3847
Peekamoose	3843
Sugarloaf	3810
Wittenberg	3790
Southwest Hunter	3750
Balsam Lake	3730

Appendix B

Accident Report

Your Name_____Date_____Time_____

DESCRIPTION OF LOST OR INJURED PERSON:

Name _____Age/Sex_____

Address_____Hair: _____

_____Fac. Hair: _____

Phone: _____

REPORTING PERSON:

Name _____Phone: _____

Address _____

WHAT HAPPENED:

_____

_____

_____

_____

_____

POINT LAST SEEN:

Car Description _____Date _____

Car Location _____

Itinerary _____

WEARING (color/style/size):

Jacket _____ Shirt _____

Shorts/Pants _____ Hat/Gloves _____

Glasses _____ Pack_____

Footgear _____ Crampons _____

CARRYING (color/style/size/quantity):

Map _____ Sleeping Bag _____

Tent/Bivy _____ Rain/Windgear _____

Flashlight/Batts _____ Extra Clothing _____

Food/Water _____ Ski Poles/Ice Axe _____

Experience _____

Physical/Mental Conditions _____

ESSENTIAL PATIENT INFORMATION

PROBLEM AREAS/INJURIES

❏ Head   ❏ Neck   ❏ Shoulders   ❏ Chest
❏ Abdomen   ❏ Back   ❏ Pelvis

❏ Left Upper Leg   ❏ Left Lower Leg   ❏ Left Foot
❏ Right Upper Leg   ❏ Right Lower Leg   ❏ Right Foot

❏ Left Arm   ❏ Left Hand   ❏ Right Arm   ❏ Right Hand

Chief Complaint and Plan

_____

_____

_____

Problem 2 and Plan

_____

_____

_____

Problem 3 and Plan

_____

_____

_____

BACKGROUND INFORMATION

Allergies _____

Medication _____

Previous Injury/Illness _____

Last 24hr food/water intake _____

Medical Conditions/Other _____

_____

FOR BACK, CHEST, OR ABDOMINAL PAIN, DETERMINE:

History _____

Duration _____

Intensity _____**Changing +/-** _____

VITAL SIGNS

	ESSENTIAL			HELPFUL		
TIME	**LEVEL OF CONSCIOUSNESS**	**BREATHING RATE**	**PULSE**	**BLOOD PRESSURE**	**SKIN**	**PUPILS**

NOTES

DATE/TIME	WEATHER/LOCATION AND FINDINGS	ACTION TAKEN

Bibliography

Bierhorst, John. *The Ashokan Catskills, A Natural History.* Fleischmanns, NY: Purple Mountain Press, 1995.

De Lisser, Richard Lionel. *Picturesque Green County.* Kingston, NY: Styles and Bruyn Publishing Co., 1896. Hope Farm Press, Saugerties, NY. 1998.

—.*Picturesque Ulster County.* Kingston, NY: Styles and Bruyn Publishing Co., 1896. Hope Farm Press, Saugerties, NY. 1996.

Evers, Alf. *The Catskills: From Wilderness to Woodstock.* Woodstock, NY: The Overlook Press, 1982.

Haring, H. A. *Our Catskill Mountains.* New York, NY: G. P. Putnam's Sons, 1931.

Kick, Peter; McMartin, Barbara. *50 Hikes in the Hudson Valley,* Woodstock, VT: W. W. Norton & Co., 1984.

Kudish, Michael. *The Catskill Forest, A History.* Fleishmanns, NY: Purple Mountain Press, 2000.

Long Path Guide. New York, NY: New York–New Jersey Trail Conference, 1996.

Longstreth, T. Morris. *The Catskills.* New York, NY: The Century Co., 1918.

Van Loan's *Guide to the Catskills.* Astoria (Reprint) 1879. Hope Farm Press Saugerties, NY. 1998.

Van Zandt, Roland. *The Catskill Mountain House.* New Brunswick: Rutgers University Press, 1966.

Index

Note: **Boldface** type denotes trail name
ALL CAPS denotes section name

About the Author

Peter W. Kick holds degrees in forestry and education. A New York State liscensed wilderness guide, he is also a former Boy Scouts of America national canoe base director and the author of several outdoor guidebooks. Currently he is a teacher, guide, and freelance writer.

About the
Appalachian Mountain Club

Since 1876, the Appalachian Mountain Club has helped people experience the majesty and solitude of the Northeast outdoors. We offer outdoor skills workshops, guided trips, and lodging options for all levels of outdoor adventuring. Our programs include trail maintenance, air and water quality research, education, and conservation advocacy work to preserve the special outdoor places we love and enjoy for future generations.

Join the Club!

Take a hike, ride a bike, paddle a canoe. We believe that people who enjoy climbing mountains, splashing in streams, and walking on trails have more fun and take better care of the outdoors. Join the fun today. Call 617-523-0636 or visit www.outdoors.org for membership information. AMC members receive discounts on workshops, lodging, and books.

Outdoor Adventures

From beginner backpacking to advanced backcountry skiing to guided hiking and paddling trips, we teach outdoor skills workshops to suit your interest and experience. Our outdoor education centers guarantee year-round adventures. View our entire listing of workshops online at www.outdoors.org.

234

Huts, Lodges, and Visitor Centers

The Appalachian Mountain Club provides accommodations throughout the Northeast so you don't have to travel to the ends of the earth to experience unique wilderness lodging. Accessible by car or on foot, our lodges and huts are perfect for families, couples, groups, and individuals. For reservations call 800-262-4455.

Books and Maps

We can lead you to the best hiking, biking, skiing, and paddling destinations from Maine to North Carolina. With more than fifty books and maps published, we're your definitive resource for discovering wonderful outdoor places. To receive a free catalog call 800-262-4455 or visit our online store at www.outdoors.org.

Contact Us

Appalachian Mountain Club
5 Joy Street
Boston, MA 02108-1490
617-523-0636
www.outdoors.org

Leave No Trace

The Appalachian Mountain Club is a national educational partner of Leave No Trace, a nonprofit organization dedicated to promoting and inspiring responsible outdoor recreation through education, research, and partnerships. The Leave No Trace Program seeks to develop wildland ethics—ways in which people think and act in the outdoors to minimize their impacts on the areas they visit and to protect our natural resources for future enjoyment. Leave No Trace unites four federal land management agencies—the U.S. Forest Service, National Park Service, Bureau of Land Management, and U.S. Fish and Wildlife Service—with manufacturers, outdoor retailers, user groups, educators, organizations like the AMC and the National Outdoor Leadership School (NOLS), and individuals.

The Leave No Trace ethic is guided by these seven principles:

- Plan ahead and prepare.
- Minimize campfire impacts.
- Travel/camp on durable surfaces.
- Respect wildlife.
- Dispose of waste properly.
- Leave what you find.
- Be considerate of other visitors.

The AMC has joined NOLS—a recognized leader in wilderness education and a founding partner of Leave No Trace—as the sole national providers of the Leave No Trace Master Educator course through 2004. The AMC offers this five-day course, designed especially for outdoor professionals and land managers, as well as the shorter two-day Leave No Trace Trainer course at locations throughout the Northeast. For information about these Leave No Trace courses visit www.outdoors.org. To register for a course, call 603-466-2727.

Contact Leave No Trace at:
P.O. Box 997
Boulder, CO 80306
800-332-4100
www.LNT.org